ADVANCE PRAISE

In quiet, lovely prose, Julie Brill has delivered a powerful reminder of why our stories—personal, familial, historical—are so crucial. A moving excavation of a family story.

–Menachem Kaiser, author of *Plunder: A Memoir of Family Property and Nazi Treasure*

Hidden in Plain Sight stands out among Holocaust memoirs. It focuses on Belgrade, a Sephardic community whose horrific experience during the Shoah is often overlooked. [...] It provides an object lesson in how to carry out research, what it takes to recover lost family secrets. Finally, it shines a bright light on the children of survivors, providing an intimate view of the deep trauma inherited and internalized by them, and translated in this case into an extraordinary book.

–Jonathan D. Sarna, University Professor and Joseph H. & Belle R. Braun Professor of American Jewish History, Brandeis University

Julie Brill's family memoir *Hidden in Plain Sight* is about her Holocaust-survivor father and her experiences learning about his life.

Brill's father was young when the Nazis attacked Belgrade. [...] Brill knew little of his story during her own childhood in the United States: "I matter of factly learned my father's war stories as simply the stories of his childhood." Later, she spent years doing extensive research into her family history. In the process of her quest to learn about her father, she also learned about the history of Serbia's Sephardic Jewish community, whose members became early victims of the Nazi genocide.

Descriptive prose is used to draw distinctions between Brill's American upbringing and the horrors her father experienced: "Throughout my childhood, I had considered which, if any, of the Gentiles I knew would hide me in their attics." Her grandfather was taken to a camp and his fate was never confirmed, with his wife holding out hope after the war that he might return.

As Brill's research raised more questions, she traveled with her father and her daughter to Belgrade. Locations she'd seen only on Google Earth become real to her, while her father's memories flowed as he returned to familiar places. They visited sites from his former home to the city's Jewish cemetery and the local temple, which the Nazis had disgraced by making it a brothel. "Emotion is a glue that cements memory," Brill writes, and her father's recollections answered questions that she'd carried her whole life.

Recounting a search for a father's memories and family history, *Hidden in Plain Sight* is an excellent memoir that bears witness to the loss of a community.

–*Foreword Review*

In *Hidden in Plain Sight*, Julie Brill does a fascinating deep dive into her family's past, unraveling the secrets of the Holocaust in Serbia. A poignant, heartfelt, haunting story of loss and legacy.

–Susan Shapiro, NYT bestselling author/coauthor of *Unhooked, Bosnia List & The Forgiveness Tour*

Julie Brill's *Hidden in Plain Sight* is a heartfelt journey that beautifully intertwines personal anecdotes with the poignant history of a lesser-known chapter of the Holocaust. Julie dives right in with caring and thoughtful storytelling, reclaiming her family's memories and showing us how important it is to share our own stories to uphold the promise to "never forget." Her vulnerability and creativity make the past come alive, bridging generations and drawing readers into a world that feels both deeply personal and universally resonant. Julie's memoir is not just a book—it's an empathetic bridge to history that speaks directly to the heart.

–Dave Reckess, Executive Director, 3GNY-Descendants of Holocaust Survivors

Part Holocaust family memoir and part exploration into the absence of Holocaust memorialization in Serbia, *Hidden in Plain Sight* is a captivating and emotional book. Julie Brill embarks on a multigenerational quest to find out what happened to her grandfather, murdered in the Holocaust. She finds previously unknown family members, documents about her grandparents' prewar life, but also grapples with the general indifference and lack of knowledge about the Holocaust in Serbia today. It is a powerful and important book.

–Jelena Subotic, author of *Yellow Star, Red Star: Holocaust Remembrance after Communism*

Hidden in Plain Sight is one of the rare books that sheds light on the Holocaust history of a once relatively small but flourishing community, often overlooked in the broader narrative of the European Holocaust. It speaks on behalf of and in the name of the fragmented family histories of many of us descendants of Holocaust survivors in Serbia. [...] This book should become mandatory reading in both primary and secondary schools.

With this book, Julie Brill, much like with the Stolpersteine (stumbling stones), ensures that her family's story and the Holocaust history of Belgrade are not forgotten. For this, we are deeply grateful.

–Sonja Viličić, Executive Director of Haver Srbija

Hidden in Plain Sight is a remarkable account of one woman's quest for her family's past. In moving, concise prose, Julie Brill recounts years of meticulous research filled with twists and turns, taking her to her father's homeland of Serbia, discovering long-forgotten relatives, uncovering stories and secrets about the family's complex origins, and confronting the improbabilities of death and survival in the Holocaust. A powerful, highly readable book taking the reader into the depths of the largely unknown, fascinating, and tragic tale of Jewish-Serbian history.

–Omer Bartov, Samuel Pisar Professor of Holocaust and Genocide Studies, Brown University and author of *The Butterfly and the Axe*

An eye-opening portrayal of the little-known history of Nazi Germany's near-eradication of Serbia's Jewish community, and a daughter's quest to reclaim her family's heritage.

–Karen Kirsten, author of *Irena's Gift: An Epic WWII Memoir of Sisters, Secrets, and Survival*

In *Hidden in Plain Sight*, Julie Brill reflects on her lifelong quest to uncover her Jewish family's history in Belgrade. Growing up with a father who survived the Holocaust, she weaves together her own childhood memories with his often fragmented and silenced recollections. This emotional imprint, combined with her later research, leads her on a journey through archives, documents, and places of memory to piece together the story of her family's fate during the Holocaust.

Brill's postmemory quest is a deeply moving account of reconstructing a history that was never fully spoken, highlighting the powerful tension between what was lost and what endures. In this rare work of postmemory literature connected to Serbia, the gaps left in family narratives come to light as she uncovers how silence has shaped her family's legacy.

–Dr. Katarina Melić, Director of the Center for Memory Studies, University of Kragujevac, Serbia

HIDDEN IN PLAIN SIGHT

A FAMILY MEMOIR AND THE UNTOLD STORY OF
THE HOLOCAUST IN SERBIA

JULIE BRILL

ap

ISBN 9789493418066 (ebook)

ISBN 9789493418059 (paperback)

ISBN 9789493418042 (hardcover)

Publisher: Amsterdam Publishers, The Netherlands

info@amsterdampublishers.com

Hidden in Plain Sight is part of the series Holocaust Heritage

Copyright © Julie Brill, 2025

Cover design: Peter Selgin

All Rights Reserved. No part of this publication may be reproduced or transmitted in any form or by any means, electronic or mechanical, including photocopy, recording or any other information storage and retrieval system, without prior permission in writing from the publisher.

CONTENTS

Chapter 1	1
Chapter 2	8
Chapter 3	14
Chapter 4	21
Chapter 5	25
Chapter 6	32
Chapter 7	40
Chapter 8	45
Chapter 9	52
Chapter 10	56
Chapter 11	61
Chapter 12	65
Photos	71
Chapter 13	78
Chapter 14	86
Chapter 15	95
Chapter 16	105
Chapter 17	117
Chapter 18	126
Chapter 19	132
Chapter 20	138
Chapter 21	147
Chapter 22	152
Chapter 23	159
Chapter 24	166
Chapter 25	173
Chapter 26	178
Epilogue	185
Photos	189
Notes	197
About the Author	201
Acknowledgments	203
Amsterdam Publishers Holocaust Library	205

For my family; for all those who descend from survivors and victims of the Shoah, who are the keepers of the stories; and for everyone who wants to remember. May this book honor my grandfather Alexander and all the dead I was able to name— and the many more I couldn't—and the survivors, especially my beloved father and the grandmother I never got to meet, but who I sought to know on my research journey. All errors are my own.

"What is a home if not a place where the stories sound familiar?" –Jordan Salama

"Never go on trips with anyone you do not love." –Ernest Hemingway

THE BRILL FAMILY

- Unknown
- Dr. Bernhard Brill/Brül 1832-1905
- Rozalija/Rosa 1840-1890
- Baruh Ruso
- Rivka

- Malvina 1852-?
- Vladislav 1854-?
- Adela 1857-?
- Julius 1858-?
- Henrietta 1859-?
- Johanna 1872-?
- Herman Vajntraub
- Heinrich 1876-1941
- Regina Ruso 1888-1930
- Filip 1876-?
- Evgenija/Jenni Schwartz 1881-1941?

- Hanna 1919-2011
- Aci/Alexander 1909-1941
- Delpha/Regina/Jelisaveta Franczci 1914-1964
- Danilo 1913-1915?
- Solomon/Monika 1915-1984
- Zora/Zoritza 1922-1999
- Zil 1921-1941
- Hypolyte Kramer 1898-1976
- Helena/Jelena 1910-1976
- Jordan 1912-1966?
- Simon 1911-1942?

- Bernhard 1907-1984
- Lonni 1948-
- Haim/Heinrich 1938-
- Martha Harrison 1942-
- Shoshana/Ljiljana 1942-
- Aci/Alexander 1947-
- Rachel 1951-
- Bentzi 1949-
- Rina 1951-
- Dorde 1931-2020
- Marija 1936-2011
- Viki 1953-

- Zil 1946-
- Paul 1970-
- Julie 1970-
- Alexander 1974-
- Johanna 1974-

- Rebecca 1996-
- Sophie 1999-
- Rachel 2002-
- Jonah 2004-

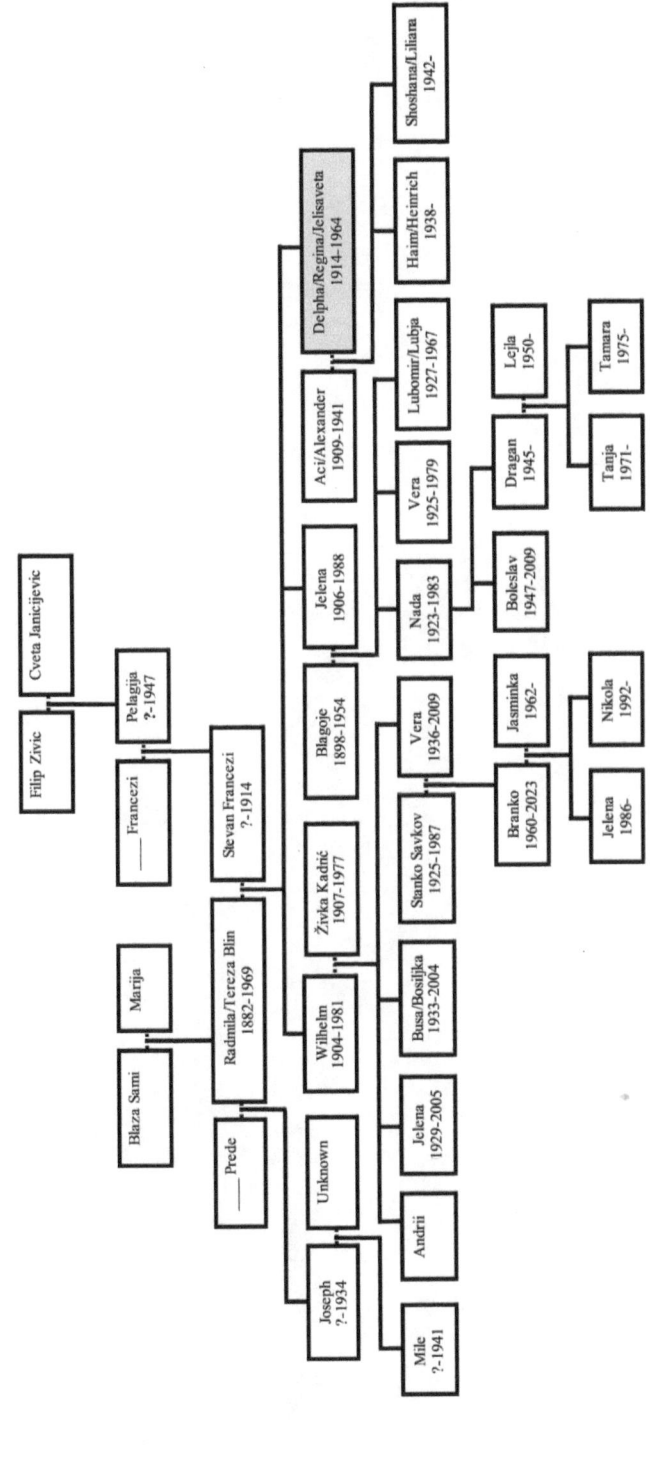

1

We cruise down the narrow street of Dorćol, Belgrade's Jewish neighborhood, with Google Earth Street View, searching for the house where my father lived before World War II. His family stretched back at least four generations in that Serbian city until the Holocaust snapped the links in our chain. My 20-year-old daughter Rebecca sits on a tall chair at the kitchen island of my parents' home, navigating on her laptop. My father sits beside her, leaning in to see the images. I stand behind and look between them. The back of my father's head is gray, but not balding, shaved military-short by my mother—a contrast to Rebecca's long, dark curls.

Although my father left the country almost 70 years ago, he is sure of the address. He remembers the two-story row house he lived in with his parents and his uncles at Solunska Ulica 8. From the front window, the three-year-old boy—who would grow up to be our family's patriarch—could see the tops of the helmets of German soldiers patrolling his neighborhood in pairs. I imagine a dark-haired boy standing on tiptoes, lifting a corner of curtain to peer out wide-eyed at the scary sight of armed occupiers goose-stepping past. His mother had forbidden it, so it was a naughty thing to do.

We are in Falmouth, Massachusetts, at the shoulder of Cape Cod's bent arm, in the familiar kitchen where we've shared many summer breakfasts, birthday cakes, and late-night bowls of popcorn in our pajamas. Behind us are floor-to-ceiling windows offering a view of the salt marsh, and beyond that Waquoit Bay. I was married on that deck, and Sophie, my younger daughter, took her first steps there on the July 4th before she turned one.

Rebecca leads us virtually up and down the street, but we can't find my father's childhood home. Looking at the computer screen, it's as if I'm in Dorćol, a Jewish neighborhood now stripped of its Jews, watching out the window of the Google car. I see pedestrians and parked vehicles that happened to be there in a moment and now dwell there permanently. We spot Hebrew writing on one building and a Star of David on another; we roll by the synagogue and the Jewish Community Center where my father, grandmother, and aunt lived after the war in a single room in an apartment with four other survivors, including a rabbi. Back and forth, but the home my father remembers seems no longer to be there. It almost feels like technology should allow us to scroll—not just across the world—but across time. There should be a button to click for a street view of Dorćol circa 1938.

To know my father better, I've researched his hometown to give context to his story. To my surprise, Belgrade had a flourishing Jewish community before the war, with three synagogues and 12,000 Jewish inhabitants.

Emotion is the glue that cements memory, so my father can remember fragments from the war: running down the street during the surprise German bombing of Belgrade; his mother chopping up furniture for firewood; being told never to pee anywhere but at home so his Jewish identity wouldn't be revealed, to wet his pants if he had to.

It feels as if I have always known my father's stories of surviving the occupation and its aftermath. He repeated them throughout my childhood, and they held my full attention. His foundational stories became mine—his memories almost like my own. This phenomenon of inherited memories is common in the children of Holocaust survivors.

As a child I wanted to learn more, to absorb what my father experienced in a world so different from suburban Boston in the 1970s. I needed to understand how he was able to survive. Though I knew my father had somehow lived through the Holocaust in Belgrade, I also felt the Holocaust hadn't really come to Yugoslavia. Because if it had, why did no one outside our family speak of it? My Hebrew school curriculum and the books I read focused on what happened in Germany and Poland.

Now I understand this reflects Timothy Snyder's Auschwitz paradox: Auschwitz is a prominent symbol of the Holocaust, although more Jews were murdered outside camps than in them. Most Jews, including members of my family, "had already been murdered further east by the time Auschwitz became a major killing facility."[1] In Eastern Europe, most Jews were shot at close range near their home. "Almost literally no Jew who stood at the edge of a death pit survived."[2] Over a million of the murdered are not named; when whole families were killed, when all the Jews in a town were wiped out, no survivors remained to identify the lost. They are, to use Wendy Lower's term, "the missing missing."

In comparison, there were a lot of Auschwitz survivors because the chance of survival was higher there since it contained work camps as well as the gas chambers. And those survivors could tell their stories and be remembered.[3]

My father retains details clearly and with certainty. His aunt Jelena's address was Mačvanska 32. The Serbian name rolls out his mouth, though I've never heard him speak his mother tongue. He only remembers fragments of the language.

Rebecca scrolls out of Dorćol and south to find Jelena's house. An address my dad has remembered for 70 years can now easily be plugged into a search bar. The building he recalls, an apartment facing the street connected through a storage area to a second unit behind it, has been replaced by a modern dwelling. The digital map brings close an imposing Serbian Orthodox Church, Saint Sava, up the street from his aunt's home.

My mother has been washing dishes. She dries her hands on her checkered apron and comes over to see the building. "Remember this, Haim?" she asks. "You must have gone by it when you visited your aunt."

He pauses to inspect the massive, traditional-looking structure, searching his memory. "No," he says finally. His face is relaxed. His voice is certain.

What she's referring to is one of the world's largest church buildings. It was dedicated to Saint Sava, the founder of the Serbian Orthodox Church. Although work began in 1935, only the foundation and some walls were built before World War II. Construction didn't resume until 1985. While Saint Sava is constructed to look as if it's stood for centuries, permanent and enduring, my father is correct. It wasn't here in the postwar years when he took the streetcar to visit his aunt. Again and again as I try to match family stories with historical fact, his memory seems infallible.

My father spent much of the war on his grandmother's horse farm on the outskirts of Belgrade, living in a substantial wooden structure that was both house and eight-stall barn. It sat on elevated ground to protect it from seasonal flooding by the brook that marked the property's edge. When it overflowed, his family would use a rowboat to get to the local train. We've heard the stories, but when my father reminisces, I listen hard, hoping to catch new details.

"It was a great place for a child to live. There was a large vegetable garden with many chickens and pigs, so the farm was self-sufficient. I remember catching little fish and scooping crayfish with a net."

I see my dad as a small, dark-haired boy, scattering kitchen scraps to the hens surrounding him, as my daughters did with our backyard layers. I envision a sort of Serbian Tom Sawyer, his face tan, his feet bare and dirty, blissfully catching fish for dinner.

"My grandmother would force-feed the geese with corn to make their livers grow," he adds. I try to conjure a great-grandmother I've never even seen a photo of with a goose under one arm. I picture her in an apron and leather boots, stout, no-nonsense. She was a woman used to getting her way, whose geese would eat whether they wanted to or not, who would make sure her grandchildren survived the war. I feel certain there was nothing delicate about her because my father believed so fiercely that she would keep him safe. I imagine she could have slaughtered a goat or a Nazi.

"There were German officers coming to ride and Partisans hiding weapons in the sawdust between the stalls." My dad's voice doesn't hint at the drama his words reveal.

I summon a black-and-white war film: the good guys, cunning and scrappy, hiding until dark so they can store their guns practically under the noses of the Germans. I see the bumbling soldiers from *Hogan's Heroes*. Lying on my belly on the orange-and-brown shag carpet in front of the black-and-white TV in our family room, I watched American soldiers, the good guys, held prisoner by inept Nazis. Our soldiers, though not able to free themselves from the prisoner-of-war camp, were constantly outsmarting their captors. Even then, I somehow knew this show had something to do with my father's childhood. Victors write history books and television series, and it was clear why the Germans lost the war. How had they ever managed a genocide? In my pre-adolescent mind, I tried to make sense of the Holocaust—the incomprehensible.

In my parents' home, Rebecca continues to scroll through Belgrade on her laptop. "My grandmother had a German Shepherd who would bark at the Allied bombers before the siren at the mint on the nearby hill would sound," my dad says. The mint on the hill, the railroad tracks, and the brook are all clues. In aerial view, starting at the Mint of Serbia, Rebecca searches in radiating circles for an area enclosed by a brook and train tracks. We spot a green space in a park, a bow-shaped lot bordered by a brook and train tracks that could be the site of my great-grandmother's farm. How I wish there were a Google Earth for 1944 that would allow me to fly above Belgrade like in a Chagall.

We know the wooden house and barn burned to the ground after the war; a passing train stopped so passengers could disembark and fight the blaze. My great-grandmother's German Shepherd died in the fire, attempting to guard the property from the strangers who were trying to put out the flames.

Two soccer fields occupy the spot where we think the farm was. Just as my father remembers, it is outside the central part of the city, a bit past Topčider Park, and accessible by tram. From the farm, he watched at the end of the war as Allied planes flew overhead towards Belgrade, the only city bombed by both the Germans and the Allies.

After the Allies blasted Belgrade, most of Serbia was liberated by the Russian Army. But Stalin let Tito and his Partisans free Belgrade.

It's unsurprising a horse farm on the outskirts of a capital city would, 70 years later, be soccer fields. My whole life, I have sorted the normal passing of time, normal bad luck, even the death and destruction inflicted on soldiers and civilians by war, from the evil inflicted on Jews for being Jews.

Growing up, I asked my father questions about his childhood, listened carefully to stories that played like movies in my brain, and tried to piece together his timeline and how it fit historical events. I wanted to know him better and understand what happened to him, his parents, and his sister. I wanted to know more about my grandparents.

My father's oldest memory is the Nazi bombing of Belgrade on April 6, 1941. The event ended the Kingdom of Yugoslavia and marked the beginning of the demise of most of the Jewish community. My father was a mere two years and eight months old; any younger and he surely would not remember the whistling sound the bombs made, how he ran in the street with his mother and older cousin towards his grandfather's basement. There, people were sitting together in silence. He does not remember his father who was arrested shortly after. For Belgrade, for Yugoslavia, the bombing divided the before time from the after time. What does it mean to have your first memory be that event?

When the attack was over, my father and his mother returned home. A plate with cookies had fallen and cracked in two. My father marveled that it hadn't shattered like a glass he remembered dropping. It's a child's memory —the profound, the horrible, and the ordinary wrapped together. His memory is so vivid, so cinematic.

As a child, my father's memories felt important to me, precious and meaningful. I listened to his childhood stories, trying to order them sequentially and make sense of it all. I worried I would forget the details. I wanted to ask questions but often didn't know what to ask. This type of transgenerational transmission, described by Marianne Hirsch as "postmemory," is common for the children of Holocaust survivors.

Postmemory describes the relationship we have "to the personal, collective, and cultural trauma of those who came before, to experiences (we) 'remember' only by means of the stories, images, and behaviors among which (we) grew up. But these experiences... seem to constitute memories in their own right... To grow up with overwhelming inherited memories, to be dominated by narratives that preceded one's birth or one's consciousness, is to risk having one's own life stories displaced, even evacuated, by our ancestors. It is to be shaped, however indirectly, by traumatic fragments of events that still defy narrative reconstruction and exceed comprehension. These events happened in the past, but their effects continue into the present."[4]

My dad didn't seem to mind talking about his war experiences, and in the retelling sometimes different facets would emerge. At times, he too seemed to be trying to make sense of the war. I think he has watched every World War II movie ever made in an effort to understand the incomprehensible or at least put an adult perspective on his childhood experiences. There are so many of these films about the good war, where good and evil are clearly defined, and who will win now seems predetermined.

Improbably, growing up I had a friend whose father was also a Yugoslavian Jew. Our fathers were both a minority within a minority. In 1978, only two percent of American Jews were Holocaust survivors.[5] My friend's father survived in a displaced persons camp in Italy. We met for coffee a few months after the 2016 election. She asked if I had started thinking about how to hide or run when Trump won. I hadn't, feeling safe in our liberal northeast corner of the country, but I completely understood her question. From the time I was little, having a passport meant I could flee the country if the need arose.

Throughout my childhood, I had considered which, if any, of the Gentiles I knew would hide me in their attics and if my light hair, which led strangers to speculate when I was a toddler if I was adopted, would allow me to pass. The six million were all Jews like me. Every Passover, our Haggadahs instructed us to imagine we ourselves had been brought forth from Egypt by

God. As a child whose father survived the occupation as a child, that made perfect sense to me.

2

On Sunday mornings when I was barely old enough to read, my dad and I would sometimes walk the mile to the center of town to buy a thick *Boston Globe* for him and some penny candy for me. The curb near the playground doubled as a balance beam to walk on carefully, one foot in front of the other. One hand held my dad's; the other was out to the side for balance. He would push me on the swings while I practiced pumping: legs straight out in front on the up, then at the top bent knees for the ride back down. A few quick trips down the metal slide so hot in summer it could burn my bare legs. Then on to the store, our main destination. On the way, we'd pass the fire station, and I'd let go of my dad's hand to run past it, in case the firefighters had to turn on their sirens and race their shiny red trucks to a fire.

The man behind the counter took my candy order seriously. He'd bend to open the jars he kept behind glass, but right at my eye level, beneath the register. I'd choose a few pieces to be rung up with the paper. There was Bazooka bubble gum wrapped in a tiny comic, candy cigarettes, and Tootsie Rolls. But my favorite was the button candy, drops of brightly colored sugar hardened to strips of white paper. I licked it with my tongue or pulled it off with my fingers. Either way, the price of the sweet treat was the dry taste of that paper in my mouth.

Soon we'd be home. My dad would settle into his chair in the family room with a cup of espresso and the Sunday paper with its tiny black letters and grainy gray photographs. Huge and serious, it was for grown-ups to decipher. But it came wrapped in colorful comics. Stretched out on the floor, I could copy them onto wads of pink Silly Putty, which I kept in plastic eggs on my dresser.

My mother and brother were waiting at home. But for the whole walk, it was just my dad and me. I recall the feeling of having his undivided attention as I told him about whatever came into my head.

Sometimes it was a chance to hear my father's childhood stories. I never asked for them, but sometimes one would just pop out.

"I remember the long walk I took with my mother, my Aunt Jelena, and my cousins," my father might say as he carried me on his shoulders. "When I got tired, my cousin Ljuba would carry me just like this."

Poor Daddy, I would think. Where was his father? But somehow, I knew not to ask.

"We followed the railroad tracks to a village where my grandfather owned land. We needed to get out of the bombed-out city," my father continued. "Life there was fun. The mattress was a big bag filled with corn husks. The outdoor toilet was a hole in the ground. I didn't want to fall in."

I imagined my dad as a little child like me, away on an adventure in the country. But what were they doing there?

"The farmers lived like they always had. They couldn't read, so at noon a man would walk through the village, beating a big drum and reciting the news of the day."

Little though I was, I understood that within these stories were clues to who my dad was and why he was different from my friends' dads. Growing up, he did not seem really American to me despite his citizenship. He never understood football. He rarely watched sports on television, but if he did it was tennis. And he hated the most American of holidays, Halloween.

At five, I dressed up as Raggedy Anne with a red yarn wig. I wiggled excitedly as my mother drew red circles on my cheeks with lipstick. My dad thought nothing could be more American than grasping gangs of kids ringing doorbells and demanding candy. Halloween is the opposite of Purim, a spring holiday when generous Israeli children leave baskets of treats anonymously for friends and neighbors. My dad took me trick or treating because the alternative, answering the door, annoyed him even more.

The trees had deserted their leaves in preparation for winter. In a few hours, it would be November, and in a few weeks, our lawn would be covered with snow. Our group of neighborhood kids rang doorbells up and down our street. My dad stood back with the other parents in the driveways, his ungloved fists jammed in the pockets of his orange ski jacket against the cold. He kept his commentary on greedy Americans to himself, an act of love for his American daughter. Between houses, I held his bare hand and clutched my plastic pumpkin, the candies inside crinkling as we walked.

My dad couldn't wait until the night was over and he could turn off the front door light. He'd yell at any wayward teens who dared to knock after nine. In the morning, I will head for the school bus down a driveway painted with shaving cream, past our cherry tree dressed in strands of toilet paper. My stomach will feel queasy at this reminder that turning kids away without candy breaks our neighborhood's rules.

To me, Halloween was a magical night that went on and on. We were answering the door when we were usually eating dinner. We were out in the dark when we were typically watching television. We ate candy when it was past our bedtime. After trick or treating in our neighborhood, we drove 30 minutes to my grandparents. Usually, we went right in, but this was different. We'd ring the bell like regular trick-or-treaters, and they wouldn't recognize us. There was time to sit cross-legged in my grandmother's deep red and white armchair and sort my loot into piles: candy to eat tonight, candy to save, candy to trade. Halloween meant face paint and costumes and your own grandparents not knowing who you were.

My dad's childhood ran like an underground river deep below my own and sometimes bubbled to the surface. Every year, he looked at my birthday cake and remembered his childhood disappointment when he watched rationed chocolate disappear into the cake batter. "I would always say to my mother, please can I have my chocolate separate?"

This ritual felt as much a part of my annual celebration as blowing out candles or carefully opening presents so we could reuse the wrapping paper, a family trait left over from my maternal grandmother growing up in the Great Depression. It reminded me how lucky I was there was unrationed chocolate and, by extension, plentiful food.

"I don't like my chocolate mixed into a cake," my father said every year before digging his fork into his piece. And I would know in that way that children know things in their bodies that I couldn't possibly be grateful enough for this abundance.

Every birthday my father reenacted the ritual of retelling my birth. "June 12 was a Friday," he'd remember. "Your mother's water broke early in the morning."

I'd envision them in their small apartment, excited and nervous. I was two weeks early and my mom, a teacher wanting to be able to finish out the school year, had fudged her due date with the principal. She told him the baby would come in July. I was born on the last day of school. My mom was ready: in her classroom desk drawer were the completed report cards for the substitute to distribute; in her bag, she had packed a wrap-around skirt she'd sewn to come home in, since she didn't know how big her belly would be, and two hair ribbons, one pink and one blue. She would choose which one to wear when she knew the sex of her baby.

"We went to the hospital. The doctor tried to tell us it was too early and we should go back home."

I know every detail, but I love the repetition, hearing the love in his voice as he remembers the day we met and he became a father.

"I told that doctor there was no way I was going back home with a woman in labor. And I had made a promise to your mother that I would stay with her until you arrived."

This was 1970 Philadelphia, when a father in the delivery room was a rare occurrence. But my parents had taken a Lamaze class together and they had a plan.

"So, the doctor took me out to lunch in the hospital cafeteria. He thought if he bought me a meal, I'd agree to miss the birth." The doctor didn't know who he was dealing with. My father was in the Israeli Defense Force (IDF), where officers and enlisted soldiers called each other by their first names. I doubted that my father thought he was outranked by an obstetrician.

"In the end we made a deal: I would stay near your mom's head, and he would stay on his end. But then right before you were born, he started reaching for that tool. What do you call it?"

This is my least favorite part of the story. I supply the word my father each year can't remember. "Forceps," I say reluctantly, thinking of the aggressive instrument doctors use on babies' heads.

"Yes, forceps," my father agrees. "When I saw that, I started to come towards him to see what he was doing. And the doctor said…"

"'We had a deal. Stay on your end,'" I'd crow, beating my father to the punchline, a native English speaker able to outmaneuver him with my rapid-fire barrage of words.

This favorite story, familiar and polished, was somehow still fresh for my father. It is the story of a father being born, a moment when he abandoned his designated post to help me if I needed him.

My parents gave me a name, Julie, that didn't sound Jewish. My dad chose it, he says, simply because he liked it. It's an American name that links me to the year I was born, 1970. The Bobby Sherman song "Julie, Do Ya Love Me?" was released a month after I arrived. Julie is so linked to the 1970s that I share it with the American Girl Doll representing that decade.

I'd think of the photos in my baby book that showed a young father in love with his infant daughter. In one, we sleep together cheek to cheek, me snuggled on his chest.

"I thought about how you'd been tightly squeezed inside before you were born," he'd told me. "I figured you'd be happier with less room to move, so I tried to do that with my arms."

When I was born, he was 31, a decade older than many of his IDF buddies who'd had babies right out of the service. He might not have known much about babies, but his love for them was already there.

"We took you home on a rainy Tuesday. There were no car seats then. Your mother sat in the front seat of my Triumph and held you in her arms. And then she carried you up to our apartment and laid you on our bed. I looked at how close to the edge of the bed she had put you. Then I picked you up and put you in the middle of the bed. So, if you rolled, you'd still be safe. I didn't know then you wouldn't roll for months."

In the 1970s, before VCRs were widely available, watching an old movie was possible only if you stumbled upon it or read it was coming in the *TV Guide* and planned your schedule accordingly. There were a few movies I watched every year in this way. I saw *The Wizard of Oz*, *Mary Poppins*, *Fiddler on the Roof*, and *Oklahoma*. But the one I remember most vividly is *The Sound of Music*.

I was five or six the first time I saw it. I had to go to bed after the first half, so I only knew the joyful beginning where Maria and the children sing merrily in their matching clothes she sewed from old curtains. Their life is full of play: picnics in the mountains and Liesl, the oldest daughter, sneaking out to meet with her boyfriend. The next day I'd walk around singing "Do Re Mi" and "My Favorite Things." As I grew older, I moved up from identifying with Gretl, the adorable baby of the family, to Marta and Brigitta. The scariest thing that could happen was a thunderstorm. Having Julie Andrews as your nanny in Austria in 1938 looked so fun!

One year, my whining and pleading to my mother to "please let me stay up and see the rest of the movie, please, please," worked. I came back after a commercial break in my nightgown with my teeth brushed to see the full horror of the swastika that Marta described as "the black spider that makes people nervous" devolve into Maria and the Von Trapp kids running for their lives. It was the most terrifying film I'd ever seen in my short, sheltered life. And it seemed to echo back to my father's war experience. One minute he was a round-cheeked baby being held proudly by his father—the only photo we have of them together. And in the blink of an eye, his father was gone, and he was a wide-eyed toddler sneaking a peek from behind the curtains of his front window down onto Nazi soldiers with the black spider swastika on their uniforms.

The Von Trapps survived by hiking into the Alps. How had my dad lived through the war in occupied Belgrade?

3

When I was growing up, my dad had four black-and-white photographs from Serbia. A camera was a luxury in interwar Belgrade and it's unlikely that my grandparents owned one. Instead, portraits were taken by professionals who would shoot in public places and then hand out their cards so the subjects could return to their shops another day to purchase the developed pictures. The precious images somehow survived the war.

My parents kept the photos casually tucked away in an envelope in a drawer with other papers. Periodically, my mother would be looking for something, and they would surface and get passed around. I felt every time she was surprised to find them; their importance as a window into a world I would never see was belied by where they were kept. My parents, my younger brother Alex, and I would all look, holding them by their yellowed, curling edges so as not to mar them with our fingerprints. No picture frame or album protected them.

One photo was my paternal grandparents' formal wedding portrait, taken in interwar Belgrade. I knew nothing about their wedding: not the date, not who was there, not what the wedding was like, or if there was a honeymoon. Alexander Brill, nicknamed Aci, and Regina Francezi, known as Delpha, posed, elegant and young. My grandfather has removed one white glove to hold my grandmother's arm with his bare hand. From a white cap that sits on top of her short dark hair, a veil flows down my grandmother's back and pools on the floor behind her. She was stunning in her long silk dress. During the war, she will cut up its train to make clothes for her children.

I studied the faces of these grandparents who were strangers to me. Like all brides and bridegrooms, they stand together, ready for an unknown future—for better or worse. I tried to imagine what their lives were like, what they were like, from the crumbs I could gather. They were established in Belgrade where they had been their whole lives. Where their families were. Where likely they expected to live and die.

My father's second picture was taken in the winter of 1938-39, after Kristallnacht in Germany. Translated as the Night of Broken Glass, the pogroms destroyed thousands of Jewish stores, buildings, and synagogues. Attackers, often neighbors, injured and killed Jews who they frequently knew by face, if not by name.

In the image, my father is a round, rosy-cheeked baby, well-bundled against the snowy Serbian winter. Did my grandmother knit his hat and mittens? My grandfather held the baby against his long, dark coat. He had dark hair, a mustache, fine features, and a satisfied expression. This young father looked so proud of his firstborn. When this image was captured, did he envision a future with albums and frames filled with photos of him with his growing son and the other children he likely expected to follow?

In the background, a pair of wooden skis rest beside an open-air structure. It looks as if they are on vacation. An optimistic image that doesn't foreshadow the coming World War. Visual proof my father had a father and that there was a prewar period when everything was in order, though he doesn't remember the man or the time.

My dad and his mother posed on a park bench in a third picture. It's probably an ordinary day in the last months of prewar Yugoslavia. Because the image survives, so does the moment, representative of many that are lost. Photographs were more valuable when people had to pay for film and developing.

My grandmother was slender and stylish in a short-sleeved, polka-dot blouse and short solid skirt, one ankle crossed over the other. My father wore a collared shirt with broad horizontal stripes, shorts with suspenders, and leather shoes with white socks. He half stood on the bench, half sat on its back, while my grandmother secured him with one hand behind, the other on his bare knee. I studied it, looking for clues, signs of my father in the little boy's face.

They gazed at the photographer. Their faces were close but not touching. The family resemblance is striking; they had the same eyes, the same nose, their hair is parted in the same spot. Did my grandmother see and appreciate their similarities? She gave a slight smile, but the little boy who will become my father is somber. Next to him is a toy metal pail with Disney's Snow White and the Seven Dwarfs; American culture has somehow found its way to the Balkans.

And then there is the photo I could never understand. My dad and his little sister stood on a city street during the German occupation. In the black-and-white image, my aunt wore a light summer dress she told me her mother sewed, her legs bare, with short socks and leather shoes. My dad must have been five or six. He wore short pants with suspenders, knee socks, and laced leather boots. This image clashed with my understanding of that period, gathered from reading survivor accounts of the Holocaust from the tiny temple library during my pre-adolescent Hebrew school years. These children are not hiding.

As soon as I could read, books were my loyal companions, coming everywhere with me like the puppy who can't bear to be left alone. They waited in a pile on the table next to my bed while I slept. Some had paper bookmarks holding my place; others were still unopened gifts. They went to school with me, staying in my desk until my purple mimeographed worksheets were completed. I read them in the backseat of my mother's red Chevy station wagon, at the bus stop in the morning, and during television commercials.

I read every book on the Holocaust shelf of my temple library including *Summer of My German Soldier*, *I Am Rosemarie*, and, of course, *Anne Frank's Diary of a Young Girl*. Anne was beautiful in the black-and-white photo on the cover, a special child who would never grow up, who shared my birthday.

I searched these books for clues, imagining I was the narrator and knowing it all somehow had something to do with my father's childhood. I wanted to work out how my dad's story fit in with what I was reading, but it seemed he wasn't the right kind of survivor. It was confusing since not only had he not been a prisoner of the camps, he didn't even seem to have been hiding. His father had been in a camp, but right in the city, not the kind you traveled to on a train. Somehow, his mother had been able to visit him and leave unharmed. My family was part of a Holocaust that I couldn't find in books, a version that no one seemed to know about.

As I aged, the vantage point from which I viewed the horrors of the Holocaust grew up beside me. As a child devouring young adult Shoah literature, I could see myself as a young character. Reading *The Upstairs Room*, I was in the burning sun in the middle of a Polish cornfield because the kind farmer who hid my sister and me, who had snuck me out of his home under a feed sack in a wheelbarrow for what was supposed to be a little break outside, couldn't return for me due to the unexpected arrival of visitors. I read *I Never Saw Another Butterfly*, a title I could never forget, and placed myself behind barbed wire in a camp where a single raspberry was something to be saved and divided among my siblings. When I failed to spoon up the last milk at the bottom of my cereal bowl or left behind a tiny bit of apple flesh clinging to the core, I thought of those starving children in concentration camps a generation before and my own father during the war and after when he never had enough to eat.

As a teenager, I walked the mile to my high school every morning. Sometimes I was in a mini skirt and pumps, both the soft pink color I hadn't yet outgrown, with just L'eggs nylons and thin bobby socks between my legs and the New England winter. That I had chosen to wear this outfit that was better suited to June than January was no comfort as my nose ran and my toes grew numb. But this cold could never compare—I reminded myself—to what Jews endured on forced marches, with leaves stuffed in their ragged boots to keep out the weather. Cold could never belong to me.

In public school we learned nothing about the Holocaust. In fourth grade, Miss Kieley, who I knew was Irish, pulled the big world map down over the blackboard and asked where our families were from. I was surprised to be the only one raising my hand.

Most of my classmates were Irish Catholic and had lots of siblings. They believed in Santa Claus, the Easter Bunny, and Jesus Christ, three imaginary creatures I'd lumped together. My mother had warned me not to tell them Santa wasn't real, and I assumed that went for the other two as well.

Churches were everywhere. White-steepled ones in the center of every Massachusetts town, modern ones further from the common. They were not mine, not ours. The crosses kids wore around their necks were also not mine, not ours. Being Jewish meant feeling uneasy walking by the Christmas tree in the school lobby. I knew about the separation of church and state. This felt like a violation to me. My father disagreed. "It's a Christian country," he reminded me. "Of course, they will have their holidays."

Being Jewish meant being uncomfortable singing Christmas songs. It meant being uncomfortable singing Hanukkah songs too, which I felt had been added on for my benefit. Couldn't school be a place where we ignored holidays altogether, I thought.

In Hebrew school, "Never Again" was drilled into us. Retelling the Holocaust story seemed the most fundamental part of Judaism, superseding the Exodus story as the primary tool for explaining to Jewish children who we were. The whole time my child's mind wondered how these victims couldn't have seen the future that was so clearly coming. The curriculum, intended or not, seemed to be teaching the inevitability of the Holocaust, not how it could have been prevented. The downfall of German Jews, who had the longest warning, seemed to lie in their not realizing how Jewish they were. They thought education, assimilation, intermarriage, and Gentile friends would somehow save them.

In my Hebrew school choir, the Makhaylah, we spent my fifth-grade year rehearsing and performing songs about the Holocaust that our director had written. Eventually, we made a record, which might still be in my parents' basement. It had our photo on the cover. We wore white shirts and dark blue pants and skirts and stood in tiered lines on the steps leading up to the *bima*, a synagogue platform. The songs got progressively darker, following the arc of history. We started by singing that "our town is burning, brothers burning" and ended with the *Shemah*, the prayer that Jews traditionally recite daily, but also at the moment of death. One song contained Anne Frank's words, "I still believe that people are really good at heart." Shortly before his death, Anne's father Otto had written a letter giving us permission to use her words. Our director showed it to us. He took explaining the Holocaust to preadolescents seriously, covering the history and the meaning behind the songs thoroughly.

When I was very young and asked where my other grandparents were, my mother explained that they had died a long time ago. "Daddy's father was killed in the war," she said, her face sad and still. "He was a soldier. He hadn't wanted to go and fight, but he had no choice," I think she said. But perhaps my young self added that later, to try to make sense of what had happened, to try to put the piece I'd been given into a greater puzzle. I know I pictured my paternal grandfather in a soldier's uniform, like my other grandfather who had posed in his, complete with the cap, and my grandmother and aunt, and my tiny mother, who was too little to look at the camera, sitting in his lap. My mother and aunt wear matching dresses in that photo on my mother's dresser.

"So, Daddy's an orphan?" I asked. Orphan was probably not a word I'd said out loud before. Orphans were in storybooks like *Pippi Longstocking*, *The Little Princess*, and *The Secret Garden*.

"Not exactly," my mom corrected. "Grown-ups can't be orphans."

But I still believed my dad to be an orphan, and I was sad for him. It somehow explained why he'd had to come to America and have my mother's parents be his parents too. Why else would he talk to them with such respect, drive an hour to bring them over for dinner, and get in the car at ten at night to check on them when my grandmother hadn't hung up the phone correctly and couldn't be reached? Of course, he had to be part of my mother's family, our family, since he didn't have his own.

That drive that got him here propelled him on—through engineering school at Northeastern University when he hardly knew the language. It got him to write papers after work that my mother typed while he knew that some of his classmates could pull a term paper out of a filing cabinet in their fraternity house closet. It got him to start his own business in our basement after a full day at work, applying for patents for a data storage drive. "I've wanted to invent something since I was very little," he told me. "But as a kid it seemed like everything I thought of had already been invented."

I got more puzzle pieces the day we performed those Holocaust songs for the first time. My mother explained: "Daddy's father wasn't killed fighting in the war. He was a victim of the Holocaust." She seemed both sad to have to tell me and surprised I didn't already know. Now the songs we sang were personal. The tears streamed down my face as we sang.

For Hebrew school students in the early 1980s, learning about the Holocaust was as much a rite of passage as learning about sex. No one seemed to question the appropriateness of this content for ten-year-olds. I don't think anyone would have their children sing such songs now or that such choirs still exist. Who would even come to listen?

In Hebrew school, we learned about Hannah Senesh, a paratrooper who the Germans captured in Hungary, tortured, then executed by firing squad when she was 23 years old. We sang her haunting poem, which was set to music after her death, called "Eli, Eli." It took up residence in my brain, alongside the Folgers commercial ("The best part of waking up is Folgers in your cup") and the theme to the 1980s sitcom Facts of Life ("You take the good, you take the bad, you take them both and there you have, the facts of life").

Banal and profound lyrics swirled around my head. Sometimes walking to middle school, brushing my teeth before bed, or putting away my laundry, Hannah's words would be the ones to surface unbidden: "Oh Lord, my God, I pray that these things never end: the sand and the sea, the rush of the waters, the crash of the heavens, the prayer of the heart." Suddenly, I'd be thinking about the Holocaust and Hannah's bravery. She had eagerly left the safety of Palestine, my Hebrew school teachers had explained, to return to occupied Hungary with the British Army to try to save Jewish lives. She had been murdered for trying to rescue Jewish children like me, like the boy my father had been. There were one and a half million Jewish children from our parents' generation who should have been alive but weren't. No matter how hard we paid attention, how deeply disturbed we were by what had happened to our people, we would never be grateful enough for our safe, comfortable American lives.

My Hebrew school classmates, mostly from the wealthier suburb where the synagogue was located, bewildered me with their fascination with designer labels like Nike and Calvin Klein and their obsession with status symbols like Rubix cubes and Walkman. Our teachers, primarily young Israelis born in the decade or so after the war, in a new Israel struggling to get out from under the weight of recent genocide, had just finished their compulsory military service. They seemed tough and Jewish in a way we could never be. They made it clear through their condescending tone that we were overprotected and needed to be shown the hard truths of what the world thought of Jews. Everything in their accented English sounded harsh to my American ears. They told us about kibbutzim, where Israeli parents were happy to have their children live separately in dorms and spend only an hour or so a day with them. The children never complained about this arrangement. If a child was an artist, the whole community would vote whether there was money for art supplies. I already knew I was spoiled from hearing my father's stories of his childhood. By age ten, he was working to help support his family.

The message was that since Jewish children had died in the Shoah, the least we could do was learn about it. Our Hebrew school curriculum emphasized the murder of six million Jews. We learned that being Jewish is tied up with persecution and genocide and the state of Israel, founded too late to protect Holocaust victims. It was only as an adult I learned there were millions of other victims, including those murdered for being Roma, Jehovah's Witness, gay, resistors, or disabled.

Despite the Holocaust being at the center of our Hebrew school curriculum, we learned nothing about Yugoslavia. The stories I heard from my father didn't match what we learned in class about ghettos, trains, and far-away camps. So even though I knew my grandfather lived in Belgrade and was a victim, I simultaneously somehow also believed the Holocaust hadn't really come to Yugoslavia. It would be years before I could sort out the truth.

4

After I left Hebrew School behind at age 13, I actively tried to avoid the topic of the Holocaust: I didn't see movies or read books about it. In college at Tufts University, I saw a class on it in the course catalog and questioned why anyone would sign up to spend a semester immersing themselves in the details of such horrors. As a young adult, I intentionally avoided the new US Holocaust Memorial Museum when I was in Washington DC and Israel's Holocaust museum, Yad Vashem, when I was in Jerusalem.

I chose a career as a doula and childbirth educator, and later a lactation consultant, gravitating to working with new babies and their families, to what I thought must be one of life's happiest times. My partner Paul and I decided to start a family, and our first daughter Rebecca was born when we were 25. Sophie was born three years later.

When I was pregnant with Rebecca, I framed old black-and-white family photos and hung them along my stairs. A connection with past generations felt critical as I moved into motherhood. I felt myself in a line, with ancestors in one direction and descendants in the other. Understanding family history was more important now that I had someone to pass it on to.

I passed my stoic ancestors heading downstairs for breakfast or up with a load of laundry on my hip. Photos of my mother's family, Jews who fled persecution in Ukraine and Poland, watched me go. I often studied the copies of the photos of my father's family I had stared at as a child, including the only two that existed of my grandfather: my grandparents on their wedding day and my grandfather holding my infant father.

Two pictures of my grandfather were not enough. Images of him should extend through my father's whole childhood. There should be a photo of my father and grandfather on the day of my father's bar mitzvah and another on my father's wedding day. I wanted albums full of yellowed pages showing the progression of his life, his frame filling out as black and white turns to color. My grandfather should have been allowed an aging, wrinkled face and the wisdom that can come with it. I wished for a photo of the two of us, him with the sideburns and tapered collar that were stylish in the early 1970s, me a round-faced baby like my father. I imagined an image that never happened where he looks at me with the same expression of pride he once had for my infant father.

I'd search my grandfather's face for family resemblances. Could I see my father's face in his angular features? Could I see myself? I questioned if my father also examined these images for clues about his family and himself. Similarities reinforce our sense of belonging. A smiling new mom I worked with pulled the cap off her baby's head, showing me how her daughter's newborn ears were a tiny copy of hers.

When Rebecca was born, I didn't just start family photo albums, I became a Creative Memories consultant, attending home parties where I taught scrapbooking and sold scrapbooking supplies for a multi-level marketing company. I have an unusually strong love for photographs and captured as many moments of my children's childhoods as possible. In every room of my home there are framed photographs. More than once, a parent sitting in my living room for a childbirth class or a lactation consult has wondered aloud how many children I have. It's hard for them to believe I've taken so many shots of just two daughters.

I have a photo of my second daughter Sophie as a toddler playing in the surf, flirting with the waves, her mass of blond curls caught in mid-bounce as she runs. The little pendulum would chase the receding tide until it turned, then shriek and run on sturdy legs toward the beach as the water washed away her tiny, flat footprints. Like the plovers dancing in the intertidal zone, she belonged to the ocean. She loved water as a toddler: puddles, baths, pools, the cold Cape Cod Atlantic. Her hypnotic, golden hair could draw in strangers—like mine when I was little. She was the first person in my family who looked like me.

While I gave birth with midwives at home to Sophie, my father waited downstairs. As soon as she was in my arms he was there, leaning in close for a careful look, his face joyous. Not long afterward, he said, "The baby's coloring reminds me of my grandmother's." It did? For as long as I can remember, I was always grasping for a wisp of a story about my father's family. "Yes, she had the same red cheeks and blond hair." So, there were three of us who resembled each other. Had it just skipped two generations? We didn't have any pictures of my great-grandmother.

As a child, I knew that my blond hair and blue eyes made me look like a transplant in my own family. My parents repeated a story of a stranger in a restaurant loudly declaring I must have been adopted. But as I got older, I could see my face in my father's, especially when it is captured in a photograph.

In my twenties, I looked so young people sometimes mistook me for my daughters' nanny. At times, I felt physically weighed down by my children when doing something as simple as navigating the supermarket parking lot on the way back to my station wagon. One arm balanced Sophie on my hip, while the other carried cloth bags of groceries while still holding Rebecca's hand. Moving across the pavement required strength, stamina, patience, and a sort of faith. A magnet on my fridge reminded me that "Mother is a verb" every time I opened the door to pull out eggs to scramble for breakfast or apples and cheese to slice for a snack.

The rule I had made for myself, though no one ever said it to me outright, was that nothing for me could be hard because I had a golden life. I had been lucky enough to be born safely in America after the war. And so, weighed down by my children and the responsibility of their care in turn-of-the-century suburbia, I imagined the impossibility of keeping them alive while fleeing war and genocide. I felt nauseated thinking of the movie *Sophie's Choice*, in which Meryl Streep's character must choose which child to save from Hitler. "How could anyone decide?" my father had said. I thought of my grandmother with children around the ages of my own and a murdered husband she still hoped was alive, somehow feeding her Jewish children and keeping them safe in occupied Belgrade.

When my kids were little, I tried attending the same synagogue again, thinking that perhaps there was some value in it for them. I took my four-month-old daughter to Rosh Hashanah services, knowing that I could keep her quiet by breastfeeding her if she woke, and was met by a daycare woman who tried to wrest her away from me.

Later I took my kids to a kids' service for Sukkot. During this fall harvest holiday, the young rabbi managed to sit in a sukkah, the temporary structure built for the celebration, with a group of children and never mention the harvest, the full moon, or the purpose of the celebration. When he made a joke about Jews building a sukkah, although we were not "a handy people," some parents booed him. I wanted my kids to know and be proud of their Jewish identity, but not there, and we never went back.

But we continued celebrating Jewish holidays at home, and I taught my children some Jewish history. Perhaps because I felt I carried the knowledge of the Holocaust with me too closely as a child, as a mother I wanted to protect my children. I hoped to preserve their sense of safety. I made a conscious decision to shield them from the scary stories and images of death camps and ghettos until they were old enough to keep from being personally terrorized. And in the process, I was able to shield myself as well.

5

When my daughters were little, they needed new shoes every year and, on some level, I couldn't foresee a time when they wouldn't. When they would leave home on their full-grown feet. And then Sophie, my baby, was 17 going on 18 and we were shopping for furnishings, preparing her for dorm life with extra-long twin sheets, extension cords, and a reading light. But there was nothing to prepare me for an empty nest.

With Sophie living at Brandeis University, I tried to adapt to my new life. At first, this involved crying at unexpected moments, long walks with my dog, meeting friends for dinner in the middle of the week and making my way through the tall stack of books I'd accumulated on my nightstand.

My new reality hit me hard. I'd been divorced for over a dozen years, and now with both kids out of the house, I suddenly had hours to fill. I started doing internet searches on the Holocaust in Yugoslavia, saving fragments and photos to my laptop, and sometimes sharing stories I learned with my dad. We both wanted to know how the fragments of his childhood stories fit into a broader historical context.

I thought about what it means to prepare children to function in their adult lives. I homeschooled my kids partly because I believe this gives children the space to discover who they are, which is the job of childhood. Part of knowing who you are, what you want to do in and for the world, and what your strengths and passions are, is knowing what you come from. Part of why I always wanted to know more about my father's childhood and his family, I could start to see, was to know more about myself. I shared my discoveries with my kids so they could know more about themselves too.

Growing up, I felt as if Yugoslavia was as unknowable, as unvisitable, as utterly inaccessible as Mars. Now I could read online and in the ominously named book I'd managed to find, *Until 'The Final Solution': The Jews in Belgrade 1521-1942*, about the brutal reality of the Holocaust in Yugoslavia. I tried to splice in the historical facts I learned with the fragments of family stories I'd carried since childhood. I was eager to know more, but the available information still felt limited. For every paragraph I scavenged on Serbia, there was screen after screen on Poland and Germany.

I began to understand the improbability of my existence. My family is the exception. Two of my father's uncles, my father's mother, my father's sister, and my father all survived while most of Belgrade's Jews were murdered.

Almost all Jewish men, approximately 8,000[1] including my grandfather, were murdered by mid-December 1941; that was more than one month before the Wannsee Conference near Berlin, where the "Final Solution of the Jewish Question" was officially decided[2] and just as the United States was entering the war. The remaining Jews, about 6,000 people, mostly women and children, were imprisoned at Sajmište, a former fairground just across the Sava River from Belgrade. In the spring, those who had survived the bitter winter, starvation, and disease were murdered in a mobile gas van.[3] On May 10, 1942, an SS leader reported to the German commander of Serbia, "The Jewish question, as well as the Gypsy question, has been completely solved. Serbia is the only land in which the question of Jews and Gypsies has been solved."[4] Belgrade was the first city to be declared by the Nazis to be *Judenfrei*—free of Jews. This was an early Nazi triumph during a time when most of the Jews they would murder were still alive.

The Holocaust came early to Belgrade. Jews there were caught unaware. Many tried to flee, but the mandatory yellow Stars of David patched onto their clothing marked them. The Germans prohibited all travel by Jews and had border crossings and railway stations under surveillance. Some Jews tried to get false papers, but this was expensive and sometimes they were betrayed and turned in to authorities.[5]

My grandparents could not foresee what was coming. They might have had the resources to get out, but couldn't imagine in time the danger they were in. The term genocide didn't even exist until 1944. Raphael Lemkin, a Jewish lawyer who had fled German-occupied Poland and lost at least 48 members of his family, coined it as part of his work to prevent it from happening again.[6] Killing all the Jews of Europe wasn't Hitler's explicit policy until late 1941.[7]

My grandmother told my father a story about my grandfather trying to procure false papers to escape occupied Belgrade. I picture late-night whispering when they planned as my father slept. Did my grandmother beg my grandfather to go or plead with him to stay? My grandparents paid a significant sum to my grandmother's relative by marriage, a Muslim who was going to help. But my grandparents never saw the money again or got the papers. Where would my grandfather have run if he'd procured papers as rumors swirled, panic rose, and borders closed? What if it had worked and he'd escaped?

There are no gas chambers or trains in the Serbian story. Most Jewish men were shot by firing squads in retribution for Nazi soldiers killed by Partisans. The order was 100 civilians—Jews, but also Roma and Serbs—executed for every Nazi killed; 50 shot for every Nazi soldier who was wounded. Once the men were dead, the Jewish women and children were held in Sajmište, across the river from Belgrade, in full view of the city, to serve as a warning to the rebellious Serbs. A baby who was smuggled out was the only survivor of the camp. Those who didn't die of malnutrition, disease, and the cold over the winter of 1941-42 were murdered in mobile gas vans—known as soul stealers—that drove the streets of Belgrade.

Ninety percent of the approximately 33,000 Jews of Serbia were murdered within a year. That probably included 90 percent of my grandparents' wedding guests and 90 percent of the family and friends who gathered for my father's bris, or ritual circumcision. Before the war, 12,000 Jews lived in Belgrade, which has a Jewish population of about 2,000 today. At the start of the war, there were about 80,000 Jews in the Kingdom of Yugoslavia, including 5,000 refugees from Central Europe. Less than 15,000 were alive in 1945. In contrast, in the Netherlands, where Jews suffered the greatest losses in Western Europe, 75 percent of 140,000 were murdered.[8] The vast majority of Jews in Serbia were killed, while in Belgium and Germany, with more warning, 50 percent survived.[9] Murder rates in Yugoslavian Jewish communities were among the highest in Europe.

No wonder there were no books in my temple's children's section on Jews in Yugoslavia. There were hardly any survivors left to tell their stories.

I reached for my phone. My dad answered on the first ring.

"How are you, my love?" he said.

"Hi Dad, I'm looking at the statistics of Jewish survival rates in Belgrade. I hadn't realized how few made it through the war. I still don't understand how you survived."

"You didn't know my mother and my grandmother. They were such tough women they wouldn't let anything bad happen to me. But you know I was so young; there's a lot I don't remember."

The more I hear this familiar answer, the less sense it makes. But I appreciate my foremothers who succeeded in installing this sense of safety in the young boy my father was and so preserved his childhood. It's such a strong sense that his answer has remained unchanged since his childhood; he's never had reason to reexamine it. A child can face grave danger and be protected for life by even the illusion of safety.

Now I realize that he worked to pass that same sense of security down to the little girl I was. My father's constant love made me feel safe.

"Put on a sweater," he'd say sometimes at dinner, looking at my skinny bare arms.

"I'm not cold," I'd protest.

"But looking at you makes me feel cold," he'd say as if he couldn't distinguish between his physical sensations and mine.

When I skinned my knees and elbows from a fall off my bike or bruised my butt from a hard fall when skiing, he'd say, "That hurt me more than it hurt you." When he saw me in bed with a paperback, he'd say, "Don't read in the dark," as if his own middle-aged eyes were being strained. But if I didn't like what was for dinner or finish the portion on my plate, he never said a word. He felt he'd manipulated his mother by eating or not eating during those lean years of his childhood and he wasn't going to have those battles with me. Food was my own business.

In an interview with American journalist Dan Rather, Geddy Lee talks about growing up with his mother's stories about surviving the Holocaust as a child. "She told them quite matter of factly, because then I realized later: these are her childhood stories. That's all she's got." The same is true for me, I matter of factly learned my father's war stories as simply the stories of his childhood. In *After Such Knowledge*, Eva Hoffman writes that those of us born after the Holocaust "sense its inward meanings first and have to work their way outward towards the facts and the worldly shape of events." I have grown up with the details, and now the greater context was giving those details a home to live in.

The year my father was born, 1938, marked the last moments of an old world. Europe was in an anxious, fragile peace. The German Anschluss of Austria and the immediate state-sanctioned antisemitism had occurred a little more than six months earlier. The occupation of the Sudetenland, the Czechoslovakian border region, was less than two months away. In a year, Germany would invade Poland and World War II would begin.

When my father was born in Belgrade, there were two Jewish communities. The Ashkenazi were relative newcomers. They lived separately, prayed in different synagogues, and were buried in different cemeteries than the Ladino-speaking Sephardic majority. Belgrade was the center of Sephardic civilization after Jewish culture declined in Turkey in the 18th century. Ladino presses in Belgrade kept "the Spanish component of Sephardic culture alive."[10]

Jews predate Serbs in Serbia. The first Jewish community in Belgrade dates to Roman times, prior to 610 C.E., long before the Slavs settled there in the 6th and 7th centuries. Sephardic Jews expelled from Spain settled there in the early fifteenth century. My family lived in Dorćol, the Jewish neighborhood, alongside their Gentile neighbors: Serbs, Turks, Roma, and Albanians. Dorćol was never a ghetto surrounded by walls and it never experienced a pogrom. Belgrade was once the edge of the Ottoman Empire, where Muslims lived alongside their Jewish neighbors. At the same time, in intolerant Christian Europe, there were gated districts where Jews had to live and curfews to ensure they were confined before dark. The Muslim empire, which extended north to the gates of Vienna, "was the bright light of the Dark Ages, the one place where science and poetry still flourished, where Jews, tortured and killed by Christians, could find a measure of peace."[11]

Many American Jews have little understanding of Jewish cultures that aren't Ashkenazi. Most Americans see Judaism as a monolithic tradition when, in fact, our culture is rich and diverse. At Ellis Island, all Jewish immigrants were termed "Hebrew," regardless of how they identified. Starting in 1910, the US Census listed the mother tongue of foreign-born Jews as either "Yiddish" or "Hebrew," and so Ladino, Greek, and Arabic-speaking Jews were not included in Jewish immigration statistics. This contributed to the exclusion of non-Ashkenazi experiences from the mainstream American Jewish narratives. This is ironic since the earliest Jewish immigrants to North America were Sephardic. In 1654, they founded Shearith Israel in New York, the first synagogue in the American colonies.

Sephardic history stretches back 500 years, to the expulsion of Jews from Spain in 1492. For Columbus Day in elementary school, we colored pictures of Christopher Columbus on bended knee in front of King Ferdinand and Queen Isabella, asking for permission to set sail to India to find spices. We looked for the names of his ships, the *Nina*, the *Pinta*, and the *Santa Maria*, in purple mimeographed word searches. We learned that in 1492 Columbus sailed the ocean blue, but there was no mention of Ferdinand and Isabella casting out Jews who refused to convert the same year. After the expulsion, Spanish Jews went in all directions, including the New World, some living as clandestine Jews—their stories lost to history.

Sephardic Jews were united by Ladino, just as Ashkenazim were joined by Yiddish. Ladino, historically called Judeo-Spanish, was the 15th-century Spanish spoken in Spain at the time of the expulsion. It has some Hebrew terms and is written with Hebrew letters. Over time, pronunciation evolved to reflect the local languages of the new lands where the Sephardim lived. Through language, Sephardim maintained a connection to Spain. When Yugoslavia was dissolving into seven countries in the early 1990s, 57 Sephardic Jews in Sarajevo petitioned for asylum from King Juan Carlos and returned to Spain, while many others went to Israel to escape the Balkan Wars.[12]

The Sephardim were a global majority in medieval times. In the 12th century, as many as nine out of ten Jews were Sephardic. But by 1700, only half the Jewish population was Sephardic, and by 1930, less than one in ten Jews were, or slightly greater than one and a half million people out of 16 million. Before World War II, 200,000 Sephardim lived in the Balkans, compared to millions of Ashkenazim in the north. After the murder of six million Jews in the Holocaust, the balance shifted again. Today, Sephardic and Middle Eastern Jews make up 25 percent of world Jewry and 60 percent of Israelis.[13][14]

"Are we Sephardic?" I asked my dad. Before I began obsessively researching, I knew very little about Sephardic Jews. I thought they lived mostly in Africa or the Middle East. I always assumed my father's family was Ashkenazi like my mother's. Jewish meant Ashkenazi in America. Childhood foods I associated with being Jewish were matzo ball soup, latkes, my grandmother's mandel bread, and bagels with cream cheese and lox. We drove 40 minutes to Brookline because bagel chains in the suburbs didn't yet exist. Only the hummus my mother whipped up in her blender because America hadn't discovered it yet was Sephardic and more broadly, Middle Eastern.

"No," my father assured me. "We aren't Sephardic."

"Ok," I responded. "Did you ever hear anyone speaking Yiddish?"

"Not until we got to Israel." These details seemed unimportant to him.

I considered how he was named for his living grandfather, a tradition among Sephardic Jews but believed to be an invitation to the angel of death by Ashkenazi. On a trip to Israel, I'd asked my dad's cousin Aci, the son of my grandfather's brother, the same question. "Yes, of course," he said, "but don't bother your father about it." So when I mapped my genome with 23 and Me, and my results were 60 percent Ashkenazi, I assumed the rest was Sephardic, which they don't test for. I was not surprised to see no ancestry from the Balkans.

Now, in a role reversal, my dad is learning our history from me. At Shabbat dinner at my parents', I ask my dad, "Do you remember the name of the neighborhood you lived in Belgrade?" I watch his face as his thoughts search through almost 70 years of files.

"No," he says after a moment.

"Was it Dorćol?" I ask and instantly see his recognition.

"Yes, that's it," he confirms.

My history obsession, a way to give background to my father's stories and to connect me with him, starts to feel boundless. Alone at meals, there's no reason not to scroll down one more World War II rabbit hole on my phone. With no kids waiting to be chauffeured and so little laundry to do that I have to buy more socks to make it from one clean load to the next, there's nothing to stop me from clicking on one site after another in the hours between dinner and bed.

In my twenties, I taught myself to be lucid when dreaming, a technique that allows me to be aware that what it feels like I'm experiencing is actually a dream. With that realization, I can change the course of the events. But in my Holocaust dreams, as I run through open fields from soldiers or try to find the children who have been stolen from me, my brain can't come up with a way out. The only solution it can find is to wake up. I lay awake in the dark, with my eyes wide open and my heart pounding as if I really have been running for my life. After waking up to a flood of adrenaline and a sweaty pause before I realize I'm safe in my bed one too many times due to nightmares, I institute a no-genocide-reading-before-bed policy.

6

I stand with a friend before the wall of black-and-white pictures at the Boston Museum of Fine Arts' exhibit "Memory Unearthed." There are photographs of the Lodz Ghetto which Henryk Ross risked his life to take with the help of his wife Stefania. But I am fascinated by the photos of the Lodz community from before the war. Ross's subjects look like they could have come out of an album of my family on my mother's side.

I gaze at the people who are focused on Ross's camera. I wasn't expecting this connection. I make eye contact with an older woman in an image who could be my maternal grandmother's sister. This photo could slip undetected onto the wall of family shots that hung in my grandparents' den. The woman who could be an auntie looks back with warmth and intelligence; maybe she has just told Ross a clever joke in Yiddish. Photos from my mother's and aunts' childhoods would not be out of place here. One little girl with two dark braids could be my Aunt Louise's twin.

Ashkenazi Jews, including my maternal grandparents and the Jews who lived in Poland, descend from what is called a bottleneck of 350 people. This suggests a small group of Jews, with 350 members of reproductive age, migrated away from a bigger group, and their descendants all intermarried. All Ashkenazim are as related, on average, as fourth or fifth cousins are in the general population. Perhaps this explains what feels like family resemblances, but it could be more. My maternal grandfather was born in Lodz, so I can't help questioning if some of Ross's subjects are blood relatives.

Ross and my grandfather Jack were born in the same city in 1910, so possibly their paths crossed. They could have been in the same class at school. If my grandfather's parents—pharmacists educated at the University of Moscow—hadn't been so driven and so lucky to be safely in Boston by 1922, Ross and my grandfather could have wound up in the ghetto together. My grandfather and his parents could be on this wall.

Ross had an official camera because he was tasked with documenting Nazi propaganda. He buried canisters of film and was able to return after the war and excavate them. The result is our access to some of the few images of the Jews of Europe in the interwar period. Ross's acts of bravery connect us to our past.

Although growing up I had my mother's family nearby—aunts, grandparents, cousins—I was always fascinated by my father's family. My paternal grandmother died in her sleep at age 50 in Israel, where the family emigrated in 1948. My father was a student in Massachusetts when she died, and she was buried before he could fly back. I had an aunt in Israel who came for occasional visits and then disappeared for years. In addition, my father had a few cousins in Israel and California whom I did not know. My father arrived in Boston alone as a 25-year-old engineering student, but what about his family and life before that? I always felt like something was missing.

Why are some people obsessed with genealogy and family history while others are bored by photographs of long-dead ancestors, old documents, and rumors that can't be substantiated? Maybe we search because we dream of finding keys to who we are and how we fit into the world. This knowledge is a way to find out crucial knowledge about ourselves we can't discover any other way.

I'd look at my grandparents' wedding portrait and try to focus not on what is about to happen but on these newlyweds who are not yet victims: here are two young adults starting out on their new life together, looking forward to setting up house, raising children, and one day playing with their grandchildren. They are marrying for romantic love, unlike my grandfather's parents, whose marriage was arranged, as was typical for the time.

My grandfather lived the last months of his life under Nazi occupation, doing slave labor until his death. But he was much more than the way he died. He was a father, husband, son, brother, and friend. He worked as a clerk and collected rent on properties his father owned. He was tall. But I don't know if he liked to sing, or draw, or read, or pray. I don't know if he was gregarious or shy. He's reduced now to a thin drawing of the man he must have been. While my grandmother filters down to me through my father's memories, my grandfather is more removed and harder to envision. He'd only just begun to parent when he was murdered. He comes only through stories my father heard about him. I've never known anyone who remembers him. I know hardly anything about his life, but that doesn't mean that the 31 years he lived before the Germans arrived weren't full.

I don't want him to be defined just by the tragic bit at the end. I want the same for the rest of my Serbian family and the entire Serbian Jewish community, vibrant in Belgrade for 400 years. They deserve a view encompassing more than what happened during World War II.

I began to see an alternate reality where my grandfather survived, and my grandparents were reunited and moved to Israel as a family. Or the prophecy a Roma woman in Belgrade told my grandmother came true and my grandfather found her and their children there. Was that why she went there, leaving a European capital city and her family for a developing country at war with its neighbors? Did she think she was going to meet her destiny?

I imagined how on the edge of war, my grandfather could have acted sooner, been less trusting maybe, or less indecisive, if perhaps he'd thought less about his wife, his young son, his father, his home. But doing so would have meant believing that Hitler was so dangerous that fleeing to the unknown was the safer option. It would have meant leaving his wife and young son to face an enemy occupier without him. He could have procured false papers and run to Italy, possibly his best chance of survival, or fled to Budapest with a fake identity, like his brother Bernhard. Or he could have joined the Partisans with his younger brother Monika, lived in the woods and beat the odds, to return a hero. Instead, he seemed to be caught in indecision, and that hesitation, ambivalence, and disbelief cost him the time that might have saved him.

In my fantasy, feasibly like my dad's and grandmother's, he returns after the war, not just physically unscathed, but mentally well. In this fantasy, he looks as young and healthy as he did in his wedding photo.

When I was a child, my dad always referred to him not as my grandfather but as his father. So I did as well. Now I see how in the alternate reality where my grandfather survived, I refer to him as casually and intimately as I do my maternal grandfather, my papa. This grandfather could have been my *saba*, the Hebrew word for grandfather. Or perhaps my *deda*, a Serbian word I had to look up and have never heard said aloud.

The story is my grandmother's early death at the age of 50 was from a heart condition. I think it was related to the violent loss of her husband. Grief is literally heartbreaking and possibly it indeed cut short her life. Europe had betrayed her. Her handsome young husband was never coming back.

If my grandfather had survived, maybe they both would have lived into old age. I would have known them, my Israeli grandparents. Likely, I would have learned Hebrew, listened to their stories, and known my family in the flesh instead of through old documents, sepia photos, and perhaps-ing.

"Little children, little problems, big children, big problems," my dad would quote my grandmother. A grandmother like that would have welcomed me onto her lap, stroked my hair, sung to me. I see her bending down to listen to my toddler self tell her something very urgent, the words coming out in an earnest rush, stored up for our reunion and now tumbling free. I saw my parents do this with my children when they were young. I hope someday to do it for my children's children.

When I do in-home lactation consultations, I notice what the new baby's grandparents are doing. The grandmothers are usually in the kitchen, trying to be helpful. The grandfathers often watch TV or read the paper, wanting to be out of the way, perhaps feeling uncomfortable about breastfeeding. I picture my grandparents like the new grandparents I see. My mother and my foreign grandparents would have needed my father to translate their communications. But there would have been no language barrier with the baby, their first grandchild.

What if—instead of asking my dad about his father, a person not in our living memories—we shared recollections to look back at together?

I kept circling back to the website for Belgrade's Jewish Museum, learning bits about the history of Jews there. I studied the photos of the Jewish community in interwar Belgrade, dressed in their finery, trying to see if I could find any family resemblances. Could I see myself, my brother, my dad in anyone's eyes, the profile of a nose, the jut of a chin? The black-and-white faces stare back at me, unsmiling, unaware they are living in the fleeting safety of what will turn out to be the last days of the Kingdom of Yugoslavia. I worry over the fate of each of them.

When I showed my father the photograph of the museum's exterior on my iPhone, he nodded and said nonchalantly, "Oh yes, after the war I lived there with my mother and sister. We had one room in an apartment we shared with a rabbi and his family and another single woman."

"The rabbi had a wife and a teenage son," he remembered. "He got two rooms because he was the rabbi while we were crowded into one. I don't know what happened to that single woman in the war. But when we lived together, she never left the apartment. She spent all day obsessively cleaning. Our kitchen must have been the cleanest in all of Belgrade." My father paused to collect his thoughts.

I waited quietly as questions swirled in my brain. My father continued: "That building was the Jewish center then and now. It was a distribution point for meals after the war. I was the one who would go and pick up food when I was six or seven. I would go with metal containers for meals. The containers could stack and there was a handle. We ate better than most non-Jews in Belgrade because of those meals funded by American Jews."

My father's memories place him front and center in the tiny postwar Jewish community in Belgrade. Most of that community would migrate together to Israel in late 1948. Three years later, the rabbi they lived with in Belgrade would bar mitzvah my father in Tel Aviv.

Early one morning I met my friend Janet, just as we did most weeks. As we walked with our dogs through my neighborhood, the day's promise of the heat to come made me appreciate my water bottle and shorts.

I caught Janet up on my research and the surprising new information that my dad had lived in the building that now housed the Jewish Museum.

Janet and I had been friends since our daughters, now in their late teens and early twenties, had been small. Even before we came to know each other, several people had told us that we were so alike we had to meet. In our suburb, we were even sometimes confused for each other, although Janet is five inches shorter and slender.

We pushed our toddlers in strollers down these roads and later walked behind our kids as they biked or rollerbladed. Those kids were then in college as we walked down sleepy streets with just our dogs panting alongside us.

We shared similar parenting philosophies, politics, and lifestyle choices. We both leaned way left, sought to reduce our environmental footprints, and wanted to raise our children to be passionate, independent thinkers. When our kids were young, we limited their screen time, protected them from early academics and processed food, and gave them lots of time for independent play. We often collaborated on homeschool projects. Our kids grew up together, playing at each other's homes, doing Waldorf-inspired crafts, practicing pieces from their Suzuki violin lessons, and staging elaborate plays they wrote, directed, acted in, and rehearsed for weeks.

Janet got chickens first, that gateway farm animal, and answered my questions when I took the plunge into poultry stewardship. Then, to the horror of some of my neighbors and the fascination of others, I got backyard goats, Janet's dream too, and she came over to see their newborn kids and milked the mama goats when we were away. It's almost like we had a little kibbutz in the suburbs. When my father told one of his friends in Israel that I had goats, the friend was confused. "Does your daughter live in Israel or the States?" he asked.

As we walked past the site of my elementary school, though the building I went to was razed to make way for a more modern one, and by the house where my best friend in kindergarten lived, I chatted about what I knew about my family in Serbia.

"You know I still have family there," I said. "The descendants of my grandmother's brother and sister live in Belgrade."

"You've never mentioned that before," Janet said. "I had no idea. How did her siblings survive the war? It seems like some sort of miracle that so many family members survived."

"There is nothing about my grandmother's family that makes them seem like they were Jewish," I answered slowly. "It's something I wonder about. Certainly, that would explain their survival."

Saying this aloud crystallized it as a possibility for me. I can't remember the moment I started to suspect my grandmother's family wasn't Jewish, but I had questioned it since childhood. I didn't have any clues that they weren't Jewish, but neither did I have anything indicating that they were. My grandmother's mother and siblings stayed in Yugoslavia in 1948, when most Jewish Yugoslavians immigrated to Israel. None of their children and grandchildren considered themselves to be Jewish.

"Are you saying your grandmother converted to Judaism?" Janet asked.

"You know, it's possible," I said. "Although my parents have never said anything about it."

"Maybe the Jewish Museum has records and would know," my friend said.

"Oh, I doubt it," I said. "I've been over and over their website and it doesn't say anything about having records on Serbian Jews. It's a lost cause."

But when I returned home that morning, I sent the museum an email titled "Searching for information about my Jewish family from Belgrade." I knew it was a long shot. I had no reason to believe they knew anything about my family or would even respond to my request.

"I am wondering if the museum could help me find more information about my father's family," I wrote. "I would very much like to share information with my father and my daughters." I summarized what I knew about the Brill family for the first time, sharing details with a stranger. "Do you know if the family was Sephardic?" I asked.

In my email to Belgrade's Jewish Museum, with both trepidation and relief, I laid bare to strangers the questions I had only told close friends a few times but which had echoed in my head for so long. "I am also looking for information about my father's maternal family. He is sure that they were Jewish, but his story of how they survived part of the war living on his grandmother's horse farm makes me doubt if this is true. How common was intermarriage in the 1930s?"

An employee named Barbara wrote back almost immediately, "Dear Mr. Brill, We checked all available databases stored in the Jewish Historical Museum and found the following documents regarding Brill family..."

Her response was like a gift. It contained my grandparents' marriage certificate, my father's birth certificate, my grandfather's birth certificate, the birth certificates of three of my great-uncles, and my great-grandfather's birth certificate. She also sent me an address where my father lived with his parents from the book of tax records from 1938-39. And she attached photos of the graves of my great-grandmother and my great-great-grandparents. I was amazed. But like an addict, the more glimpses of my family's past I got, the more I wanted. And now that I knew where to go and that the graves still existed, I wanted to stand in the cemetery where our dead were buried.

Growing up, I was jealous of Protestant friends with family trees stretching back generations across the New England landscape. The ones who could casually point at a cemetery as we drove past and tick off the layers of great-grandparents who rested there. I loved to watch *Finding Your Roots* on PBS and fantasize that Henry Louis Gates Jr. would hand me a book with my family mapped out, old photographs carefully curated alongside detailed bios of long-dead ancestors, and birth and marriage certificates in the languages of the old countries, together with their English translations. I longed to find a mythical file that would include everything I wanted to know about my relatives. I had never seen a single object or document that had belonged to my paternal grandparents or their parents. Knowing who they were, I believed, would help me understand more about who I was. It would give me something tangible to pass down to my daughters, something their children could hand down the line.

When I was a child, the Holocaust seemed to live in the long ago. Paradoxically, as I have gotten older—and 20 or 30 years no longer seems a lifetime—the past is not as far away. The trial of Adolf Eichmann in Israel was in 1961, nine years before I was born. While the genocide quickly became known as *Shoah*, catastrophe in Hebrew, the term Holocaust wasn't used until the 1960s. Just as I was starting to study it, the term entered common usage in 1978 with the miniseries starring Meryl Streep called *The Holocaust*, which was watched by an incredible 60 percent of Americans.[1] The United States Holocaust Memorial Museum wasn't opened until 1993, the year after I graduated from college. European nations are still sorting out restitution for property that was seized. Through new movies and books, we still struggle to understand what happened and what it means to us now.

My father is aging well; he's still strong and active, but my sense of urgency is growing as time passes. There will never be a better time to try to collect the missing jigsaw pieces of our past. If I'm ever going to make sense of wartime events and how they shaped my father and me, it should be now, while he's fit enough for international travel.

"Do you want to visit Belgrade?" I asked my father.

7

My father was ten in December 1948 when he and his family made *Aliyah*, or immigrated to Israel, along with 4,200 others who arrived that month.[1] Why did my grandmother take her two young children to Israel? My father said she wanted no part of a country, of a continent, where people could execute such tragedy.

My family was lucky to get there early as resources for arrivals were increasingly overwhelmed. Jews who came later spent months in more crowded camps, with living conditions deteriorating to the point where hunger strikes were held to protest. Between May 1948 and the end of 1951, more than 684,000 Jewish refugees from around the world caused Israel's population to more than double. Jews from Yugoslavia and Bulgaria were among the first to arrive in the Great Aliyah. They came en masse; almost all Holocaust survivors emigrated.

In the early years, there was more shame than pride in being a survivor, in having lived when so many died. Most people just wanted to go forward, not dwell on traumatic pasts. At any rate, my young father did not consider himself a survivor and likely those around him did not either. Survivors were those who lived through ghettos, camps, and forced marches. It would be decades before the definition was expanded to include all Jews who lived in German-occupied Europe or who escaped to avoid the occupation.

My father remembers saying goodbye to relatives in Belgrade and an overcrowded ship, the *Kefalos*. The journey was supposed to last a week, but they hit a storm, causing it to take an additional six days. They ran out of food, and everyone was seasick. But he doesn't remember learning Hebrew or changing his name from Heinrich to Haim.

After a short time in a refugee camp, my father's family moved into an apartment in Old Jaffa, above the seaport overlooking the Mediterranean. The government wasn't facilitating newcomers relocating into these shelters; Jews found and moved into dwellings left vacant because the Israeli military had expelled the Arab occupants. My father's uncle Monika, who had come ahead on an earlier ship, had a better spot, which included a courtyard.

Life in Israel was hard. My grandmother didn't speak Hebrew, of course, but unlike many refugees, she also didn't speak Yiddish or Ladino. And their Serbian-speaking community was tiny. In my family's new neighborhood, there were open sewers and sex workers walking the streets. In shock, my grandmother was unable to work the first several months.

But my family was better off than refugees who arrived later and spent months in camps with no place to go. By May 1949 there was no more empty Arab housing remaining unoccupied. In January 1949, after eight months of independence, 100,000 immigrants had arrived. By the end of that year, 90,000 refugees lived in seven camps. Those who came later, after the former British army camps were full, lived in new camps that lacked appropriate infrastructure.[2]

By the memorable snowstorm of 1950, my father was living with his mother and sister in the Blockonim, a neighborhood of cinderblock duplexes, a single room with a toilet in the yard. There were dirt roads and a septic system that overflowed. It has since been razed. At some point, my grandmother paid a local handyman to build an asbestos shelter over the walkway to the toilet. While the internet has given me the name of the Jewish neighborhood in Belgrade where my father was born, the name of the ship he sailed to Israel on, and details of the German bombing that killed his grandfather, my searches for "Blockonim" turn up empty.

An elderly couple from Turkey with grown children lived in the other half of the duplex; my father learned Ladino to talk with them. He commuted by bus, hitchhiking, and walking back to his old school in Jaffa, where his friends were. His friends were Bulgarian, so he picked up that language as well. Israel didn't have enough food, so austerity rationing was introduced in March 1949. My father worked odd jobs and raised rabbits to eat.

They had the furniture they had shipped from Belgrade in huge wooden crates, the cost covered by Jewish aid organizations or the young state of Israel. There was a wardrobe, a painting of fruit, a large table on which my grandmother would lay out her sewing fabric, and numerous chairs, which guests would sit on when they came for potlucks. My grandmother's sewing machine, which my father later modified from manual to electric, also made the journey. The crates were enormous; some people used them as an additional room. The rabbi they lived with after the war in Belgrade put the piano he had shipped to Israel in his crate. His son, who would one day be a general, would play it there.

When he was 15, my father felt there was no room for him in their one-room home. He decided to go live on Kibbutz Beit Oren. He learned to drive farm machinery on the country roads. He loved the people, but living there he didn't have his own socks. He realized he didn't want to live communally. After a year, he went back to living with his mother and sister.

My grandmother applied for and received German restitution money equal to an estimated portion of what my grandfather should have been earning. The German money survivors received was important for impoverished Israel as a whole. My grandmother used her funds to move with her children to a larger rental apartment and then purchased a new one-bedroom apartment that was to be built in Holon.

As long as I can remember, I've wanted to speak Hebrew. It was a code I wanted to crack when I heard my father speaking it to his Israeli friends. My mother learned quite a bit in the early years of my parents' marriage when it was still possible they would make a life in Israel. My parents spoke it when they didn't want me to understand what they were saying. I managed to pick up a few words. *Glida*, for example, is ice cream. But for the most part the language was a mystery. No matter how hard I listened when I attempted to eavesdrop, I didn't understand. This belief was reinforced during my years at Hebrew school where, despite its name, we only learned to read prayers, not speak conversationally. I developed a stubborn childhood belief that I didn't know Hebrew because I couldn't know it.

When Sophie started college, I realized I finally had time to learn. The previous two decades had been a whirlwind of homeschooling my kids, mainly as a single mother, and working part-time teaching childbirth classes and training childbirth educators and doulas. But with both kids launched, I enrolled in beginner Hebrew at Hebrew College.

I was unprepared for how rewarding class would be. There was a system to the code! I was learning words and speaking sentences. I could do this. It was the opposite of Hebrew school. Here was a group of adults I had something in common with. We helped each other and it was fun. It made me want to turn over every other unexamined childhood belief.

"H'kadur gadol," I repeat after the recorded voice. The ball is big. "H'kadur h'gadol," I say. The big ball. I'm 48 years old and finally speaking Hebrew. I have stacks of flashcards helping me ask where the bathroom is, tell time, comment on the weather. The surprise is not that it took this long. It's that I'm actually learning it.

My dad is pleased I'm learning Hebrew. My mom tells me she hears him bragging about it to his friends on the phone. "I was too focused on learning English and becoming an American to teach you when you were little," he tells me. "I guess I should pay for your classes," he jokes.

When I was a kid and he was busy running his business, he was sometimes impatient with me. In retirement, he has had unlimited time for his granddaughters. Waiting for Rebecca to be the last one out of the dance studio after class was no problem. Driving four hours round trip to bring a forgotten part of a homework assignment to her at her dorm at Connecticut College was not an inconvenience. Now I am also the recipient of this patience when I ask him for a word in Hebrew and 20 minutes later ask him again. "Learning a language is hard," he says sympathetically. I think of him twice immersed in a language he needed to learn rapidly to survive, trial by fire.

When we meet with his best friend Alex over Skype, my dad proudly tells him in Hebrew that I am learning to speak the language. "I really want to speak Hebrew," I say in Hebrew slowly, self-consciously. I am learning, but very slowly."

Meeting with my dad's old friend from Israel is my mother's idea. "He knew your grandmother," she tells me. "He might have stories. She sewed his wife's wedding dress."

Alex and his wife Vickie left Israel years ago and resettled in Brussels, where Alex had a photography store before retirement. My dad's old IDF buddies are all over the world now: Belgium, Australia, Israel, and the US. For years distance and their busy lives raising and supporting families separated them, but in retirement technology and a shared past reunite them. My dad arranges a three-way Skype call with Alex and me.

I haven't seen Alex in years, but it's the same smiling face, only older, looking back at me through my laptop screen. It's good to see him.

"I have nothing too much to tell you about your grandmother," he says. His English is halting but clear. It's one of his four languages. He was born in Bulgaria and came to Israel after the war. Then he learned French in Belgium. "She was a wonderful woman."

I wait in the not uncomfortable silence, hoping something more is coming.

"She was beautiful, and she smoked a lot," he says about my grandmother. "That's all I know. Really, I have nothing more. I'm sorry. Tell me about this book you are writing."

"I'm writing about my dad and what happened during the war," I explain to Alex. "But also about the Jews of Serbia because no one seems to know that."

"Ah yes," he says and smiles encouragingly on my screen. I feel close to him although we are thousands of miles apart. "Then you must tell it. It's just like that with the Jews from Bulgaria. No one knows how we suffered." And then he changes the subject and we are catching up about our families.

My dad stays on the call after Alex has hung up. "He told me he didn't remember anything," he says. "It was a long time ago and he only met her a few times. But it was because of him my mother had a proper burial."

Wait, I think here's the story. Let's call Alex back. But now my dad is telling the story. He wasn't at his mother's funeral. She died suddenly shortly after he came to the US to study. His friend Moshe's uncle, who had been his visa sponsor and hired him at his factory, told him she was gravely sick, gave him a plane ticket, and got him on a flight. Later my dad realized that this uncle must have known she was already dead to have moved so quickly and decisively. At that time in Israel, following Jewish custom, people were buried soon after death, the same day when possible. A son flying from America was no reason to wait. My father boarded a flight in Boston believing that his mother was sick, and when he landed in Tel Aviv, she was already buried. My aunt, who had lived with her mother and found her dead, dealt with funeral arrangements.

"Aunt Shosh hadn't donated to the Chevra Kadisha," my dad says, referring to the Jewish Burial Society. "A donation wasn't required, but the rabbi was stalling, trying to get one. Shosh told me that my friend Alex told the rabbi that if he didn't start the service right then, he'd put him in the grave with my mother."

8

My Serbian grandparents' family histories had been the most obscured of all my family lines. My efforts to uncover their stories were blocked by not knowing my paternal grandparents who might have told me stories and passed on details, by distance and then the Balkan Wars, and because I don't speak Serbian. Ashkenazi Jews who sought out their roots in Poland, Ukraine, and Germany laid the path for others to follow. Guides there knew the history and could pull documents and translate them. My Serbian family history felt more challenging to access.

Thanks to Barbara at Belgrade's Jewish Museum, a stranger I had met online, I had birth and marriage certificates and photos of long-hidden family graves. I was able to do as Noah Lederman describes in *A World Erased: A Grandson's Search for His Family's Holocaust Secrets*: "to rebuild that family that had completely vanished one summer day, to rescue something from the carnage... [it felt] like watching a coveted image develop in a darkroom."[1]

The 22 family documents Barbara sent stretch back to the mid-1800s. My great-grandfather Heinrich's birth certificate is dated May 14, 1876. My grandfather Alexander's is dated July 5, 1909. His *dat.orbez*, which I learn means the date of his bris took place as expected eight days later on July 12. Yugoslavia would not become a country for another nine years; they first had to survive World War I. Only then would US President Woodrow Wilson orchestrate the union of the southern Slavs.

My father's birth certificate is the last in the 22-document multigenerational succession. I am floored by this document, written proof he was the last link in a now-broken chain. He is rooted in that old world more than I or even my daughters now belong to the new country.

My dad's younger sister, my Israeli aunt, was born improbably in May 1942, after their father had been enslaved, imprisoned, and disappeared, after the Nazis declared Belgrade one of the first cities to be *Judenrein*, cleaned of Jews. She has no birth certificate at all.

I enter words and phrases from the documents into Google Translate and slowly puzzle out the broken English it spits back. I puzzle over how my grandfather and his brothers can all have different grandmothers until I realize *babica* isn't grandmother in Serbian, as Google insists, but midwife.

In addition to the three paternal uncles my father had known, I discover a fourth, Danilo, who died in early childhood, something no living family remembered. I learn my father's paternal grandmother, Regina, who died before he was born, came from a Sephardic family in Šabac.

For the first time, I can see my grandparents' marriage certificate documenting the union of two people I've never met. Now I know my grandparents' birthdays and the names of their parents. I can put a date to their wedding portrait: January 27, 1935. Hitler had been in power for two years.

My grandfather's name is Alexander Brill. If I had been a boy, it would have been mine. Instead, my younger brother inherited it, just as my father's paternal grandfather's name was passed on to him. But my grandmother's name is that of a stranger. I've never heard it before, and neither, it will turn out, has my father. He had told me it was Regina, but the family called her Delphi. Her birth name is Rene Jelisevata rebukes the certificate—one piece of paper, so few words, so many revelations.

I had never been satisfied with my father's survival story. "You were just living on your grandmother's farm?" I would ask. "You weren't hiding?" And he would shrug, implying that was all he remembered. As my critical thinking developed, I sometimes pressed him when the story came up. "But how did you survive the war?" His answer gave me a glimpse of the little boy he had been. "My grandmother and my mother were tough women. They weren't going to let anything bad happen to me."

I had thought my question about if my grandmother was born Jewish was unanswerable, but now, thanks to these documents, it's clear my grandmother converted. Laid bare, on my grandparents' marriage certificate is her Christian name: Rene Jelisevata. It's the name she was probably baptized with before she converted, married, bore two children, lost a husband to genocide, survived a world war, and emigrated to Israel. This evidence is more validation than surprise.

Barbara writes that my grandmother was born to a Christian family and likely converted before her wedding, though no documentation of a conversion is in their archives. I write back and ask why she might have changed her name. Barbara speculates my grandmother took her dead mother-in-law's name when she converted. Choosing Regina was a way for my grandmother to honor my great-grandmother.

After I've had time to absorb all this new information, I reflect on how my parents raised me to believe that being Jewish was special. I sensed that it connected me to other Jews around the world, not quite like extended family, but with a feeling that we were all related. At the same time, I felt separated from most of the world, who were Gentile. My security in feeling Jewish persists; it's the faith and culture I've been raised in. Besides that, Jewish lineage is passed from mother to child and my mother's heritage is secure. Because my grandmother converted, my father's Jewishness is also not in doubt. But now that I have learned that a quarter of my relatives and ancestors weren't Jewish, I share family in the wider world. Discovering that my family is less Jewish makes me feel more Serbian.

The documents raise as many questions as they answer. Where is the birth certificate for my father's cousin Simon? Why is my grandmother's mother's name listed as Tereza when my father remembers it was Radmila?

My father's birth certificate confirms his birthday as August 23. It reveals the date of his bris: September 4, and the name of the mohel: Ruben Sabitaj. The Jewish circumcision ceremony is usually performed on a baby boy's eighth day of life. According to Jewish law, illness is the only acceptable reason to delay a bris. My father's bris was four days late.

In 1938, under totalitarian rule, Hitler was building the German army and making clearer the danger he posed to peace. *Time Magazine* made the controversial choice to name him their Man of the Year, saying he was "the greatest threatening force that the democratic, freedom-loving world faces today." Five months before my father was born, Hitler invaded Austria and incorporated it into the German Reich. The following month, the Nazi government began seizing the property of German Jews. Two months before my father was born, Germany saw the first mass arrest of Jews, who were imprisoned in concentration camps. During the last days of my grandmother's pregnancy, in the heat of summer, as she watched her belly, wondered what labor would be like, and waited to meet her baby, SS authorities opened the Mauthausen concentration camp in Austria. That summer, 32 countries met in Evian, France, to discuss how to resettle German-Jewish refugees. However, most countries, including the United States, were unwilling to ease immigration restrictions.

My father remembers his mother told him she was uncertain if the bris would happen because of heightened antisemitism. His parents were likely concerned that in the future being marked as a Jew by circumcision would be dangerous. My grandfather considered himself a Serb first and then a Jew. A "Serbian of Moses' religion," I have learned was the expression used in legislation and widely accepted by Jews of my grandfather's generation.[2] Probably my great-grandfather, the child of a prominent Ashkenazi leader, considered a bris to be the covenant between God and the Jewish people. Maybe he and my grandfather argued. If so, my great-grandfather prevailed, but my grandfather was right about the imminent danger: during the German occupation my grandmother would tell my father he should never pee anywhere but home, even if it meant wetting his pants.

The bris may have been at my great-grandfather's home. My father's birth certificate tells us the street where his bris occurred is called Knjeginje Ljubice. On a map of Belgrade, my father and I can see this street. It is in the direction he remembers running with his mother during the German bombing, while the bombs overhead made that whistling sound. They were seeking the safety of his grandfather's basement.

Did my great-grandfather Heinrich hold his first grandson, my father, during the circumcision as is traditional? Did he feel satisfaction and relief that my father was being circumcised, despite the danger spreading in Europe? I've never seen a photograph of my great-grandfather. Perhaps, he looked like my father did almost two decades ago, when he was in his early sixties. I try to imagine my great-grandfather beaming when it is announced the baby is named Heinrich for him. I envision my grandfather standing near the mohel, a yarmulke on his usually uncovered head.

My father's parents were following the Sephardic tradition of naming the first son after the father's father, living or dead. If they had continued to follow this custom, the first daughter would have been named for her father's mother, Regina, the second son for his mother's father, Stevan, and the second daughter for her mother's mother, Radmila. But when my aunt was born after my grandfather disappeared, my grandmother named her Ljiljana, which translates as Lily. In May 1942, it was best to have a Serbian name.

"May this small infant Heinrich grow and become great. As you have come into the Covenant of Abraham, so may you come into Torah, into marriage, and into good deeds." My grandfather would have prayed in Hebrew. Born in 1876, my great-grandfather was just 62 and could reasonably hope to be an honored guest when my father married. Was he thinking about other grandchildren who would surely come from four healthy, grown sons? Was he looking forward to watching my father grow up, attending his bar mitzvah, and one day seeing him as a bridegroom under the chuppah? Being sandek, the one who holds the baby during the bris, is an honor and a blessing for long life.

The future was uncertain in 1938, but the coming horrors were unimaginable. It was impossible for my great-grandfather to foresee my father's bar mitzvah in Tel Aviv or his wedding in Boston. Even if I could reach across 80 years and 4,000 miles, what advice could I share from the safety of hindsight? If I could travel back across time and space, the sad truth is that even with almost three years' lead time, there was still almost no place in Europe where a Jewish family would be safe.

Recently my father told my squirming teenage nephew Jonah, "Holding you during your bris was both an honor and a very hard thing to do." Likely his grandfather felt similarly. I think of my father, standing in my kitchen, holding his first grandchild, my two-day-old, seven-pound daughter Rebecca. He asked my mother if he would get to dance at her wedding. My father cried when Rebecca was born, heaving sobs of relief and joy. A grandchild, especially the first, is a new generation going forward, a connection to the future. How far into that future does a grandparent, even a healthy one in middle age, dare to hope he will get to see? As my father held Rebecca's soft newborn cheek against his own, perhaps he looked back as well as forward, thinking of his parents who never got to hold a grandbaby of their own.

My great-grandfather was alive in 1938, but my father barely had a life with him. Heinrich was killed in the Nazi bombing in April 1941. My grandmother later speculated to my father that rather than stay in the safety of his basement shelter, Heinrich was heading out to help her and my father when the stairs collapsed and he was killed.

My midlife probing of my father revealed this information, and it becomes the most important thing I know about my great-grandfather. He has no grave, no surviving photographs, or letters. Nothing he owned has endured. My father is the only living person who remembers him, and that is with the haziness of a toddler's recollections. But now this idea survives. He was the sort of man who, even in his later years, ran toward his family in danger.

I imagine looking down from above, watching the scene. I see my great-grandfather as a portly man, like my father has become. Had the war not come to Belgrade, he might have matured to look something like my dad does now, his hair gray but still full, his cheeks broad and his brown eyes lively. The early morning surprise attack wakes my great-grandfather. First, he thinks the Yugoslav Air Force is performing aerobatics. There has been no declaration of war, after all. There's no way to know that in his fury, Hitler will delay attacking the Soviet Union for a month to punish and destroy Yugoslavia, starting with its capital which has no anti-aircraft defense. My great-grandfather gets an adrenaline surge as he realizes his neighborhood is under a surprise attack; he moves more quickly than his shape suggests is possible. He flashes back to the Austro-Hungarian bombing of Belgrade during World War I, when he was the father of young sons. Hurriedly, he laces his shoes and races out to help his namesake, my toddler father.

But that is in the dark future. I return to the happier moment in the summer of 1938. We have no photograph from the day of my father's bris, but I conjure up a black-and-white image of my grandmother holding her newborn while guests all lean in to admire him, and I wonder if there were any survivors beyond mother, child, and the two uncles.

The documents, though sparse, yield a depth of information, things my dad would have known if the war hadn't stolen them. The marriage of my great-grandparents, Heinrich and Regina was a mixed one, uniting the Ashkenazi and Sephardic communities, unusual for the time. Regina's parents, my great-great-grandparents, were Baruh and Rifka, the Hebrew version of my daughter's name: Rebecca. Danilo, my great-uncle who died as a toddler, had a bris that was delayed for two months, suggesting he was sickly from birth. My grandfather's profession on his marriage certificate is *poreznik*, which Google Translate tells me is exciseman, someone who collects a tax on goods. It's a definition that sheds no light on what my grandfather did for a living.

We're Sephardic and one of our family names is Ruso. Many Ashkenazim only took last names when the Habsburg emperor Joseph II required it in 1787. But Sephardic Jews often had family names that dated back to before their expulsion from Spain in 1492. Familytreedna.com tells me there are two Sephardic groups named Ruso; the smaller one is likely mine as they settled in northern Greece and Macedonia.[3]

That my grandmother's family was Christian was a secret hidden in plain sight. Her name on the marriage certificate, the name we had never heard before, Rene Jelisevata, is Christian. I feel relief to know the truth and the weight of knowing a secret. Does my dad know? Should I tell him?

9

Now I want to know more about my grandmother, whose childhood is suddenly so different than I had understood before. I have always pondered why she left Belgrade when her family was there, heading out with her husband's family to a new and developing country.

But now it seems more mysterious. Did she feel Jewish? Having a grandmother whose family wasn't Jewish anchors me more in Serbia, since Judaism is an ethnicity as well as a religion. Jews lived all over Europe while maintaining their own separate identity, languages, and cultures. But suddenly I was rooted in a new way in Serbia. I've discovered that I'm more Serbian than I understood before.

When I find this out, I know immediately I will tell my kids. I want to give them this piece of history they hadn't known was missing. This is their story too. Once you have your family history, it can't be taken away from you. To withhold it would be to keep a secret. I'd tried to raise them without secrets. Children sense when information is withheld, and it makes them doubt their instincts about the truth. They need those instincts to navigate their own lives.

I call my mother. "I hope you're sitting down," I say.

"Is it the kids? Is everyone okay?"

"Nothing like that, Mom," I said. "You know how I wanted to find out more about Dad's childhood? Well, the Jewish Museum in Belgrade just sent me an avalanche of information. I've got the birth certificates. I've got his parents' marriage certificate. I know when his bris was. And you know what else? My grandmother's family wasn't Jewish!"

In the silence that follows, I feel like I can hear my mother thinking, trying to fit this piece of information into everything she knows, into what she has learned from living with my father for half a century. I know she will be initially resistant to me rocking the boat. She seems to have never questioned the stories my father told her. She has seemingly skipped over the incongruous parts, the pieces that I couldn't let go. Could accepting the news somehow change something in her view of my father after over 50 years of marriage?

But the new information helps complete a mystery for her.

"Oh," she says. "Aunt Shosh told me a story once, years ago when we were first married, about fighting to get her mother buried in a Jewish cemetery in Israel. Now that makes sense."

Family secrets are missing pieces in a puzzle we convince ourselves aren't there. I wanted to believe what I knew fit together perfectly, that I was seeing the whole picture. But like a tongue working a rough spot on a tooth, I kept coming back to certain things. I find relief in knowing the truth because, in some way, I always knew the pieces didn't fit.

The missing piece has come in that email from Belgrade, and now the puzzle does fit together. We can see where the gap was. The existing pieces rearrange themselves to allow room for this piece of truth. The surface is smooth now, the puzzle is whole, and it's already hard to remember how it was without the new addition that completes it.

"We should tell Dad," I say. "Secrets are a burden. Let's get it out in the open. I'm going to tell my kids what I've learned. It's not my secret to keep. They should know about their history. And I think they will be interested and not upset."

My mom has the opposite reaction. She wants to bury the news; she doesn't want me to tell my kids or talk to my dad. Is it due to differences in our generations? She grew up in the sweep-everything-under-the-carpet 1950s, while my childhood in the 1970s was a time of more openness. Maybe all those years that I had been trying to figure out the mystery of my dad's survival, she had been actively trying not to. Knowing it now, it's hard to believe we all didn't see it before. It's what Christopher Bollas calls the "unthought known."

For a few days it seems constantly in my thoughts whenever I can let my mind wander. It's there as I walk my dog, drive, make dinner. I come to see her point.

My dad has carried this secret for his half-century-long marriage. Why make waves now? He is proud of being Jewish. "Jews are smart," he boasted to me many times when I was a child. He once told me a story of his uncle fighting as a Partisan outside Belgrade. They were preparing a roadside ambush of Germans. The Serbs were tough, but they needed a smart Jew to tell them not to shoot at the soldiers from opposite sides of the road. I have an urge to give the documents to my dad as a present for his birthday. But I don't want that present to include telling him he's Serbian. I want to protect him from possible disappointment.

A few days later I call my mom. "I've thought about what you said, and I agree now. Dad is almost 78. Let's leave his identity alone."

My mom says, "Actually, I think we are weakened by carrying secrets. So I talked to Dad. It turns out that he's known about his mother's conversion all along."

I feel relieved. My dad has been unburdened of his secret.

My dad and I never discuss that a truth has been revealed. While he's always been open about his childhood, in contrast to some survivors who never speak about what happened, there has always been a line that I haven't wanted to cross. He's alluded to seeing the horrors of war, and my research has fleshed out what he might remember by reading other survivor accounts that talk about bodies hanging from lampposts and stacked at the sides of Belgrade's streets. It's never been clear to me whether my father is protecting me from hearing about such horrors, or whether I have protected him from having to articulate them. I fold this untold story about his mother's Christian past in with the rest of what he prefers to remain unsaid; it's all part of the explanation of how he lived when he should have died. It's enough that we all know now that we know. From now on my father and I discuss our Christian family as though I've known about it all along.

I'm curious if he's relieved to be unburdened. Maybe he'd never intended to hide it exactly, but because he didn't tell my mother immediately, it became harder and harder to disclose. Perhaps it was something he never thought about; he knew who he was.

But knowing the truth changes who I know myself to be. I don't feel less Jewish, but now I am something else as well. Because my family history is different than I thought, I am different. My kids are different. I am a person with Christian ancestors. I am connected to another history. I am more deeply entrenched in Serbia.

Looking at the documents on my computer and scanning the photos of my relatives' graves and the whole Jewish cemetery, I begin to be able to put my father in context. It's fascinating to see he came from a long line of ancestors in a long-established Jewish community. He belonged in and to his birthplace. I begin to picture standing at the graves of my great-grandmother and great-great-grandparents and navigating the streets of the Jewish Quarter.

Barbara at the museum asks me to ask my father to record his memories, "if it's not too painful." He is one of the few now living with memories of prewar and occupied Belgrade. He says he will, but he's busy. He's retired, so I wonder if this is code for, *I will do it never.*

10

My father's earliest memory is the German bombing of Belgrade Hitler called Operation Retribution and Operation Punishment. The fierce attack was punishment for the coup against the government that had signed the Tripartite Pact, acquiescing to Germany in return for peace. When that agreement with Berlin, Rome, and Tokyo was signed on March 25, 1941, citizens protested in the streets. The largest demonstrations were in Belgrade. Protestors carried signs that said, "Better war than the pact" [*Bolje rat nego pakt*] and "Better the grave than a slave" [*Bolje grob nego rob*].

"There's no war without the Serbs," I read somewhere. Their huge losses in World War I, nearly half a million soldiers and another 700,000 civilians, almost 30 percent of the total population, were proportionally greater than any other country's. My grandmother's father Stevan was among these soldiers who never returned. Many men marched off to war in *pentafallas*, one of the few Serbian words I know, although until recently I assumed it was Hebrew. Originally Turkish, it means soft-soled shoes or slippers.

In World War I, Serbia's citizen soldiers were woefully undersupplied and unprepared, contributing to the devastatingly high loss of life. But that didn't seem to make the Serbs hold back from another world war. They overthrew the Royal Regency of Prince Pavle Karadjordjević and replaced him with the heir Prince Peter Karadjordjević, who was still underage. Air Force General Dušan Simović replaced Prime Minister Aleksandar Cincar-Marković. The new government declared Yugoslavia would remain neutral, but sent a message to Berlin on March 30, which tried to reassure Hitler that they would honor the Tripartite Pact.[1]

On March 26, *The New York Times* ran on page one an article entitled "CROWD ASKS FOR ARMS: Opposition Leaders Are Rounded Up in Capital—City Heavily Guarded." The *Times* reported an armed "irate peasantry," numbering in the thousands, from Central Serbia and the Montenegrin mountains were marching in their capitals, demanding arms and leadership to fight Germany. In response, the government banned the singing of war songs, "but the people sang their forbidden songs with a will and without interference." Serbian priests and monks had "fought with the peasants against suppressors and invaders for nearly 200 years" and now distributed pamphlets in cafés calling for revolt.

Three days before the bombing, Major Vladimir Kren defected and disclosed not just locations of military assets but bomb shelter locations as well. This worsened the civilian death toll, which included my great-grandfather. Lebel writes it was a revenge bombing with no military targets. "Two hundred forty-three bombers and 120 fighter planes performed 980 sorties and dropped about 440 tons of bombs. The number of victims was estimated at 3,000 dead and 15,000 wounded and tens of thousands of homeless people." Belgrade became a heap of ruins, with both living and dead trapped underneath.[2] Sources vary widely on the number of civilians killed. Ernest Powel puts the number at 20,000.[3] Perhaps there will never be an accurate estimate.

The Germans particularly targeted Dorćol, the Jewish Quarter. After the war, my father's uncle Bernhard listed my father's grandfather, Heinrich Brill the elder, in the victims' record at Yad Vashem. Does the targeting of the Jewish neighborhood make Heinrich a victim of the Shoah? It felt that way to Bernhard.

Hitler wanted Yugoslavia destroyed "with merciless brutality" because it had reneged on the Tripartite Pact.[4] He reportedly told his senior officers on March 26, "I have decided to destroy Yugoslavia." The bombing went on for three days. My father remembers sitting in the shelter with his mother, cousin, and strangers, all quiet and still.

Over one-third of the total housing stock and at least half of all buildings in the center of town were destroyed in the devastating Nazi air raids."[5] The National Library of Serbia, containing hundreds of thousands of rare books, maps, and medieval manuscripts was demolished. So were the royal palace, the military headquarters, the telegraph office, and railway and power stations. The Belgrade Zoo was hit, and frightened animals ran in the streets.

Dušan Makevejev, who was six years older than my father, remembers the bombing and occupation. He wrote that "buildings were cut in half. Once they were opened up, you could see dining tables, chandeliers, pictures untouched on the wall, here a dentist's surgery, there a bathroom with its tub." Without water or electricity, the smells were horrific. In the center of the city, a temporary public toilet was built in some bomb craters. There was a fence and separate entrances for men and women.[6]

The bombing began around 6:30 a.m. with hundreds of planes attacking. My father remembers the horrible sound dive bombers made as they closed in on their targets. The Royal Yugoslav Air Force was no match, and after the first round were no longer a threat to the Nazis. There was a second wave at about 10 a.m., a third wave around 2 p.m., and a final one at four. More attacks followed the next day. The attack on civilian targets, with no declaration of war, was a war crime. General Alexander Lohr was captured by the Yugoslavs at the end of the war and tried and executed for war crimes, including the bombing of Belgrade.

Was my dad sleeping when the first bombs were dropped? Was it their sound and vibration or his mother who woke him? Was he still in his pajamas when they ran? Charles Simic, a Pulitzer-Prize-winning American poet and former poet laureate, was born in Belgrade three months before my dad. He was two kilometers away from my father when the bombs started falling.[7] His poem "Cameo Appearance," about watching war footage of the bombing with his children and catching a glimpse of himself in a window reflection, captures my attention. Simic's words are lyrical and the sentiment he beautifully captures is the same as my father's, as he recalls standing "dazed in the burning city."

When I heard the story throughout my childhood, I imagined a night-time bombing like the Blitz. But Belgrade was attacked in broad daylight. If my great-grandfather was killed when the stairs collapsed, I realize now that the building had probably already been hit when my dad and grandmother took shelter in its basement.

The bombing lasted all day. My dad must have grown restless in the crowded shelter. Did he whine for something to eat? Relentlessly ask why they had to stay in the basement or when they could leave? Was my grandmother patient, crying, short-tempered? He remembers someone finally coming to tell them they could go home.

Did my grandmother cover my father's eyes as they walked through the streets, past the dead and the bombed-out buildings? Or is it his protective memory that allows him to retrieve the image of the shattered plate they found when they returned home, damage on a scale a child could understand, but nothing more? As a child, I imagined the plate was all that was destroyed. Understanding now the scale of the damage, knowing the synagogue directly behind his house was demolished, I consider what else was shattered. Were the windows blown out? Mirrors cracked? Picture frames broken?

"Fear, the most instantly communicable of viruses, spread in a city that only days earlier had been full of defiant demonstrations against the Nazis that displayed a typical Serb bravura,"[8] Roger Cohen writes about Belgrade in *Hearts Grown Brutal: The Sagas of Sarajevo*. I researched survivor accounts to try to recreate the images my father can't remember. Irena Damon, a young girl during the bombing, remembers running to a basement. The room was "already full of clusters of families huddled on the cold, damp, cement floor... The air was foul and full of dust. Children were screaming with fright and adults prayed. Some softly, and some screaming at God. Each person reached across their own bridge of faith to the depth of their belief in God. 'Shema Yisrael!', 'Jesus Christ!', 'Allahu Akbar' were some of the sounds that emanated from the mass of bodies on the floor."[9]

Another survivor remembered a strong wind fanned the flames as everyone fled in the same direction. "Through the chaos and smoke, I saw a man on the third floor of a building whose facade had been demolished. He was sitting at a piano, playing something. His playing could not be heard at all above the general confusion and the fire, but I've carried this image with me all my life."[10]

The image of a freshly ironed party dress flapping on its hanger where bombs had torn the walls open imprinted on a young girl: "It fluttered in the wind where three of our apartment walls had been as an enormous cloud of dust carried our hope and youth irretrievably away."[11]

Like me, Serbia is not finished dealing with its past. They are still unearthing unexploded German bombs. In June 2017, the government announced it would turn the site of the ruined National Library into a memorial garden.

When my father finally sits down to record his memories, he is focused. He reworks drafts with my mother and adds newly remembered details until he's satisfied. After several weeks, he emails his account to me. He's never written down his memories before. No one had ever asked him to.

I'm thrilled to be able to see his recollections laid out sequentially. Here are all the stories I had tried to piece together now neatly ordered. I email Barbara at the museum. I'm proud to know his experiences will now be permanently recorded in the museum's archives.

"Your father is a hero," she emails me back. He has shared his personal memories with a historian and been validated. His early childhood recollections fit into the outline of her understanding of the war in Serbia. I know my father is too modest to consider himself a hero, but I appreciate Barbara's recognition all these years after the fact. My father says he wouldn't wish a childhood like his on anyone. But he knows it taught him how to navigate through the world and made him who he is.

11

A trip to Belgrade is something I've thought about for years. Now it feels more urgent. My father is 78 and I want us to travel together before it becomes too difficult for him. I want to make my research more real, give it context, and get at more than I can find in a book or my computer. I want to walk down the streets we saw from the Google car's perspective months ago.

Place can elicit memory. Maybe as I stand with my dad at Solunska 8, where his earliest recollections took place, something new will bubble to the surface. Since I was little, I have imagined this city. Now I hope to see for myself. There will never be a better time. My dad feels the same. He has thought about going back for a long time. Though I have never been, I too talk about "going back to Serbia."

We begin planning a trip to the place my grandmother defiantly turned her back on in 1948. She turned away from Eastern Europe just as my mother's grandparents all had a generation earlier. Growing up during the Cold War had cemented for me that part of the world as an austere, vaguely threatening place. It was ingrained in me that Eastern Europe was a place Jews fled, not vacationed in.

Until I was ten, my father drove a yellow Triumph convertible he called the Zoom Zoom. The year before I was born, my parents picked it up in England, my dad navigating British roads that required him to hug the left side, while sitting on the left side of his car that he'd had specially constructed for the roads back home in the States. Then they sailed on a ferry across the English Channel so they could drive throughout western

Europe on a sort of belated honeymoon. Afterwards, they shipped the car home. I rarely got to go in that sports car. I rode in the backseat of my mom's red Chevy station wagon with her at the wheel, unless it was a family trip, in which case my dad drove. Sometimes he'd thread his right arm back to me so we could hold hands.

The few special times I went some place alone with my dad, it was in the Triumph. It was exciting sitting in the front seat, watching him shift, chewing sticks of his Wrigley's spearmint gum, not the sugar-free stuff my mom gave us. I felt grown up when we raced down the highway with the top down, my dad driving fast and fearless. The wind made my curls fly straight back and cooled the ink-black seats that had been hot to the touch. It seemed like we were getting away with something that wasn't quite allowed. The journey itself was the adventure. Now I am the one making an adventure together happen.

It's not the first trip I've taken as an adult with my father. A single mom from when my kids were four and seven, we often vacationed with my parents to share the responsibility of traveling with young children. We hiked with alpacas in western North Carolina, sunned ourselves on Florida's beaches, soaked in hot springs in Banff, and walked on a glacier in Jasper. We toured Buckingham Palace and straddled the Prime Meridian in Greenwich. We celebrated my mother's 70th birthday in the Caymans.

Five years earlier, we'd traveled to Israel to visit my aunt and cousins, climbed Masada at dawn, floated in the Dead Sea, and waded through the ancient Hezekiah Tunnel by flashlight. We'd visited the old port city of Jaffa where my dad lived in former Palestinian Arab housing in 1949 when he, my aunt, and my grandmother first left the refugee camp. My dad remembered visiting his old neighborhood once before, in the 1980s, when he'd been in Israel with his friend Phil. That time they'd knocked on the door of his old home. They initially mistook the Canadian teenager who answered as American.

"Dad," she'd called. "There's another man at the door who says he lived here."

The girl's father welcomed them in and explained that they'd once been visited by an Armenian who lived in East Jerusalem. He had been the owner until his family fled in the 1948 war. Now the state owned these homes, but they could live here on a long lease.

"I've never understood this odd archway," he said, pointing to a jagged shape overheard.

"Oh yes," my father remembered. "My uncles took down a wall here. Be careful, I doubt they considered if it was load bearing."

Standing by the Ben and Jerry's cart in present-day Jaffa, watching well-dressed people walk down clean streets, past well-kept homes with flower boxes, I'd tried to envision the open sewers and streetwalkers my dad remembered. I could imagine Israel and my father's life, but the deeper layer of his Serbian beginning was much more opaque.

"Are we really going?" my father asks repeatedly as I confirm dates, research flights, and read about hotels and restaurants, just as I do for any vacation. Is it as hard for him to believe this trip will happen as it is for me? He has only been back once since he moved to the States. He and his old friend Alex, who lives in Belgium, had driven to Belgrade from Brussels. I try to see what this must be like for him, to return to where he lived in three different worlds: the pre-war monarchy period when the old world was intact and his family was relatively affluent, the war when he lost his father and grandfather and lived on a horse farm, and the early Communist period when, with his mother and sister, he shared an apartment with four other survivors. In a sense, everyone's childhood is a lost country, but my dad's was literally lost. Now we are flying there on Air Serbia.

I assure him we are going, but none of it seems real. In my mind, my dad's childhood is inaccessible not only in time but in space. But Belgrade is a real place; Expedia sells plane tickets to its Nikola Tesla Airport. I read about general tourist sites: Kalemegdan, a prominent fortress my dad remembers from his childhood and Saint Sava, the giant church near where my dad's aunt lived that we saw on Google Maps. I examine Trip Advisor comments. I study US State Department travel warnings, relieved to see that Serbia looks pretty good if we avoid political demonstrations and sporting events. I look up if you can drink the water (no), do you need a visa (no), is there much street crime (no). I buy *A Travel Guide to Jewish Europe, Third Edition* online. This turns out to be a 752-page tome that doesn't mention the Balkans at all: Temple Isaiah Hebrew school all over again.

My dad emails his cousin Dragan who lives in Belgrade. Dragan's grandmother and mine were sisters, making us second cousins. He's as closely related as my mother's cousin who we see on holidays. He was born after the war but before my father left for Israel. I've known vaguely of his existence, although I'm not sure I've heard his name before. My aunt in Israel has kept in touch and visits periodically. She has kept up her Serbian. My father understands some but speaks less, although he believes if he were immersed in the language it would come back after a few weeks. Because

Dragan speaks little English, they have not had much contact, although Dragan has made many attempts. He seems to not believe that my father is no longer fluent in their mother tongue. While my father has been twice an immigrant, Dragan has lived his whole life in Belgrade. My grandmother's decision to convert has set her children and their families on a vastly different path.

When my 20-year-old daughter Rebecca hears about our trip she wants to come too. My dad and I are thrilled. She will see my dad's hometown. We will make discoveries together. My trip will be even more meaningful. The next generation will be learning this history firsthand from my father.

Through Barbara at the Jewish Museum, I connect with a Jewish scholar and licensed tour guide who tells me, "Aside to Serbian and Slovenian language, I speak English, Hebrew, and Spanish. So communication problem is solved."

Via email we discuss our itinerary. He will show us the remaining vestiges of Belgrade's Jewish community: the one remaining synagogue, the cemetery, and Dorćol, the Jewish neighborhood. We will visit Barbara at the Jewish Museum, which preserves what it can of a 500-year-old Jewish community that is now a shadow of its former self. At the cemetery we will see for ourselves the graves in the photos Barbara sent.

I make a reservation at the Hotel Moskva, the oldest hotel in Belgrade, located in the city center. It's a landmark; everybody there knows it. My dad remembers walking by it as a kid and seeing people eating in its café. Now we get to stay there.

I pack maple sugar candies to give to our Serbian cousins, our guide, and Barbara from the museum, as well as small stones so I can leave something from home on my family's tombstones. I look at the pebbles I've gathered to place far away; there are local family graves I've never visited. My maternal grandmother's family is buried 20 minutes away in Woburn in the Pride of Boston Cemetery, but I have never been. Suddenly, before I travel over 4,000 miles to find my father's family, it seems important to see the ones who are so close.

12

On a cold February day, my teenage daughter Sophie, my parents, and I visit my mother's family's graves. Sophie is surprised to learn we have family graves nearby we've never seen. She is happy to go and learn a bit of our history. We struggle to find the cemetery even with my phone's GPS, which seems ironic given that we could easily stroll along streets in Belgrade via Google Maps. The discomfort of the biting wind seems appropriate.

Over 100 years ago, when Woburn was the countryside, Jewish congregations and landsmanshafts, organizations of people from the same town in Europe, bought land and started walled cemeteries. Each one is compact. They line up shoulder to shoulder with each other against what is now a busy road. We park on a side street and cars stop to let a small family, bundled against the cold in hats, scarves, and bulky coats, cross to the cemetery.

We have no map of grave locations, so will need to go up and down each crowded row. But almost immediately my mother spots the grave of her grandfather Louis Silverstein.

"Do you remember him?" Sophie asks. A gray hat I knit her sits on her light-brown corkscrew curls. Her cheeks are flushed with cold.

"No," my mother says. "He died in 1938, four years before I was born. He came from Ukraine with his sister Leah just after the turn of the last century. They came through Ellis Island and settled in Boston. He made deliveries for a bakery with a horse and cart."

Louis left his wife Rebecca and four children, who would join him when he was settled and able to send money for the passage. This was the typical Jewish migration pattern across Europe. I have an 8x10 inch sepia photograph Rebecca sent him of her and the children during their separation that lasted several years. The boys are holding their prayer books and wearing hats. All four children look solemn, and Rebecca seems stern and matronly. I suspect they are dressed in their best clothes in this please-don't-forget-us picture. No one smiles, as was the custom, but it felt to me as a child staring at their young faces like they were looking back across their struggles in the old country or forward to an uncertain future in a strange land.

What gave Louis the strength and conviction to get up one morning and leave their home forever? I imagine him walking away down a dirt road or perhaps catching a ride in a farmer's wagon, his family standing in the yard, watching him go. They were the only Jews in their Ukrainian village, where they supported themselves by running a store. Did he doubt if he'd ever see them again? Second-guess his decision? Pogroms, organized attacks against Jews and their homes and businesses, happened in waves with relative calm in between. Still, antisemitism must have been much worse than an uncertain future thousands of miles away.

In 1905, when Louis likely began to plan to emigrate, there was a wave of pogroms across the Pale. Hundreds of Jews were killed, and thousands injured. I think of Somali Warsan Shire's poem, "No one leaves home unless home is the mouth of a shark... you only leave home when home won't let you stay."

A family recording of Rose, the oldest sibling and my great-aunt, includes a story about the journey that involved sneaking across a potato field that was a border (what border?) at night because Kyiv was too far for them to go for passports. One of the brothers carried Mina, the youngest. Were they shot at, or was that from my grandfather's story of a border crossing?

The family made their way to Boston, where they lived first in Malden and later in Dorchester and Roxbury. They lived in triple-deckers alongside their immigrant neighbors, many of whom I can see from census records were also Yiddish-speaking Jews from Eastern Europe.

My grandmother Sophie was the fifth and final child, born in 1910, a year or two after the family reunited. Her mother died when she was six, so she was raised mainly by her sister Rose, who was 16 years her senior. I vaguely remember Rose who died in 1979 and is buried here.

My grandmother didn't learn English until she started school, but she had clearly mastered it quickly. She tested into Girls' Latin School, the first college preparatory high school for girls in the country. Every day she walked into the school under a sign that read in Latin, "Here is an open field for talent; appreciative recognition is assured to the deserving; diligent application is honored with due rewards."

Those words proved true for my grandmother. She studied at Jackson College, then the women's college of Tufts University. She went back and forth between the campus and her home in Dorchester by trolley car. She majored in biology and went to obligatory chapel masses on Sundays. While working in a lab, she met my grandfather. Perhaps by then she thought she might never marry; she was 29. A generation later, she likely would have become a doctor like her brother. Instead, she married one.

In the early years of their marriage, my grandfather was a general practitioner for the Boston suburb of Dedham. His office was on the first floor and the family lived upstairs. My mother remembers coming down from dinner to let in a patient who had arrived early for evening office hours. My grandfather made house calls as well and delivered babies at home. When they could afford it, the family moved out of the building where my grandfather worked, three and a half miles away to a brand-new home in Chestnut Hill, where they would have Jewish neighbors. It was roomier, though modest by today's suburban standards: three bedrooms, two and a half baths, a one-car garage, and an unfinished basement. There was also a one-story summer beach cottage in Scituate. A few years before she died, my grandmother, not wanting to face living alone through another New England winter, moved to an assisted living facility in Jamaica Plain. She lived her whole life in Boston and the neighborhoods just a few miles beyond its borders.

We stand in front of my great-grandfather Louis's grave. He is buried so far from Ukraine where he was born. Somewhere in that distant countryside are the graves of his parents, grandparents, and great-grandparents, but the locations and even their names are lost to history. He broke that line when he left for America, a decision that saved his life and his children's lives. A generation later, Nazis would occupy Ukraine, which in 1941 had the biggest Jewish population in Europe. Most were shot near where they lived and buried in mass graves. We don't know the names of Louis's siblings, besides his sister Leah who came to Boston. Who was left behind and is now lost in an unmarked grave?

We place pebbles on Louis's grave, observing the Jewish tradition of marking we have been here. We split up to continue searching. Up and down the crowded rows, reading stones, each hinting at its own story. Two generations of Jews who left Eastern Europe around the turn of the last century, seeking better lives for their children in the New Country. We are the only ones here today looking for clues about them.

I call out, "I found Rebecca!" I can see my breath in the frozen air.

My parents and Sophie make their way along the narrow paths to see. My mother stops to bend over. Her gloved hand picks up a pebble from the pathway to place on the grave. Rebecca was my great-grandmother, Louis's wife. My oldest daughter is her namesake. I am sad she is not buried with her husband, but the graves are ordered by date. It seems they were purchased individually when there was a need. In 1916 Rebecca died at age 45, about the age I am now.

We find my grandmother's brother Henry, his wife Anna, Louis's uncle Abraham, his wife Mary, and their daughter Bessie. They are buried together, perhaps a sign of a level of prosperity that allowed them to purchase graves in advance. We speculate Louis came to Boston because Abraham was already here. There is no one alive who knows.

I named my younger daughter after my grandmother Sophie, who is buried with my grandfather, his parents, and my aunt and uncle in a greener, more spacious cemetery in Sharon, Massachusetts. My grandfather's parents had the foresight and funds to purchase a group of plots in the 1950s. They were pharmacists who met at the University of Moscow. My grandmother, Sonia, who my middle name Sarah is after, was from Lithuania and her husband was from Romania. After they married, they lived for a while in Lodz, then Russia, now Poland, where my grandfather Yacov, later James, was born in 1910. After living in Odessa, they immigrated to Boston in 1922 when the borders of the United States were already closing. They were coming in under three different quotas, and the Lithuanian one was full. So they waited on a Boston harbor island while Sonia's brothers, who were already here, got help from a Massachusetts senator from Lithuania.

My grandfather seemingly lived the American dream, arriving speaking "only" Yiddish, Russian, and Polish. He was put in the first grade at 12—too big for the desk—until he learned English. He graduated from Boston Latin High School, Clark University, and Boston University Medical School. He served as an army doctor in World War II.

My grandfather, who my brother and I called Papa, was a gentle man who liked bird watching and gardening. At home, even in the garden or relaxing in the backyard on a lawn chair, he wore the dress shirts, slacks, and leather shoes he saw patients in. He seemed to have only one type of clothes—work clothes.

Papa would call me Shorty and place me on top of the refrigerator when I was tiny enough to fit there if I tucked my head. I loved the view from beside the cardboard cereal boxes; I could look down on the heads of the grown-ups. It seemed slightly absurd to be so tall, a joke the two of us shared. The game was he would look for me in kitchen cabinets, under the table, behind cookbooks, in drawers, and everywhere but where I was while I giggled and called to him.

My grandfather was an only child, unusual for the early 1900s. When I discovered I was a Tay Sachs carrier before I conceived my first daughter, I speculated if the gene had been passed down from him. Tay Sachs is an extremely rare genetic disorder in the general population but carried by about one in thirty Ashkenazi Jews. Carriers are unaffected, and one theory posits they are provided some protection against tuberculosis, but when a child is conceived with two genes, they usually don't live past toddlerhood.

When I was little, we'd have dinner at my grandparents' and before we left for the half-hour drive home, my mother would change us into pajamas in their living room. I hated it. It seemed appropriate for my little brother, but at five or six I was clearly too old. So humiliating.

Yiddish was the mother tongue of both my maternal grandparents. My grandmother would stand by the door and say to my grandfather in Yiddish, "We need to go to bed because our guests want to go home." I didn't speak a word of Yiddish, but I learned to recognize what she was saying because of the setting. And I got the humor. I knew the language tied them to an Old World I wasn't a part of. Even my mother didn't speak Yiddish. It was what the grown-ups spoke around her when she was a child and they didn't want her to understand. She and I, we were American. Not like my grandparents and not like my dad.

In my quest for family information, I email my dad's sister Shoshana who lives in Holon, Israel. She sends me photos my dad has never seen. There's my grandmother. She's 46, her children also grown, smiling with her mother and sister, slender and young, just four years before her death. She had traveled home for the first time, using German restitution money for her trip, to bring her sister back for an extended visit. This was possible because it was six years before Yugoslavia would cut diplomatic relations with Israel due to the Six-Day War.

Seeing my grandmother at my age makes me feel like we could be friends, and there's so much I'd love to ask her. I want to know the details of how she survived the war, pregnant, and then with two young children. I wonder what it was like to convert and then move to Israel even though her husband was gone. How could she leave it all behind: family, culture, language?

Shosh gives me more new information. My grandmother's family came from Germany, although to me Francezi sounds Italian. My grandparents met at a dance hall. My grandmother had a boyfriend at the time, a career soldier who was often away. When my aunt visited in the 1980s that boyfriend wanted to meet her. He had never married and would leave his money to Shosh if she moved to Belgrade, but she declined.

She tells me, "My mother was like me." She means that both their fathers were killed in a world war before they were born. Belgrade is a city with layers of wars.

PHOTOS

Alexander and Regina Brill, in their wedding photo in 1935

Alexander and Haim, winter of 1938-39

Regina and Haim in a Belgrade park, 1940

Haim with Regina and Radmila, 1940

Dr. Bernhard Brill, date unknown

Twin brothers Filip and Heinrich, date unknown

Radmila, date unknown

Jewish men of Belgrade reporting for forced registration to the occupying Germans, April 1941. The author's grandfather is somewhere in this crowd. (Bundesarchiv, Bild 1011-185-0112-08/Neubauer/CC-BY-SA 3.0)

List showing Alexander Brill was registered #182 when the Jewish men of Belgrade were forced to register, April 1941

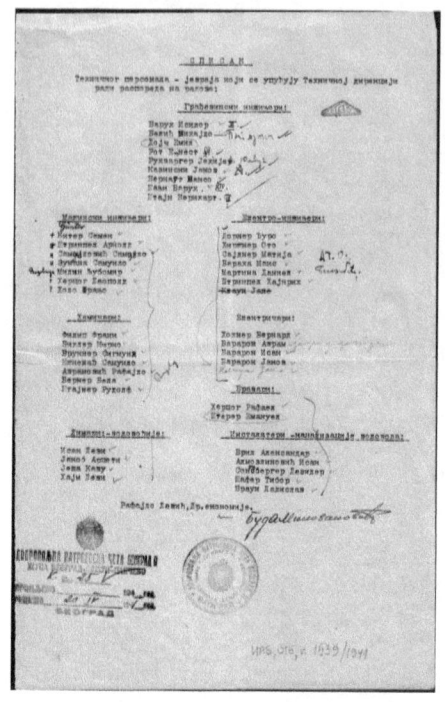

List showing Alexander and other Jewish men reporting for slave labor, April 20, 1941

Street pass giving Alexander and some of his Jewish neighbors permission to be on the street as they walked to and from work on a slave crew repairing sewer lines destroyed by the German bombing, April 21, 1941

Haim and Shoshana on the street in Belgrade during the war

Haim, Regina, and Shoshana as new immigrants to Israel, 1949

Haim and Julie, 1970

13

Rebecca and I look at the Air Serbia sign and exchange a glance that means "we are actually doing this." I photograph it for a Facebook post, to show our family that our trip is finally starting. Of course, Serbia is a place you can fly to, but it had almost felt as mythical a destination as The Land of Oz or Neverland.

In 2017, after a week vacationing in England, we're at London's Heathrow Airport, at the gate for the single daily flight to Belgrade. We are three adults, but I feel I alone am responsible for my elderly father and my 21-year-old daughter. I am the one who sparked this trip. Why am I so focused, even obsessed, with squeezing every ounce of story out of my father's childhood memories and faded foreign documents?

The waiting passengers are mostly well-dressed men, European business travelers. My dad asks one about taxis from the airport and I take a picture of a number on the man's phone. The three shiny navy-blue US passports I clutch with our boarding passes in my right hand stand out among other travelers' crimson Old-World ones. We seem to be the only Americans and Rebecca and I are two of a handful of women.

The flight attendant at the gate starts the pre-boarding announcement, asking everyone to remain seated. As one, the crowd ignores her and rises to form a line. I see this behavior again when the plane lands. The pilot makes the standard announcement: we will be taxiing, and instead of staying seated, everyone on the aisle stands in unison and begins reaching for luggage. Rebecca and I laugh. My father's tendency to elbow his way through a crowd, which sometimes feels embarrassing, reads as a national trait.

Belgrade's airport is named after inventor Nikola Tesla and a museum in Belgrade is devoted to him. He is a Serbian hero, a celebrated favorite son, although the little I knew about him before focused on his life as an American immigrant. If his Serbian origins were mentioned at all, they were a footnote. American history is one of arrival, and here it includes those who departed. Serbia still holds claim to its emigrants. They are still Serbian sons and daughters. We will see that attitude encompass my dad, my daughter, and me.

We don't have to wait for checked luggage because we have none. Traveling light is a family tradition. Since my childhood, the rule has been carry-ons only. I've taught my kids to travel with just what will fit in the overhead compartment: a week's worth of shirts and underwear, an extra pair of shoes, a raincoat, a sweater, one dress, and a toothbrush. My luxury is four 3oz bottles of conditioner for my curly hair that I filled before we left. If we haven't packed it, we don't need it.

The three of us walk through passport control and customs, which seem like nothing at all; unlike flying into London's Gatwick airport, leaving the European Union is a non-event. There, on the other side of customs, my dad spots his cousin Dragan and his wife Lejla. They have unexpectedly come to say hello. Dragan's grandmother and mine were sisters, and apparently family is family. They greet us with the traditional Serbian greeting consisting of three kisses, on the left cheek, then the right, then the left again. We don't need a common language to feel their warmth. Their car is too small to take us, but they plan to meet us later at our hotel. In an instant they have gone from being a vague idea to our flesh-and-blood Serbian family.

At the Hotel Moskva in the city center, we walk up stone steps with red carpet, through gold-framed glass doors, and into a lobby with chandeliers and uniformed doormen. The hotel is grand in both senses of the word, sizeable and sophisticated.

After almost three years of construction, King Peter I presided over the hotel's opening in 1908. It was the largest privately owned building in Serbia at the time. Built with Russian financing, it signified the government turning its foreign and economic policies away from Austria-Hungary and towards the Russian Empire.

The exchange rate allows us a two-level suite with two bathrooms and a sitting room for less than our room in London. It is a far cry from the type of place we usually stay, but here it's affordable. My dad once walked these streets; a skinny, fatherless neighborhood kid who watched diners with money in their pockets eat pastries and drink coffee. He saved his coins to buy a sausage like the ones he saw the patron enjoying Now he's an elderly American with a credit card limit that allows him to travel globally and stay in a suite above the restaurant.

During World War II, the Gestapo transformed the hotel into its headquarters; it was one of the last Belgrade buildings to be liberated in October 1944. I ponder if a high-ranking officer lived in our luxurious space. I don't know if by staying here we are ignoring the building's horrific past or reclaiming Belgrade's elegant central hotel.

Across the street is a *palačinki* stand. Palačinki, one of the few Serbian words I know, is similar to a crepe and rolled with treats like sugar, nuts, raisins, Nutella, and apples. My mother makes them on leisurely weekend mornings.[1] Each one is cooked individually, so it's slow going. I've never seen the word written down or heard it spoken outside my family. I text a picture of the stand to my mother, my brother, and my daughter Sophie, who is surprised to learn palačinki are Serbian and not Jewish as she had assumed. We know so little about our Serbian heritage.

In the morning my father moves slowly, hampered by a newly developed arrhythmia that leaves him winded after only slight exertion and by extreme swelling in his legs from a new medication. He was tired on vacation in England, complaining that 45 minutes at Stonehenge was too long. But this morning, despite his slow pace, he's as excited as the ten-year-old who left. His eyes sparkle.

At 9 a.m., the time we are to meet our guide in the lobby, my father is still sitting in the restaurant's outdoor café, cloth napkin in his lap. He is sipping the strong black European coffee he loves and eating cold meats and dried fruit from the breakfast buffet. His first plate, which he has leisurely emptied of its omelet and vegetables, waits to be cleared by one of the waiters wearing white button-down shirts and black vests. They circulate, attending to their guests, mostly foreigners on bus tours who will spend one day being shepherded through Belgrade's attractions and be across the Romanian or Hungarian border by nightfall. "Keep your passports accessible," a sign in the dining room reminds one American tour group, above a description of their morning tour of the city that includes the old fortress of Kalemegdan and the not-yet-completed St. Sava Church.

I glance at the prominent golden wall clock and then at my father's face. While I'm eager to start, my thoughts racing with everything I've planned for us to do today, my father is unhurried; his face is serene. I don't know if he could move faster, but he sees no need to. For him, breakfast in the elegant Hotel Moskva is the first thing we are doing today. He smiles across the table at Rebecca who is texting her friend. She hasn't finished her palačinki.

"I'll go meet our guide and let him know you're coming soon," I say.

On the burgundy couch below an imposing gold-framed mirror, our guide is waiting. As he rises to shake my hand, his face, middle-aged with graying eyebrows, looks familiar, although we've never met. A few minutes later, as he stands next to my dad discussing our day, I'm struck by their resemblance, their broad faces, and similar coloring and body type. They could be cousins. I don't know him but there's an immediate connection across our shared heritage. It's quite possible we share ancestors.

Our guide explains he is a Jew from Croatia. Born a few years after the war, he speaks Hebrew and has been to Israel to visit his daughter many times. He could claim Israeli residence, but he chooses to live here. His passion for history and Judaism is clear as he becomes animated describing our itinerary for the next two days.

"We will go to the synagogue," he says, "and then to the street where you lived. We will also go to the Jewish Museum, the cemetery, three Holocaust sites, two monuments, and to the top two tourist attractions in Belgrade: the ancient Kalemegdan Fortress and the massive St. Sava Church, the largest Orthodox Church outside of Russia."

We are welcomed here as Serbians, but we are also foreigners returning to our roots to puzzle out our past. As our guide lays out our agenda, he seems calm in what I realize is a familiar role. He makes his living guiding Jews, some with Serbian roots, around Belgrade and the rest of Serbia. We are not the only ones to have found our way back to this spot. Unwittingly, I understand now we are playing a part in a drama he has witnessed many times.

I want to track down information about my grandmother's family. I ask about visiting the archives. Our guide is discouraging, saying it was mostly destroyed in the war. The irony is while many of my Jewish family's records are intact and easily accessible through the Jewish Museum, my Christian family's information seems lost.

Standing under a gold chandelier in the lobby, our guide relays how the plot to kill the heir to the Austro-Hungarian throne, Archduke Ferdinand, the spark that started World War I, was hatched here in our hotel. Some of the plotters were Jewish. "Jews are the spice of every story," he says with a flourish. I can tell how passionate he is by how his hands move as he talks.

"One million Jewish soldiers served in that war and millions of Jews in Eastern Europe lost their homes," our guide says. "Jews on both sides were suspected of collaboration with the enemy. In response to Ferdinand's assassination, Germany entered World War I on the ninth day of the Hebrew month of Av, the same day the holy temples were destroyed in 423 BCE and 69 CE, and Jews were expelled from Spain in 1492."

We walk outside and stand in the sun on the sidewalk. Pedestrians pass us. The conversation shifts to the occupation. "Survival was not the norm," our guide reminds us. "Most Jews were killed; only those few who were able to get out before the war or who joined the Partisans survived."

He turns to my father. "You were lucky to get out in time."

My dad corrects him. "We survived the war here in Belgrade because my grandmother was not Jewish. My mother, sister, and I lived with her on her horse farm in Topčider. I used to watch the German officers come and ride my grandmother's horses." My father is nonchalant as he reveals the information I've only recently discovered, the story that he kept from us for decades.

How improbable it all sounds. So much had to happen for us to be standing here on the street. The most incredible events enabled my birth and my safe childhood on the outskirts of Boston. My dad, his mother, and his sister had to somehow survive the Nazi occupation, then make their way to Israel. Then my dad had to make it through his IDF service and do well enough in school, be lucky enough to have a friend whose uncle would be his American sponsor, and have the gumption to immigrate to Boston. He had to meet and marry my mother. Then one day in his late seventies, he had to agree to go on this return trip with me. I can't help but feel it's all *bashert* [destiny], the sort of impossible outcome that by its very nature implies divine assistance.

I must recognize the Holocaust itself is a part of who we are. It's the reason my father was displaced from the life it once seemed certain he would live in Belgrade. We are part of the post-Holocaust chapter. We are part of the generations Hitler tried to prevent. And yet, without the Holocaust, we would not exist.

Our guide appears unsurprised at our mixed heritage. His father was born Jewish, while his mother converted, and his wife is also a Jew by choice.

My mixed family seems to be a known part of the Serbian narrative and, more broadly, of the Ottoman Empire, which was more tolerant than Western Europe. Our personal history fits into a greater context I am just beginning to understand. Our guide and my dad share a Serbian and Jewish culture I know so little about.

We stand in our compact group on the sidewalk, trying to be out of the way of passersby. I know we don't look like locals and I feel conspicuous in our foreignness.

Our guide gestures to Rebecca's phone. He wants her to video my father. I am grateful he thought of this documentation I want but have felt awkward asking for. As my father reminisces Rebecca begins recording. There will be a record of his memories, of this piece of our family history. Elie Wiesel said listening to a witness makes you a witness, and I've brought my daughter so she can bring our family story forward to the generations that will hopefully follow.

I glance over at Rebecca. Her long dark curls are scooped off her neck in a ponytail in anticipation of the day's coming heat. I glimpse the toddler she once was who could fit underneath my pregnant belly, so close to me that she could disappear. More than once, I looked around and called her name, only to find her right beside me, looking up with bright blue eyes under long, dark lashes.

I'm so grateful Rebecca is here. In a t-shirt, denim shorts, and sneakers, iPhone in hand, she could be a young American traveler anywhere in the world. She is listening intently, her face focused with the expression she uses on museum tours and map reading.

But this isn't a vacation. I hope her attentive brain is hard at work creating an indelible recording of this moment. When she's my age, I hope she will be telling her children about this trip. I hope there will be grandchildren listening to this story when she's my dad's age. *L'dor v'dor*, generation to generation, is the expression in Hebrew. Today in Belgrade we touch both the past and the future.

On Rebecca's screen, I see my father in a short-sleeve button-down shirt and khakis. His bulky Nikon lies on his round belly; his sunglasses rest on his full head of graying hair. Like Rebecca, he looks like a tourist, but he can never be one here in his hometown.

"A relative of my mother by marriage lived here," he says, pointing across the square, his memory reaching back across 70 years. "She was the wife of my mother's brother Joseph who died before the war. She was living on the top.

The elevator only goes that far up," he gestures. "And then there's machinery." He circles his hand to show gears rotating. "And she was living alone right there. The elevator didn't go to her room."

The elevator mechanics impressed him, a boy who would grow up to be an engineer. I have lived in the same town nearly my entire life, so it's hard for me to think what I would remember from before the age of ten if I had moved away.

"Have you been upstairs?" our guide asks.

"Yeah," says my dad. "I went there with my mother and sister to say goodbye in 1948 when we were getting ready to go to Israel. My aunt was an alcoholic, which is not unusual here."

I've thought a good deal about my dad going to Israel but somehow never focused much on his departure from Serbia. For the first time, I imagine my grandmother, hand in hand with both children, visiting each family member for the last time.

My aunt Shosh told me her maternal uncle Joseph died in 1934 before my grandparents were married. My grandmother was wearing mourning clothes right up until the wedding.

The Serbs violently resisted the occupation, and the Germans responded with brutality. German soldiers forced Joseph's widow to call out to her only child, a son who was fighting as a Partisan, to lure him from his hiding place in the woods. Then they killed him. Standing here gives the story context. This broken, despairing aunt lived right over there, above the elevator. It's no wonder she drank.

One of my unanswerable questions is why my grandmother left her family and brought her two young children to Israel. She came here to say goodbye to her widowed, alcoholic sister-in-law, one of many final goodbyes. Was she trying to get away from this desperation and loss? Did Israel seem like a fresh start? "God helps those who help themselves," she would tell her kids. Was this her way of helping them? Did she believe this was what God wanted—to raise Jewish kids in Eretz Yisrael?

"Well," our guide nods agreeably. "Do you remember what she was drinking? Slivovitz or wine?"

My dad just shrugs. This detail is unimportant to him. And our guide continues with our tour.

I see now this trip is allowing us to dig down through the layers of my father's life. Before he was Israeli, he was thoroughly Serbian. I realize in this moment that we are not just from Serbia or Belgrade. We are from right here. My dad remembered a story I hadn't heard before; his memory was triggered by location. We are in a place completely familiar to him. This foreign place was his home; my kids and I are from here.

14

We head for Dorćol. Belgrade once had the third-largest Jewish community in the Balkans, after Istanbul in Turkey and Thessaloniki in Greece. Residents were mostly merchants and artisans.[1] A thriving Jewish center with the first Ladino newspaper, the city had two Sephardic synagogues and an Ashkenazi one at the start of World War II.

We stop at a traditional market. Everything here is organic by default since the small farmers can't afford to import pesticides. In a whispered aside, our guide points out who are the real farmers, rather than the middlemen. These old people look to me like the peasants in the time of the Yugoslavian kings, the proletariat under Tito. The men wear overalls, and the women wear headscarves to keep their long white hair back off their wrinkled faces. Their sunken mouths hint at missing teeth. Their gnarled hands never stop moving as they trade bags of fruit for cash, make change from coins in their pockets, and rearrange the remaining produce on their tables. We buy cherries and strawberries that drip juice when we bite into them.

We walk through a pedestrian mall, my dad sharing memory fragments, Rebecca recording them. I don't know what this day will hold, and I hope her resilience will carry her through. I shielded my daughters from this harsh history when they were children. But Rebecca is 21 and there will be no shielding her today.

My dad was a city kid and Belgrade was his city. He knows exactly where we are as we traverse neighborhoods.

"There wasn't much to do after the war," he says. "It wasn't like there were televisions. I used to go out and walk for hours."

As we cross Republic Square and pass the National Theater he remarks casually, "I saw a show here with my mother."

Our guide points out the National Museum, the oldest and largest museum in Serbia, which has been closed for 15 years for lack of funding. A sculpture of a man on a horse sits in the center of the square.

"This is a monument," our guide explains, "of Prince Mihailo. When it was erected in 1882, it was the first equestrian figure of a ruler in Serbia. Serbia had just gained independence from the Ottoman Empire four years before. The prince is bareheaded, unusual for a rider at that time."

My dad repeats a rumor, which our guide has never heard and thinks untrue: at the unveiling a child pointed out the rider had no hat, and the artist killed himself in disgrace.

There is no obvious boundary around the formerly vibrant Jewish neighborhood. Here, as everywhere else in the Ottoman Empire, there were no Jewish ghettos or pogroms. Jews were welcome to settle, free to practice their religion and live where they chose.[2] The practice of forcing Jews into ghettos occurred throughout Catholic Europe. The Venetian Ghetto is the first place where Jews were forced to live in a walled-off section of the city—with a curfew enforced by armed guards. The word ghetto is derived from the Jewish ghetto in Venice.[3]

Our guide stops in front of a gated synagogue. "Sukkat Shalom [House of Peace] is the only remaining synagogue in Belgrade and the only active synagogue in Serbia," our guide shouts to be heard above the noisy construction on the street. "This temple services the tiny remaining Jewish community, Ashkenazi and Sephardic. Once it was the Ashkenazi synagogue, the center of the city's Ashkenazi life, and there were also older Sephardic synagogues. Before World War I, the Ashkenazim wanted to build a synagogue with a school and community offices. The war delayed construction."

After additional fundraising due to currency devaluation, the cornerstone was finally laid on June 15, 1924. King Alexander signed the charter that is sealed in the cornerstone. There was a mikvah or ritual bath, a student mess hall, a gymnasium, and an apartment for the kosher slaughterer on the ground floor. Upstairs, above the sanctuary, were apartments for the rabbi and teachers. The classrooms were in the attic.[4]

Standing outside the synagogue, I feel obviously foreign, American, and Jewish, exposed in front of the construction workers and those passing by. I consider if they have a deep enough grasp of the history of this neighborhood to guess who we might be and why we have returned.

It is a relief when we pass through the front gate and have an unobstructed view of a plain-looking, five-story building with a Star of David in a circle of glass near the point of its roof. Were it not for the six-pointed star, its appearance would be instantly forgettable. The kind of bland place I would likely walk right past.

Is this where my grandmother converted? Did she purify herself for the occasion in the mikvah, with a mikvah lady helping her through unfamiliar rituals? Did she pray here? Perhaps my grandparents and my great-grandparents married here. Sukkat Shalom could have been an important place for my family before the war. Or it could have been that my Ashkenazi great-grandfather prayed with his Sephardic wife and the larger Sephardic community in one of those synagogues that no longer stand. No one alive knows.

The doors are locked and the woman who keeps the key is not in. It seems we will not be able to see the interior, but then the rabbi comes along and opens the door. It closes behind us, providing welcome relief from the jackhammer on the street. The young rabbi says hello, lifting his baseball hat to scratch his head, and we can see the yarmulke hidden underneath like the synagogue locked behind its gate. I wonder if he hides his yarmulke intentionally when he is beyond the safety of these walls. He hurries off, dashing up the stairs.

The interior is simple, a small room with hard wooden benches that look like church pews, a sharp contrast to the chairs with plush cushions in my childhood temple. On High Holidays overflow seats waited in rows stretched out beyond the opened accordion doors. A crowd of assimilated Jews, most of whom came to pray only once a year, parked on the side of surrounding roads once the parking lot filled. They would cross the street aided by a police officer who stopped drivers on their way to an ordinary day in a neighborhood that, in a few months, would shine bright with Christmas lights in the December darkness.

Our guide puts on a yarmulke and hands one to my dad. We photograph the sparse room, several electric menorahs, and a prominent Star of David. Our guide asks if we want him to take the Torah out of the ark, the holy cabinet where it is kept. This feels surprisingly casual, but we agree and photograph that too.

The House of Peace survived as a Nazi brothel. It was re-consecrated after the war by the rabbi my father and his family lived with, the one who also emigrated and who bar-mitzvahed my father in Israel. My dad tells our guide he came here with his friend Alex in the early 1990s. It was Friday night, and the congregation needed a minyan, at least ten men to recite certain prayers, so they stayed, although they had come out of curiosity and not to observe Shabbat.

Next, we head to Solunska Ulica 8 where my father lived until early in the war. Having visited the street on Google Maps, it all looks oddly familiar. The area had seemed a bit sketchy when we peered at it from Rebecca's laptop in my parents' kitchen, and I'm pleased it's not that way in person. People who live here go about their business, maybe used to the occasional Jewish tourist, though I doubt they know much about the prewar community. Standing in a clump on the street I consider how we must look to passersby: might they guess that we are from here too?

I try to imagine Dorćol as the neighborhood my father was born into; it had existed for hundreds of years and was destroyed before he was old enough to remember it. Ernest Powel, a German Jew who escaped to Belgrade in the mid-1930s, described his outsider's view of Dorćol in *Life in Dark Ages: A Memoir*. He wrote that the community, "by the desolate shore of the Danube," was rundown and "felt like a separate village." There people spoke Ladino and "cats and dogs chased chickens across unpaved streets."[5]

It is so improbable my dad could make it back and we can be together to share it. I keep watching his face, searching to see what today means to him. He is lively and focused, not overwhelmed by history and loss.

We are standing on the street where my father ran with his mother and cousin to the bomb shelter in his grandfather's basement. It is a warm day, and the street is still. The building where he snuck glimpses of patrolling soldiers during the occupation is gone.

Solunska Ulica 8 is a new building, not the same one where my father lived. Our guide shows us on a map where there was a synagogue across the courtyard. My father doesn't remember it. But he does recall his father had a Lancia, an Italian car, parked in a courtyard behind the house. "It was damaged in the bombing. There must have been an alley that allowed my father to get it back there." We walk around, speculating where the alley might have been.

My father's life was comfortable with his parents before the war. His grandfather Heinrich owned quite a bit of property, including the two-story home that stood here. My father and grandparents lived with a maid and a housekeeper, who wore the traditional Serbian dress. Although they were adults, my grandfather Alexander was responsible for his younger brothers, Solomon, nicknamed Monika, and Žil, who lived upstairs. My grandfather worked for his father Heinrich, who lived nearby and was a widower. My grandfather's older brother Bernhard flunked out of medical school, went to law school, and became a judge in Novi Sad, a city in northern Serbia.

My grandfather's youngest brother Žil was born May 17, 1921, so he would have been 19 during the bombing. My grandfather encouraged Žil to take my toddler dad places. My father remembers getting dressed up and waiting for Žil, but then spilling something on his clothes so he couldn't go. Maybe he grew restless, sitting quietly on the front stoop, all ready to go in his freshly laundered clothes. Likely he wailed in frustration when told he could no longer go with his exciting young uncle.

Žil, whose mother had died when he was nine, was a troublemaker, a wild kid. He got the maid pregnant. With his close friend, who was my grandmother's nephew, Žil was in the underground resistance and involved with sabotage activities. Tragically, they were caught, tortured, and died in prison. Rebecca and I have heard this before, but it's as important for us to receive it here in Belgrade as it is for my father to tell it.

My father remembers: "When the Germans' intentions for Jews became clear, some Jews moved away to areas where their identities were unknown. My father, with a pregnant wife, a young child, and a close friend who was not in good health, hesitated to run. But eventually he was persuaded to 'buy' a false passport and other essential documents to disguise his identity. A lot of money was gathered for the bribe. The man they paid lived in Zemun and worked with the German administration. He was not Jewish but was married to a relative of my maternal grandmother, so my father trusted him. But he never delivered the papers."

I consider the anxious waiting, disappointment, fear, blame, and anger this failed attempt must have entailed.

My father's uncle Monika was dating a non-Jewish woman whose brother, Alexander, died from natural causes. Because Alexander was secretly buried in the backyard, Monika could take his identity papers and run away. Somehow, Monika connected with the Partisans and spent the war fighting the Germans. He was wounded and rose to a high rank, apparently in charge of the Belgrade liberation. The Yugoslav Partisans were the only ones who liberated their own country.

When the occupation began in April 1941, the Soviet Union and Germany were still allies. So the Partisans, who were communists, weren't yet fighting the Germans. On May Day, 1941, the Partisans celebrated Germany's "struggle against Western imperialism."[6] But when Germany attacked the Soviet Union on June 26, the Partisans turned against them. Understanding the timeline makes the stories of my father's two uncles who escaped and joined the Partisans more confusing. It wasn't like they could run off to the woods in April and find them, as I'd imagined all these years. Where did they go and how did they evade the Germans and survive before they joined the Partisans?

I'm surprised to learn from our guide that Yugoslavia was already limiting Jewish rights before the occupation, attempting to please Hitler. In 1938, 821 Jews in Yugoslavia, 241 foreigners and 580 citizens, converted; a disproportionately high number.[7] In response, the Belgrade Jewish School Committee chose as its theme for a competition for Hanukkah 1938: "Why I must persist in these difficult times."[8] On October 5, 1940, for the first time since Yugoslavia was founded, laws were passed prohibiting Jews from selling food and limiting the number of Jewish children who could attend school.[9] In response, the Jewish communities in Belgrade and Sarajevo set up their own schools. In Belgrade, the improvised school was at the Ashkenazi temple we visited this morning. Lessons continued until March 27, 1941.[10]

My father's earliest memory, the bombing, is a flashbulb memory, a vivid snapshot created by the trauma of the moment.

"The screeching sound and images of the diving German bombers and the explosions nearby are very vivid in my mind," he tells us. "My mother's niece Vera was visiting, and I recall that my father was not with us. I remember my mother putting a crystal tray with cookies high on the wardrobe and taking my hand to run with her niece to a more substantial building in the neighborhood where my paternal grandfather, Heinrich, lived. The building had a basement used as a shelter."

As a child, I always pictured a dark wooden cabinet filled with china and my father in the short pants he wore in a black-and-white photo, looking up at the cookies, now out of reach. What reflex made my grandmother move them as they rushed for safety? Now that I'm a mother, I try to imagine the bravery and desperation that made her grab her child and run into the street, pulling him by his hand. I know nothing about being bombed. Was there a break while the planes circled that made her think they had a chance to make it down the block?

"By the time we arrived, the building had taken a direct hit and the staircase had collapsed," my father says. "We learned later my grandfather was crushed by the falling stairs and killed. My mother speculated he was on his way to get us to the shelter rather than going there directly himself." It's clear to me how vividly my father is seeing this event now two generations past.

He continues: "We proceeded to the basement where we met many others just sitting silently. I have no sense of the passage of time, but at some point we got out to the street and went back home. The crystal tray had fallen on the floor and had split in two parts with a clean break. I recall wondering how the tray did not break in many pieces as a glass or a dish that I had broken in the past."

My father pauses to see if we are still listening. "We came back here after we fled to the country. The bombing had stopped, but a lot of buildings were destroyed. German soldiers were patrolling the streets. In my mind, I can clearly see the pairs of soldiers walking in high boots with rifles and helmets. I don't know where my father was while we were away, but he returned home, and the Germans started registering Jewish men, using them as laborers to clear the damage from the bombing. My father would come home for the night and go to work for the Germans in the morning. From my mother's stories, I learned that arrangement lasted for months, until one evening he did not return. The strange feeling is I recall vividly many events from that early stage of my life, but I do not recall my father."

"My mother and I, and her sister with three children, went to live in one of the villages where my grandfather owned land," my father says.

"And you don't remember the name?" asks our guide.

My father shakes his head.

"Any kinds of documents?"

My father shakes his head again. "It's one of the reasons I will never do anything to try to get restitution. Because I will spend my life on it and it's not worth it."

Serbia has recently passed laws to restore property or market value to Jews with losses in the Holocaust and to their heirs. Their motivation, at least in part, seems to be trying to get into the European Union. My father isn't interested. It seems like too much work and he doesn't have time. Also, he doesn't need the money. Our guide wishes he would change his mind, encouraging him to "be a little less Serbian and a little more Jewish," drawing on their shared mixed heritage and the Serbian reputation for enjoying life and relaxing in cafés with a drink and a cigarette.

This is what my father wrote in a note sent to the museum:

> My mother was pregnant, and I remember her being very upset the night my father did not return. Somehow, she found out where the Germans kept the Jews, which turned out to be on the outskirts of the city. For a while, my mother would go to see him and carry a basket of food for him till one day, the gates of the camp were open, and the camp was empty. The Jews were taken away. Much later, I recall my mother telling me she went to the German administration to inquire what happened to my father. She was told he had had a heart attack during the transportation to the concentration camp. My mother never bought the story. But she never heard anything more about my father.

My dad continued to live with his mother in their home for a while after his dad was taken. Occasionally, he saw peasants in the house. "My mother was trading with them, exchanging my father's suits for food. I also recall my mother breaking furniture and feeding the stove to keep it going. I woke up in the middle of the night in my father's bed to see my mother in her bed and a baby next to her. Somehow, I knew it was a girl and said, 'Now I have a sister.' My mother named her Ljiljana. This was on May 5, 1942, and I was 3 years and 8 months old. Because of the curfew imposed, my mother could not go to the hospital, but a woman doctor was escorted to our house to help my mother give birth."

This is perhaps the biggest mystery. On December 7, 1941, the police issued an order that all Jewish women and children should report the next day to the yard of *Judenreferat*, the Police Department for Jewish Affairs on George Washington Street 21. They should take only what they could carry, including a blanket, cutlery, and enough food for one day. They had to bring their apartment keys with their name and street address attached. An itemized property list had to be left in their apartments. There would have been a stream of women and children, carrying luggage and wearing yellow stars, through Dorćol. How was my father still living at home five months later?

It is easy to see how Dorćol's current residents could be ignorant of the neighborhood's Jewish past. On the modern building that has replaced my father's home, there is no physical sign of who lived here before.

I think about Stolpersteine, literally stumbling stones, created by the German artist Gunter Demnig that mark the last voluntary residences of Jews in other European countries, so "the horror has a face to it."[11] Helmut Loelhoeffel, one of the coordinators for the programs, said, "Six million Jews were killed, murdered. The stumbling blocks make clear that it was one plus one plus one plus one. It makes clear that they were all individuals."[12]

The Stolpersteine are palm-sized commemorative plaques, but most are placed for people who will never have a gravestone. As such they often become a place for the family to pay their respects. In German the word *stolper* has a double meaning. It means stumble, but it also means that something is jolted, in this case a memory. They jolt the memory of a family reunited in this way, outside the last place they lived together, never in a cemetery. Symbolically people who were murdered and those who survived are together again.

There are almost 100,000 of these stones across Germany and 15 other countries, including Austria, Belgium, the Netherlands, Hungary, the Czech Republic, Ukraine, and Norway. But not in Serbia. No former Yugoslavian country yet has a Stolperstein. Standing here makes my family history more real, and I want a physical stone to mark these people who lived here. I want to bring Stolpersteine to Serbia, starting with my grandfather at Solunska 8.

I want the stone to read: "Here lived Alexander Brill. Born 1909. Deported 1941 to Topovske šupe. Murdered."

15

We walk around the corner, past a group of Israelis on a Segway tour. I photograph a yellow building with a Star of David and another with a star and a Hebrew inscription. A plaque on the latter mentions the history and function of the building. It held a department for the care of the elderly and ill, space for youth clubs, and a spacious hall for religious and social gatherings. It explains most of Belgrade's Jews were killed in World War II, but doesn't use the words German, Nazi, or Holocaust.

This is a Jewish neighborhood that still has a *Jevrejska Ulica*, a Jewish Street. But it has no Jews. For hundreds of years, the Jewish community was an integral part of this city. They must have seemed permanent, everlasting. And then, within a few months, they were wiped out.

We turn onto Kralja Petra. The street reflects Belgrade's unusual diversity and co-existence. It houses the Jewish Community Center, a Serbian Orthodox cathedral built in 1840, and a Turkish mosque built in 1690. After World War II, it was renamed 7 July to honor the 1941 uprising against the Nazis. Its original name honoring King Peter was reinstated after the collapse of the communist regime.

The building that houses the Jewish Museum and other Jewish community offices comes into view. I remember showing my father the museum's website and him remarking he lived in that building for a while. After the war, strangers were living in his family's house since the new communist regime claimed it was too big for just the three of them. Under communism, all religious activity was banned, including Jewish studies and the teaching of Hebrew. The Jewish Community Center served as a gathering place for displaced and returning local Jews. The center provided food and clothing.

"I remember we would come here to get food after the war. We had containers." He gestures with his hands to show they were about eight inches high. "Maybe three, four, five containers stacked together with a handle. I would come here every day to get food. And I would take it home."

"To Solunska Street?" our guide asks.

"To Solunska," my dad confirms. "At some point, we moved here. I don't know the logic. It was an apartment with four bedrooms on the third floor. There was a big laundry room. In that apartment two rooms of the four were given or belonged—don't know—to the rabbi."

"Rabbi Alkalaj?" our guide interrupts.

"No, Altarez," my father clarifies. "He bar-mitzvahed me in Israel. He had two rooms. And I was friends with his son Moshe, whom we called Mozi. He was a teenager here. And later Moshe was a big shot paratrooper. Then there was a single woman living in the other room."

"Three families in one apartment," says our guide. "And you were here until 1948."

"Right," my dad nods.

"In 1948 you made Aliyah altogether."

He uses the Hebrew word, Aliyah, for the process of moving to, literally going up to, Israel. Ten percent of Yugoslavia's population perished in the war, but 80 percent of Jews died. In the early years after the war, over 7,000 Jews, about half the survivors, left for Israel, Great Britain, North America, and elsewhere.[1]

"In December," my dad confirms. "One of my uncles made it earlier."

Our guide nods. "What happened to the house on Solunska?"

My dad has no idea. Our guide explains, "The problem is that in 1948, when many people decided to leave the country—"

My dad interrupts. "My mother wrote off everything, including citizenship." He makes a shooing motion as if he is pushing it all away.

"That's the issue," our guide agrees. "The communist Yugoslav government allowed Jews to leave for Israel. That wasn't the case in Hungary, Bulgaria, or

Romania. Here they were free. But they had to sign a special document, declining how do you call it?"

"Possession," my dad supplies.

"This process is now reversed. Now they give them. You can try now to get back the property."

"I'm too old for that," my dad says.

My father remembers life at Kraja Petra 71:

> At age seven, I started attending first grade. My sister was going to kindergarten and my mother got a job. On the way back from school I would pick up my sister and wait in the apartment till my mother returned from work. For a long time, my mother lived in hope that my father would return. Many stories circulated among desperate people like my mother. People said the Russians had moved thousands of Jews from concentration camps to Russia, from where they would eventually return. I am not sure at what point my mother gave up all hope of seeing her husband again, but she never remarried.

I reflect on what it was like in those early post-Holocaust years. Traumatized fragments of the once-thriving Jewish community made their way back to Dorćol. Jews from other places, many of whom had survived the camps, arrived as well. The monarchy was gone, replaced by Tito's communism. Private property was a thing of the past. My grandmother lost her apartment and now lived with her children in a single room. They didn't know that four years later there would be a state of Israel where most survivors would emigrate. For all they knew this was it, post-genocide, postwar communism —make the best of it here.

My grandmother worked as a seamstress. My father and his sister went to school where their lessons included Russian. There was only one other Jewish child in my father's class, a boy named Rafi whose mother was friends with my grandmother. Rafi would emigrate to Israel in the 1960s and later to Canada and the United States; he stayed in touch with my father his entire life.

My father was a member of the Pioniri, the communist youth group for all children over seven. They wore red scarves and learned propaganda. There was a red Pioneer Booklet and a loyalty pledge. Somehow there was money for him to take violin lessons.

My father went once with his uncle Monika to meet Tito and another time to meet Moses Pijade, Tito's general secretary who was Jewish and helped convince Tito to allow Jews to emigrate to Israel. My father remembers a boy in his class whose father was high up in the Communist Party. He went to his house once and was struck by the wealth; there were bowls of fruit on the table, and he got to eat his first banana.

Chaos was the order of the day. My father saw people accused of being Nazi collaborators killed in the street. His uncle Monika disappeared, which was not uncommon. My grandmother searched all the prisons in the city, and there were plenty of them, but with no results. One day a soldier came to see her. He had just been released from the prison near the Jewish Community Center and had a message from his commanding officer. Someone named Alexander, with a last name that wasn't Brill, wanted to see her in the military hospital. My grandmother's immediate reaction was that it was her husband with a false last name. But from the note the soldier handed her, she understood it was Monika, who was wounded and trying to make contact.

My father and grandmother went to meet him and bring him food. My father recalls seeing other wounded Partisans being brought to the hospital. The war was still going on in some parts of the country. Monika offered his mother a pistol saying, "You never know when you may need it." But his mother refused the weapon.

When Monika was released, he said he was incarcerated because he had never disclosed his identity to the Communist Party. All through the war he had kept the identity of his girlfriend's dead brother. In the eyes of the party, "he was not true to the party." Once Monika was back in uniform, he had to find the remaining Chetnik soldiers who were still loyal to the deposed king and were hiding in the mountains to clear his name.

By now the Partisans had become the Yugoslavian Army. They started drafting new recruits. One of the recruits was the son of the man from Zemun who never delivered the false passport to my father. The young man was assigned to the dangerous mission Monika was about to lead. His parents came to beg my grandmother to ask Monika to take special care of their son, fearing that Monika would take revenge for the loss of his brother's life. Monika agreed to protect the young soldier and assigned him as a helper to his second in command, a close friend. The second in command and the young soldier stepped on a mine and were killed. The parents blamed Monika and my grandmother for the death of their only child. After completing the mission successfully, Monika was reinstated to his original high position in the party and the Government.

Monika rose high in the Communist Party and was initially planning to stay when Tito allowed Jews to emigrate to the new state of Israel. My dad remembers something happened, and suddenly Monika was on the first ship out. We put it together when I read that 1948 was the year Tito split from Stalin and purged his government of those he considered traitors. This division is known as the "Historical No" in the former Yugoslavia. It was the first time a communist government declared its independence from the USSR. Monika must have been viewed as being too closely aligned with Moscow.[2]

My father's oldest uncle Bernhard, named for his grandfather who came from Upper Hungary and was the king's doctor, also survived. Prior to the occupation he lived in Novi Sad and was a lawyer and a judge, a rare position for a Jew. He spoke Hungarian, so he ran away to Budapest when the Germans came. He worked in a factory making wooden heels for women's shoes. There he met his future wife Hannah, a refugee from Slovakia. They could live as Gentiles in a city where everyone was a stranger. After the war, they returned to Novi Sad. There Hannah gave birth to their son Žil, named for the youngest brother who was killed fighting as a Partisan.

Most Jews remaining in Yugoslavia emigrated to Israel on two ships in late 1948. Both of my father's surviving uncles, their wives, and their young sons sailed on the first ship because families with young children received priority. My father, grandmother, and aunt were on the second ship, the *Kefalos*. Six months earlier, the *Kefalos* had been used to smuggle much-needed supplies for the Arab-Israeli War of 1948; hidden under 1,400 tons of sugar were 36 75mm cannons, 500 machine guns, 17,000 shells, and seven million rounds of ammunition.[3] My father and his family were among 4,300 refugees who arrived in boxcars from Yugoslavia and sailed from Bakar on December 15. Storms lengthened the trip and made passengers seasick. Food had to be rationed. Ten long days later they arrived in Haifa.

A woman coming out of the museum tells our guide the elevator is broken. My dad doesn't translate this but tells us she's addressing him with the formal form of you. He's catching words, but not whole concepts, like a young child learning a language for the first time. With the swelling from his medication, my dad is easily winded. The museum is on the first floor, which means a full flight of stairs in Europe. He considers waiting downstairs, but our guide convinces him to join us. He pauses several times to catch his breath.

While the Jewish Museum in New York City has two security guards standing watch and checking bags and a metal detector, the one in Belgrade has no security. Serbia is relaxed and unafraid; there weren't any recorded airport security warnings about unattended luggage and suspicious behavior.

Upstairs Barbara and her co-worker are waiting for us. Seeing Barbara is like meeting up with an old friend, someone who gifted me with incredibly intimate and important information. She is thin with curly auburn hair and bright brown eyes behind her glasses. I am surprised she is younger than me. Our presence here still amazes me. But Barbara doesn't seem surprised.

We sit at folding tables in their office, and she offers us soda and orange cheese curls set out in a bowl. Her co-worker doesn't speak English, but they confer in Serbian and produce a book on the Jews in Šabac. She shows us a copy of a deed and translates how this shows that my great-grandmother's father, Baruh Ruso, purchased a house for his minor daughter Regina and then sold it when she came of age. The money was likely for her dowry.

Barbara gives us a copy of the German property registration list, just the portion of people whose names started with B, from Bošković Franjo to Bukuša Mandila. Barbara has highlighted Bril H. Aleksandar, Bril H. Solomon, and Bril S. Žil, my grandfather, and two of his brothers, all listed as living at Solunska 8. The middle initial H for Aleksandar and Solomon references Heinrich, their father's name, and is traditional. Both Solomon and Žil are listed as *trgovački pomoćnik* [merchant assistant]. Aleksandar is listed as a *bivši činovnik* [former clerk], which could indicate he lost his job for being Jewish.

We walk through the museum, which looked more impressive online. The exhibits are faded and extend only through the end of Yugoslavia in the 1990s. There is Judaica from the prewar period and posed black-and-white photographs. I study the faces, checking to see if they look familiar, identifying with their fear, and wondering how much of what's coming they understand. We examine photos of Jews under the occupation and my father marvels people were even able to take such pictures.

I watch Rebecca. My daughter is coming of age during a resurgence of antisemitism, racism, and xenophobia around the world. She loves museums and has switched into what we call her "museum mode," studying each artifact and reading every sign. She has fallen behind us as she concentrates on the details. I search for clues to what she's thinking, but her studious face gives little away.

We say our goodbyes and leave the museum. In the hallway, we discuss going upstairs to see where my father lived after the war. I could go alone, but how would I know what door was his? The old building feels slightly intimidating. If someone questioned me, I wouldn't have the Serbian to explain. It's standing with him and hearing his memories that makes this building interesting. But I could at least take a picture to show him. Anything my dad can't do he doesn't want to. Before I can sort through my thoughts, he and our guide have decided we are moving on.

We drive to Topovske šupe, the concentration camp where my grandfather was imprisoned. It was a gun shed before the war. In 1941, this was the outskirts of Belgrade, but the city has grown around the site.

"There are plans to build the largest shopping mall in the Balkans here," our guide reveals. His tone doesn't betray his opinions on the matter. "The architect is an Israeli firm."

"The Jewish community put up a sign against the fence to mark what happened here during the occupation. But a few weeks ago, it was stolen."

You could live nearby, walk past every day, and have no idea what happened here. The weather is August hot our guide says, though it is only early June. It's cramped in his tiny Yaris. My father has pushed his seat back almost into my lap. He needs the room to help with the intense swelling in his legs. My feet crowd against my bag. I'm sweaty but too tired to work out how to rummage for my water bottle.

It's been an emotionally overwhelming day for the three of us. My dad doesn't have the energy for one more thing. He won't be getting out. Because I'm in the back seat of the two-door Toyota, if I'm to walk the camp's grounds my dad will have to get out, or our guide and Rebecca will. I can see the whole yard through the car window. Nothing beckons me as I survey it. The camp is surprisingly small, just a couple of long, low buildings crumbling into the overgrown lot. I wonder if this is how my dad has imagined his father's prison over the last 70 years, but I am too worn out to ask.

Just like a few hours ago at the museum, where we debated going to see where my dad had lived, I'm reluctant to surpass him, to go beyond him into the past where he doesn't want to trespass. It's clear, even from the car, that when Jews and Roma were imprisoned here, locals walking by would have had a clear view of the situation. Walking to work or a soccer game, or coming home from a friend's, there would have been no doubt of the terrible conditions under which these prisoners who had committed no crimes were living.

While we sit, resting and processing our day, I picture my grandmother here, wearing the 1930s print dress from the photograph. Maybe she was wearing a hat as well. To our modern eye, people then were generally overdressed for every day. How many times did she visit between August and November, as the weather turned from sweltering to cold, and the situation became increasingly desperate? Every other day? Once a week? Sometime during that period, she would have realized she was pregnant.

I imagine her from behind, facing the camp, holding a basket of food on one arm. I see her neat and composed, like in the picture from happier times. Were she and my grandfather able to talk? Did he tell her about life in the camp or try to shield her from harsh details? Did she share rumors from the city with him? Repeat cute things my father had said or done? Tell him she was pregnant? What happened the last time she came when the gate was open and the camp was empty? My father said, "There were no Germans, no prisoners, no one." Was she part of a group of women who were wailing and screaming? Or was there silence? Was she alone?

Auschwitz and Bergen-Belsen are museums. Is it size that determines what becomes a museum and what becomes a shopping mall? Or the wealth of the country? Or how much value its citizens place on events? Topovske šupe serves no current purpose and has not even a sign to clarify what happened here.

I read the camp was established on August 20, 1941—three days before my father turned three—on the site of a former Royal Yugoslav Army military base. It operated until December and was run by Serbians, the Nedic government police, who publicly hanged prisoners who attempted to escape. Over four months it housed 5,000-6,000 Jews, Roma, and Serbs who were suspected of anti-German activity. Three thousand were killed as hostages in retaliation for Nazis who were killed or wounded in Partisan attacks. Over 1,000 were killed as alleged anti-fascists. The Germans took prisoners from here when they needed victims for reprisal shootings, murdering between 150 and 450 a day, usually at the Jajinci firing range. It's the barbaric behavior of a military that never thought it could lose, never expected to be held accountable for its crimes, and expected to rule for a thousand years. Although it is known Nazis kept lists of the prisoners at Topovske šupe Camp, they have never been found.[4]

I think of a joke I know about the Holocaust, not really a joke at all.

Question: "How did you sleep last night?"

Answer: "Like God during the Holocaust."

At our guide's insistence, we go to the local registry to try to get records for the properties my father thinks his grandfather owned. They are just closing when we arrive. The clerk assures us that if we come back tomorrow, we can get the information we seek in five minutes.

We pause at a nondescript street corner. Here the truck that gassed thousands of Jewish women and children stopped to attach the carbon monoxide hose. Locals experiencing an ordinary day pass by as we take it in. They seem unaware of their history and don't look at us.

"The German soldiers complained about having to shoot women and children," our guide says. "So the military brought a truck from Germany to gas them. This was in 1941 before the gas chambers further west were up and running.

I stand here with my daughter, choked by both the heat and the horror of our guide's words. How unlikely it is that we exist at all.

Our last destination of the day is the Menorah of Flames Holocaust monument along the Danube. Wilted and overwhelmed by a day spent immersed in details of the Holocaust horrors that happened here, I strain to follow our guide's explanation. The statue was erected in 1995, half a century late. It commemorates the 9,000 Jews murdered during the occupation of Belgrade. The sculptor, Nandor Gild, was born in Subotica, in what is now northern Serbia. He was deported to a labor camp in Hungary while his family was sent to Auschwitz. He escaped the camp and joined the Partisans.

Two mothers, engrossed in conversation, push baby carriages past the statue on the paved walkway that runs along the river. An older woman with earbuds and pink sneakers jogs towards them. A dead pigeon lies near the edge of the statue's base. The normal and the horrific live together here. My father wants a picture of Rebecca and me at the monument. It's awkward. Should we smile? What is the etiquette for posing in front of a sculpture that commemorates genocide?

That night we meet our cousins Dragan and Lejla for dinner. They bring their daughter Tanja and her husband, both lawyers with conversational English. There is a round of the Serbian triple kissing while I purposefully think lean left, lean right, lean left, and try to hide my ineptness. Neither our Americanness nor our Jewishness seems to impact our warm, familial welcome.

Our cousin's husband tells us he worked on the law for Serbian restitution of Jewish property and has just been speaking about it at a conference in Warsaw. He knows the rabbi at the synagogue and has been honored by lighting a candle at Hanukkah. He has been to Israel as the guest of the Israeli ambassador to Serbia. I'm amazed that my non-Jewish cousins are so involved in Belgrade's Jewish community.

My dad gets interested in restitution, lighting up because it now seems possible with this connection. Our cousin is encouraging. I too thought it seemed impossible before, but now the idea of my dad, my aunt, and their cousins having what should be theirs returned is appealing. That we are at dinner with the lawyer who wrote the restitution law seems like a sign.

Dragan shares old photos with us, a formal one of our grandmother's grandparents and a snapshot of my grandmother. From our table on the top floor, we have a view of old Belgrade and across the Danube to New Belgrade as well. Lightning flashes across the expansive sky. A white cat wanders the room.

My dad doesn't want German restitution money which seems to attempt to place a value on the loss of human life by paying a portion of my grandfather's estimated lifetime earnings. But Serbian restitution is different. This is about property compensation. Serbia has something that is his. My dad has started to see himself as a Holocaust survivor.

16

I've always been a taphophile, a person interested in cemeteries and tombstones. I've been jealous of friends who can see how their ancestors stretch back over centuries and visit them in local graveyards. Most of my explorations have been in New England's old Protestant burial grounds, preserved open spaces that can offer a respite from what's beyond their walls. I taught my kids to drive in our town cemetery before we dared to venture onto the road. Every fall a graveyard down the road from my house is home to the riotous display of color put on by a row of old sugar maples; I always make a point of stopping by. When I wander down the rows of graves, I like to look for clues to what happened in long-dead families, children who died within days or weeks of each other, likely of an epidemic, sons named after fathers, husbands buried between two wives. I try to use my imagination to fill in the gaps.

The 17th- and 18th-century American history I learned in school and the local cemeteries from that time aren't my family's history. It's much richer to visit Belgrade's Sephardic cemetery, walk among the graves of people my family might have known, prayed with in minyans, gossiped with on the street. I think of a definition I once heard of what a true Vermonter is: someone with four grandparents in the ground in Vermont. By this definition, I am from nowhere. But Belgrade is my dad's hometown, and we've returned with him. It's so strange for me to realize that we are more rooted in Serbia than back home in America. Though Serbia is in many ways completely foreign to me, it is my home.

I've come home to where my family is buried. In my pocket are the pebbles I've carried across the ocean to leave on the tombstones. I'm building a connection from one continent to another, from the New World to the Old. I want to leave something from where I live behind.

On our second full day in Serbia, I awake from the deep sleep of the exhausted. Our guide is waiting to drive us to the cemetery. It must have been on the outskirts of Belgrade in 1888 when the Jewish community opened it, having outgrown the one in Dorćol.

"Serbia will come into the EU," our guide remarks as he navigates a rotary, "when people become polite."

I think of every passenger in the aisle rising in unison while the plane taxied to the gate.

We drive by buildings in ruins, remains of the 1999 NATO bombing. Americans did this in my lifetime. I ask if they've been left standing to make a point.

"No," our guide says. "There's just not been the money these last 18 years to fix them."

Belgrade, situated on the way of armies coming in or out of the Balkans, has been razed and restored about 40 times.[1] I've heard from the air you can see the lines of where the city was bombed in World War II, by stripes of new buildings among the old.

We arrive at the two walled Jewish cemeteries; our family is in the Sephardic one, which is still active. A smaller, inactive Ashkenazi one is across the street. The cemetery keeper opens the gate so we can drive inside. We are here to see tombstones of relatives who get graves because they were safely buried before the war: my great-great-grandfather Doctor Bernhard, who died in 1905; my great-great-grandmother Rozalija, who died in 1890; and my great-grandmother Regina, who died in 1930.

My grandfather Alexander, my great-uncle Žil, and my great-grandfather Heinrich had no funerals and have no marked graves. None have plots in this cemetery although they died in this city and must have expected to be buried here. My grandfather doesn't even have a known date of death. Is there a prescribed way to mourn, to light a Yahrzeit candle, when the date of death is unknown?

I've never been in a Sephardic cemetery before. More than 4,000 tombstones testify to my family's existence and a substantial prewar Jewish community. Many tombstones have black-and-white photographs of the deceased. I will later learn that while Ashkenazi cemeteries don't allow this due to an interpretation of graven images, pictures are common in Sephardic cemeteries. I love seeing not just names and dates but the faces of the people whose lives I am trying to imagine.

The cemetery keeper speaks only Serbian. He is a short, middle-aged man with the sleeves of his plaid shirt rolled up and his brown pants tucked into rubber boots. He chats with our guide, who translates. It is overcast, and they discuss if it will rain. The cemetery keeper is from a village 30 kilometers from here. It rained there this morning.

What is the cemetery keeper's understanding of Judaism and the people buried here? How often does he see families like us visit? Our guide will coach my father to tip the cemetery keeper. In apparent gratitude, as we are leaving this worker will answer with "Trump" and give us a thumbs-up. My father will be confused since Trump sounds like the Hebrew word for hitchhike, and the thumbs-up gesture is the sign you need a ride. The cemetery keeper is trying to connect with us, seven months into Trump's term.

Our guide explains most Serbians favor Donald Trump over Hillary Clinton. They dislike the Clintons for their involvement with the NATO bombing. They like that Melania is from nearby Slovenia.

Unlike the cemeteries at home, there is no grass here, only grave next to grave, with headstones and what I later learn are called ledgers, stones that lie flat and cover the whole grave. People were buried in the order they died, so families don't rest together. Establishing a cemetery in a new Jewish community is always a top priority, more pressing than a synagogue. It seems to me that the first death, the first grave in a new location, roots a community in a way even their synagogue won't. Here in Serbia and across Europe, in places where synagogues have been destroyed or repurposed and the Jewish communities are gone or nearly so, it is still sometimes possible to stand in Jewish cemeteries and marvel at the lives these stones with their brief descriptions represent. I've always been more comfortable in cemeteries than synagogues.

There's no record of my family in the synagogue we visited yesterday. I must question if that was even where they prayed. But I know the Nazis were there, desecrating it as a brothel, raping women. Temple Shalom, a place of peace that carried the Hebrew word for peace in its name, became a place of violence. Here in the cemetery, on the other hand, there are memories of our family, and it is peaceful. Here are the names and even the photographs of my great-grandmother and great-great-grandparents. My family's physical remains are here, rooting us here. Here the living mourned and hopefully found consolation in the Jewish rituals of mourning.

Belgrade's Sephardic cemetery dates to 1889. In 1928, the old Jewish cemetery was closed and the graves, as well as some of the bodies, were moved here.[2] The city has grown around the walls, ugly communist-era buildings in all directions. Giant cement towers, plain and uniform, dominate the near distance. We five are the only ones here.

Jewish cemeteries are easy targets for antisemitic vandals. I have also read of Eastern European Jewish cemeteries that are in disrepair. Some, like the one in Nis, 125 miles south of here, have Roma living in them. The Roma are confident they won't be disturbed because they know there is no legacy to come and protect their dead. Here in Belgrade's cemetery I feel safe. I know from the images Barbara sent that it is well-tended here. With Barbara's Excel ledger that shows what the stones look like, we start down the central walkway.

We come to a monument to Jews who died fighting for Serbia in the first Balkan War and World War I, a period of fighting that stretched here from 1912 to 1919. Serbia suffered losses in greater proportion than any other nation in the War to End All Wars. There weren't enough boots and some soldiers were marched off in their slippers. Jews fought for a country they felt a part of and accepted by. The Jewish community of Serbia suffered disproportionally higher losses than Serbia as a whole.[3] How unprepared they were to be singled out during the occupation.

The monument is a work in progress, with names still being added. My grandmother's father died in World War I before she was born in 1914. Until I learned last year he was Christian, I would have expected to find his name here.

We reach my great-grandmother Regina's grave first. Seeing the tiny image of her gray stone I saw on my phone screen at home drew me here. I knew from that picture the stone was in disrepair. Now I can see details: the long crack that runs towards its middle, the weeds that surround it. How long has it laid face down in the dirt? My father speaks to our guide but looks at the cemetery keeper, his arm gesturing toward the sky to show the direction he wants the tombstone moved.

"Can he get this up?"

His voice is the one I heard when I'd been rude as a kid. I bet it's how he talked to a supplier late with a delivery or an employee who missed too many days of work back when he ran his own business.

Our guide says something short in Serbian though it seems that no translation is necessary, and the worker heads towards his shed. I wonder at his job description; has he walked by here regularly for years, with no compunction to spend the five minutes needed to raise the stone? He comes back with a crowbar and levers it up. His action seems odd, a bit brutal. I feel self-conscious of being American, being Jewish, taking photos, but am glad later to have before-and-after shots to document this meaningful moment.

My great-grandmother's image on her tombstone has been worn away by its long contact with the earth. Our only surviving picture of her is gone, but we can see the Cyrillic and Hebrew letters. I know from museum documents she was born in 1888 into a Sephardic family in Šabac, a port city now about an hour from here. She moved to Belgrade for her marriage in June 1906, when she was 18. She died of causes unknown to us at age 42 in 1930 when my grandfather was 20 and his youngest brother was just nine. We learned yesterday her father sold a house, probably for her dowry, likely for an arranged marriage.

I read on the birth certificate of my grandfather's younger brother Monika that Regina's parents were at his bris. Did other family make the trip? I know nothing about her siblings or her birth order. Did she go back to Šabac for visits? Teach Ladino to her children? Did my grandfather know his grandparents Baruh and Rivka?

Here our guide is not our host. Seeing my great-grandmother's grave cements for me that we have as much right to be here as any of Dorćol's children. Our guide and my dad discuss permanently fixing the stone. Our visit today has accomplished something. We are doing an important duty as her descendants. It is up to us to help. Although Regina had five sons, four who survived to adulthood, no descendants remain in Europe. We are scattered to both coasts of the United States and Israel.

In Judaism, caring for the dead is the most honorable work, the ultimate mitzvah, because they can never repay you. When you do a mitzvah for another living person, even without expecting anything in return, there is always the possibility they might return the favor one day.

We don't say the Mourner's Kaddish, the Jewish prayer for the dead that doesn't mention death or grief but focuses instead on peace. We aren't religious Jews. None of us ever met my great-grandmother. There is no way to know if she would have minded that we don't pray. Surely, she would have expected us to. Born in the 19th century in a small Sephardic community, married as a teenager to a man from another city she likely hardly knew, how could she have foreseen the foreign, secular Jews her family would become?

I think about Regina's burial and the people who would have been here. My great-grandfather, grandfather, and three great-uncles would have stood by the grave, throwing the first handfuls of dirt. They would have expected to be buried here themselves. None are. No one can say with certainty where in Serbia my great-grandfather Heinrich, grandfather Alexander, and youngest great-uncle Žil are buried. My two great-uncles who survived the war are in cemeteries in California and Israel.

With their clothes symbolically torn, did the mourners go home together to sit shiva, their mirrors covered, and their meals delivered by sympathetic neighbors? I don't know how my great-grandmother died, if her death was sudden or expected. I don't know what kind of mother she was or what kind of grandmother she might have been to my father if she'd lived.

I realize that when I want to guess at what her life might have been like, what kind of home she might have made for the boy who would be my grandfather, I rely on my knowledge of Judaism, mostly learned from books. I'm taking what I learned through my fascination with religious life of all flavors, but particularly religious Jewish life, and looking through that lens at my ancestors' lives.

While my American life is largely secular, my week has a rhythm marked by a family dinner on Friday night, where we usually light candles and say a blessing. Many of my values, my family values, I associate with our Jewish heritage. Our love for family, our pride in our children, our stress on the importance of learning, our sense of humor, and our focus on food are Jewish to me, though, of course, not exclusively so. I assume my Jewish ancestors shared these values as well. I absorbed them from my parents who inherited them from theirs, and on up the line. This is part of why learning that my grandmother converted left a gaping hole.

We stand where the mourners stood. I try to picture the scene. I don't know the season. Were they sweating and yearning for a breeze as we are now? Huddled against rain or the winter cold? Was there a crowd of mourners, friends, and extended family who were able to gather quickly, as Jewish burial is usually before sunset?

I take one of the stones I carried from home out of its plastic bag. It's warm in my hand. I place it on Regina's now up-righted grave. It is a symbol of the permanence of memory. I hand one to Rebecca and one to my father, who do the same.

We move on to find the more ornate stone of my great-great-grandfather, Regina's father-in-law, Doctor Bernhard. It is imposing, surrounded by a metal fence, and faces the main central walkway of the cemetery, a sign of his wealth and prominence in the community, I assume, although in death all Jews are supposed to be equal. In 1832 Bernhard was born an Austro-Hungarian citizen in Trencin, Upper Hungary, now Slovakia. His stone says he trained at the Sorbonne, and I know from Jennie Lebel's book, *Until the Final Solution: The Jews in Belgrade 1521-1942*, that he "moved to Serbia on May 1, 1865, on the Belgrade ferry with a passport valid for three years, which he later extended. With him came his wife Rosa and five children: Malvina (13), Vladislav (11), Adela (8), Julius (7), and Henrietta (6). He received Serbian citizenship on May 13, 1875. From then on, he went abroad only once with a Serbian passport, for eight days, to the Vienna World Exhibition."

The path is dusty. My dad leans on a fencepost in a patch of shade, unscrews his water bottle, and takes a long drink.

In Lebel's book we also discovered Bernhard was a veteran of the Serbian-Turkish War of 1876. He was decorated for his medical service with the Takovo Cross.[4] That Cross was awarded from 1865 to 1903. Its name honors the Second Serbian Uprising against the Ottoman Empire, which started in Takovo, Serbia. The day I searched, one was available online for $4,800.

When I first found mention of Dr. Bernhard Brill in Lebel's book, it made my father's memory more credible: his mother had told him that his great-grandfather had been the king's doctor. His knowledge of his father's family relied on what his mother remembered his father telling her. With both his father and grandfather killed in the war, the transmission of family history was severed. Lebel had listed only the names of Bernhard's children who were born in Trencin. We didn't know yet that my father's grandfather was born later in Serbia. In the book, my father wrote mistakenly in red block letters: ONE OF THESE TWO BOYS IS MY GRANDFATHER, MY FATHER'S FATHER. He was trying to further the written record of our family in the definitive book on the Jews of Belgrade. His block lettering, the way he always wrote, echoed the Hebrew alphabet which has only capital letters.

Bernhard's photograph shows a distinguished-looking man in a suit and tie with a mustache. Rebecca goes around the side of the grave and discovers another marker. There's a sepia image of a man in his late twenties or early thirties in a suit and tie, his face in profile, his hairline starting to recede. I scan it for family resemblances. My dad translates the Hebrew inscription: Dr. Simon Brill, killed in the Shoah.

We don't know how we are related to him, but I leave two stones. No one alive remembered Simon, but he's been found now.

Lebel writes, "On many tombstones, next to the name of the deceased, the names of killed relatives are found, with the obligatory addition 'Victim of Fascism.' This is of course on condition that some member of the family has survived the catastrophe. Most of the victims have remained anonymous!"[5] The Nazis wiped out whole families, entire villages, so no one survived to record the names of the dead. Victims only existed if someone survived who could remember them.

"Why do you think your father isn't on the side of the grave here too?" I ask my dad.

He pauses. His face is expressionless, and I wonder if my own looks the same. "Likely Bernhard, my oldest uncle, put this here. I think my mother wouldn't let him mark my father. She held onto the belief he was still alive for a long time. She wanted the rumors that men had been deported to Russia to be true."

I scan his face, looking to see how he is handling this death-themed day. His father who was stolen from him will never have a marked grave. He doesn't even have a marker in this cemetery. But my father's face is stoic. In his telling and retelling of the stories of personal and familial loss, there has always been a theme of acceptance and a shrugging off of grief. No anger. No search for pity or meaning.

Lastly, we reach the grave of Rozalija, Bernhard's wife. She died when her son Heinrich, my father's grandfather, was just 16.

The cemetery keeper rubs a stone across the writing to clean it and increase the contrast. Her photo above the writing has a lightning-shaped piece missing across the side of her face, but enough is left to make out the side view of a well-dressed matronly woman with a round face, her dark hair up in a bun. A doctor's wife, obviously well-to-do, she traveled 300 miles from her birthplace and likely never saw her family again, learned a new language, and changed citizenship. Our guide tells us the Serbian translates as:

> To my sweet and loved wife
> and mother Rozalija
> 1840-1890
> Inconsolable husband Dr. B. Bril
> and God given children

I do the math and realize Rozalija would have been 25 in 1865 when they arrived in Serbia. So she must have been Bernhard's second wife and stepmother to at least 13-year-old Malvina and 11-year-old Vladislav, and possibly to some of the younger three. Bernhard, eight years her senior, seems barely old enough to be Malvina's father. He must have married his first wife as a teenager.

The older children disappear from the museum records. There are no marriage certificates for them, and they are not the parents on any birth certificates. But knowing now of their existence makes me consider the Brill cousins I may have somewhere in the world. People sometimes ask if I am related to some other Brill they have met. There are English Brills from Buckinghamshire and German Brills from the German word brul, meaning wetlands, and brill, meaning eyeglasses, feasibly referring to someone who made or wore glasses. Ashkenazic names beginning with Br or Bar are probably acronyms, although the specific family history is often lost. Brill may stand for Ben Rabbi Levi, Rabbi Levi's son. My answer has always been that I'm only related to nine other Brills in the United States, but perhaps that's not true. Could some of Bernhard's other grandchildren or great-grandchildren have made it there as well?

When Bernhard, Rozalija, and their oldest five children came here in 1865, the Jewish community was still feeling the effects of having their equal rights revoked after the war that started in 1862 between the Serbs and Austrians.[6] The Serbs renewed their rights in 1888. By 1895 there were about 3,000 Jewish citizens. There was a split between the Ashkenazi and Sephardic communities between the 1840s and the 1880s.

Bernhard was involved in this split. In 1869, he headed a group of 30 men who wanted to create a separate Ashkenazi congregation, which the larger Sephardic community opposed. They warned if a separate community was founded, they would be denied "the right to the services of the rabbi, enjoyment of the poverty and hospital funds, the preservation and preparation of the dead, and burial in the Jewish cemetery which was the property of the Jewish community."[7]

Lebel quotes David A. Alkalay, who wrote in 1939: "Undoubtedly the separation of the Ashkenazi Jews into a separate community seventy years ago came as the result of two different mentalities and educations of the Ashkenazi Jews who came from cultured Austria-Hungary, literate, often well educated, even with the title of doctor, and the Spanish Jews who lived in their quarter, which was the whole world for them, an old-fashioned life, with long, maybe century-long traditions... differences in mentality, education, the way of life, the width of perspective, as well as knowledge of languages (neither side could boast perfect knowledge of the Serbian language) lead to a certain intolerance."[8]

By the beginning of the last century, the rift was healing, partly because of both groups' shared interest in Zionism. This was reflected in the creation of "mixed" marriages[9] like that of my father's grandparents, Heinrich and Regina, whose wedding was on June 25, 1906. Heinrich's father Bernhard, who had led the separation of the Ashkenazi Jews 37 years earlier, had died the year before.

It was such a thrill when I found this information and could share it with my dad. Our family had existed somewhere. My dad seemed interested but not surprised. For me it was important validation. It proved family stories were true, backed up by names, dates, and locations. This was the farthest I could go back in any family branch, all the way to 1832. I looked up Trencin and emailed the Slovakian-Jewish organization but got no response.

We pass a *genizah*, where damaged holy books are buried. Next, there's a sizeable grave where 13 rabbis who were moved from the old cemetery in 1928 were reburied. Then we come to a massive gray stone monument with a menorah in the corner. It's a memorial to victims from the Kladovo Transport, funded by the Jewish community of Vienna because many of the victims came from there. In Hebrew, German, and Serbian, it tells about 1,100 Jewish refugees who left Austria in late 1939. Some were Orthodox, some more secular, some atheist. Surprisingly, these Jews may have a connection with my great-grandmother's family.

The Jews of the Kladovo Transport attempted to escape German-occupied Europe for the safety of Palestine by sailing down the Danube. Their efforts were illegal because the British government was severely limiting immigration into Palestine. At the Romanian border, the refugees were turned back at the request of the British. It was December 1939, one of the coldest winters of the century, and the Danube was icing up. They had to return to the port city of Kladovo to wait for a thaw in desperate conditions.

The company that owned the ships recalled them in the spring, so the refugees moved into mud huts in farmers' homes. Local Serbs were friendly, according to testimonies. In September 1940, the Jews of the Kladovo Transport moved by barge and boat to Šabac, my great-grandmother Regina's hometown, because authorities feared clashes between them and the *Volksdeutsche*, ethnic Germans. The refugees lived in a former flour mill and wheat storehouse. They received money from the Federation of Jewish Communities in Yugoslavia for their care.

Life in Šabac was more settled. The refugees held concerts and lectures, printed newspapers, and wrote letters trying to get permission to emigrate to Palestine or the United States. Several times they believed their rescue was imminent, and in fact Aliyah Bet, the organization directing illegal immigration to Palestine, bought a ship for their use. But help never arrived. In March 1941, just before the Nazi invasion, about 250 refugees, mostly young people, were issued Yugoslav passports and visas for Greece, Turkey, and Syria. They traveled by train and Jews along the way gave them food and drink.

In July, the remaining Jews from the transport were interned in a forced labor camp by the Sava River near Šabac. In August, Šabac's Jews, likely including our cousins, were sent to the camp. In early October 1941, Partisans killed 21 German soldiers, so General Bohme ordered the execution of 2,100 civilians in retaliation. On October 13, German soldiers took eight hundred and five Jews and Roma, including all the men and boys aged 14 and older, from the Kladovo Transport to the Senjak Camp and then to Zasavica. There they were shot in front of what became their mass grave."[10]

In January 1942, the women and children of the Transport and Šabac were transferred by cattle car to Ruma and then marched to Sajmište, the camp across the river from Old Belgrade. Between March and May, those who didn't die on the march or in the camp were murdered in the gas van brought from Germany for that purpose. They are buried at Jajinci.[11] In 1945, the mass grave at Zasavica was opened and the bodies moved to the Jewish cemetery in Šabac; in 1959, they were moved here to the Sephardic cemetery in Belgrade.

The Kladovo Transport is the most famous story of the Holocaust in Serbia, although the vast majority of those murdered were not Yugoslav. The victims wrote letters to family in Austria and elsewhere. Some of those family members and the youth who got to Palestine lived to tell their stories. Few Serbian Jewish victims had surviving family to record their fate.

We are surely related to some of the people who are reburied here. My great-grandmother Regina must have left behind siblings and cousins in Šabac, who were living there in 1941 with their children and grandchildren. They could never have imagined they would wind up here, in the Belgrade cemetery.

We place more stones.

Then we move on to an imposing Holocaust memorial to Yugoslavia's murdered Jews, which dominates the back of the cemetery. It's shaped like wings and formed from the rubble of Dorćol's bombed buildings. Architect Bogdan Bogdanović[12] completed it in 1952 after my father and his family had been in Israel for almost four years. I leave a stone from my bag on the monument to my family, their community, and the approximately 67,000 other murdered Yugoslavian Jews. I hand one to Rebecca and one to my father, who do the same.

In one sense, we are doing the most normal thing in the world; we are three generations visiting our dead. But the odds against this moment ever happening are phenomenal. This seemingly simple act can't be simple in this cemetery. There are few left to visit their kin. The dead here overwhelm the living.

I feel overcome by heat and history. We stop to rest in the shade of a cherry tree. Yesterday seemed about five days long with everything we did and all that I'm processing. Today seems like it will be the same. The cemetery keeper picks small, dark, sweet cherries from a tree and hands each of us a few.

17

We return to the registrar, seeking proof my father's grandfather owned their home at Solunska 8 so my father can pursue restitution from the Serbian government. Our guide fills out forms and stands in line. Bureaucracy is the same everywhere. While he goes to pay a filing fee at the post office, we sit on plastic chairs in the waiting room, conspicuous in our foreignness. This is not a place for outsiders. A man with clear English, trying to be helpful, lets us know no one will help us while we wait in this outer room. We need to stand in line to be served. Locals here are doing their day-to-day business, getting permits perhaps for selling a home or opening a store. But our business is with the past.

I try to use the bathroom but don't even know which sign indicates which gender. My dad goes with me and shows me that *mushki*—a nickname he has always used for my brother, but I never thought to wonder its meaning—means male. I need the other door.

The five minutes the clerk promised us yesterday stretches to 45. Rebecca and I head out to find food, locating a pizza place where a woman assures me the slices are vegetarian, although there turns out to be ham under the cheese. Maybe this is what passes for vegetarian in Serbia, a country that clearly loves its meat.

Our guide decides he will pursue the paperwork another day without us. We head to St. Sava, the largest Orthodox Church outside of Russia, still under construction. As a child, Dragan told us, his grandmother sent him and his brother here to pick rose hips for jam. This is the building we saw last summer on Google Maps. The one my mother had been surprised my dad couldn't remember until we read it hadn't yet been built when he lived here. Construction was completed in 1989. It was consecrated in 2004. The main floor is still unfinished but there are ornate images with golden backgrounds in the basement. My grandmother's family was Serbian Orthodox, so I stand among the beautiful images and the faithful, checking to see if I sense something spiritual. Nothing. Visiting Stonehenge the week before held more meaning.

We drive to the Memorial Park Jajinci, where we each silently read the sign at the entrance: "More than 80,000 Serbs, Jews, Roma, and other anti-fascists were executed in this area during World War II (1941-1944)." Our guide tells us that women and children who were held at Sajmište and murdered in the gas truck were also buried here.

This is probably my grandfather's final resting place. Contrary to the Holocaust history I learned in Hebrew school, Jews in Serbia were mostly murdered close to home. Our guide explains, "The memorial was opened on October 20, 1964, the 20th anniversary of the Partisan army entering Belgrade."

I have never been to Auschwitz, Bergen-Belsen, Treblinka, or any of the other camps so enormous that their names have become familiar to many. Places where the murdered were so numerous that the world could not ignore them. Now they are museums where school groups and tourists go. Guides usher crowds in orderly lines. There are signs and artifacts and brochures.

In contrast, Jajinci is parklike, an expansive mowed lawn on the side of a hill. It's easy to imagine people on their lunch break sunning on blankets, tossing a frisbee, enjoying a cigarette and a cup of coffee. Our guide sometimes reports people for picnicking or walking their dogs here. Its peacefulness doesn't hint at the daily execution of civilians by firing squad that went on for months. I think of black-and-white World War II photos I've seen of Jews digging their own graves and then lining up in front of them for firing squads.

We drive up and see a tall monument with a silver structure at the top. The vast area is empty except for a couple making out on a bench.

I look at my father in the front seat, drinking from his plastic water bottle. His father was likely murdered and buried here, but there is no monument with his name, Alexander Brill. There is no monument with the names of Holocaust victims anywhere in Serbia.

My dad looks exhausted. He's come to Belgrade willingly, but at my request, taking this trip into the heart of his family history and an untold historical genocide. A trip to a park where my grandfather was murdered by firing squad can be normalized and endured. None of us break down or express emotion. I am numb. My dad is uncomfortable from the swelling in his legs. The unseasonable heat and being folded in the tiny car must be making it worse, but we don't get out. There is nothing remarkable to see. I want out of this horrible place that looks like a peaceful park but is the opposite. None of us even roll down a window for a photo. It's a relief when our guide shifts into drive and we head down the long hill.

I left a stone from home at the winged Holocaust memorial in the Jewish cemetery, but here at the actual grave I didn't. I don't know why. Perhaps I forgot about this ritual because my grandfather's grave doesn't seem like a grave. There is some intrigue to imagining the scene when my great-grandmother was buried, to be in the place where her husband and sons gathered to bury her. There is only horror in imagining my grandfather being murdered here.

We drive to Topčider, a leafy neighborhood with grand homes set back on lawns. Here, a walk from the end of the tram line, was my great-grandmother Radmila's farm. This is where my father spent much of the war, hiding in plain sight.

My father remembers when the Germans started to search for Jewish women and children; he moved with his mother and his baby sister to his maternal grandmother's horse farm and riding school on the outskirts of the city. His mother reassured them they were safe, even though they were not hiding because his grandmother was not Jewish and the place was isolated.

His mother was very available to him and his sister. She taught him to read by age five; he read *David Copperfield* and Jules Verne's *Journey to the Center of the Earth*. He loved being with the horses and fishing in the brook. The family had a big garden and chickens and pigs. When the chickens started dying, his grandmother and mother roasted the dead chickens, and his mother sold them to the German soldiers in the train station.

Though my father has happy memories of life on the farm, the dangers of war weren't far away. Partisans were hiding guns in the spaces between the horse stalls and periodically retrieving them at night. He recalls how upset his grandmother was when they stole the horses. German officers would often come on their days off and pay his grandmother to ride in the large open field in front of the house.

In 1944, the Allied Forces started bombing strategic positions around Belgrade, starting the fight for the liberation of the capital city. Across the brook that bordered the farm, a mint was dug into a steep hill. On top of the hill was a siren, and probably radar as well; when the Allied airplanes were approaching the siren would blast. But his grandmother's German Shepherd would start howling a few minutes before the sirens.

Train tracks ran along the property. Retreating Germans cut the railroad ties using a locomotive with a saw in the rear, slowing the advancing Russian forces. My father recalls the big Russian tanks with soldiers sitting on top of them. The tanks parked on the property and did not enter the city. The Russians were waiting at the outskirts for the Yugoslav Partisans to arrive to claim the capital. Belgrade was the only city to liberate itself.

Most of the German soldiers had gone, but some remained. Maybe their retreat was blocked. They were hiding in the surrounding homes and using civilians as human shields. Some barricaded themselves in the railroad tunnel my father and his family could see from the farm. They watched as the Russians gave the Germans an ultimatum to surrender. People were saying the Germans were waiting for the Partisans, preferring to surrender to them than to the cruel Russians who weren't—in my father's words—"taking any prisoners." But the Russian soldiers were using snipers and smoke to push the Germans out quickly. My grandmother, after almost four years of war and loss, was still soft enough to comment that the soldiers were only children and so far away from home.

The war was over and my father, with his mother and sister, moved back to their house in the city.

We found where we think the farm was on Google Maps before we left for our trip. Now roads cross over and under each other. The place looks nothing like it did in the early 1940s. We pass some horseback riders in a park and a racetrack, but even with the Google Maps printout we can't find the soccer fields we think are on the site of the farm. The farm will stay lost to us.

Next is Kalemegdan, a park my father played in as a child. It is a fort that once contained the old walled city of Belgrade, located at the strategic meeting place of the Danube and Sava rivers. In *Belgrade: A Cultural History*, Norris describes Belgrade as "the gateway to the Balkans. It towers over the place where two great rivers meet... Over the centuries this meeting point has stood for the geographic and political border between the Balkans and the rest of Europe, East and West."[1] We certainly get a sense of that looking down over the old walls.

This is where Belgrade started. "Perched on a promontory high above the confluence of the Danube and the Sava, defiant outpost of the Balkans facing the hostile Magyar-Tectonic plains of Pannonia, it has since time immemorial provoked the greed and fury of countless conquerors from Visigoths and Huns to their modern-day descendants. Whether the spirit of the place shaped those who lived in it or simply attracted a special breed may be debatable; not so the generosity and sheer pig-headed contentiousness of a population that above all else was intensely and outrageously alive." [2]

While our guide parks the car, we enter on a drawbridge over a dry moat, pausing so I can photograph my dad and Rebecca at the entrance. A man in his 20s tries to scam us with some long story about how he must catch a bus and needs money immediately or he will lose some money he's already spent. At first, he seems sincere, and I struggle to understand his English. By the time I get he's playing us, he's realized he won't be getting anything from us and moves on. He's correctly pegged us as tourists, but I'm my father's daughter and nobody's fool.

Inside the walls the city is gone, replaced by a green expanse. Children play on the grass and couples snuggle on the wall. An open-air bus filled with school-aged children makes its way up the hill. Here as in other places in the city, although it is Wednesday, it feels like a weekend with everyone off work for the day. Serbs, it seems, always have time for a leisurely cup of coffee and a smoke or a saunter through the park with a friend. My dad was once a local kid playing in this park.

Our guide joins us and my dad reminisces about coming here as a child. "It was the first time I ever saw a tennis court," he said. "They were clay. They were in the moat. I used to watch this here and say, 'Someday, I'm going to play.' I never played here." But he did leave Yugoslavia and learned to play.

I've heard the story before and doubted it. It didn't make sense. Tennis courts in the moat? Having just walked in the front entrance, over a moat devoid of courts, makes the story seem even more doubtful. We stop and our guide photographs the three of us with the river and New Belgrade in the background.

We make our way through a short tunnel, following the bus with the children who are now shouting to hear their voices echo. I don't need to speak Serbian to understand the universal simple joy of calling out and hearing your voice call back to you.

We round the corner and in the moat are two perfect red-clay tennis courts; a children's tennis lesson is in session. Yet again, everything my dad remembers is accurate—no matter how unbelievable. I snap a picture and text it to my mom.

We come to a statue of a naked man holding a hawk and a sword, which was originally designed for the city square, but banished to the park, facing away from the town center, censored for nudity. Our guide tells my father the story in Hebrew, and I catch the word *tuchus*, which means bottom.

We leave the tranquil park. Our day is alternating between the normal and the horrific. We drive to Staro sajmište. A concentration camp across the Sava River but in full view of the city, it served as a warning of Nazi power to the rebellious Serbs. Before that it was the Old Exhibition Ground, the site of fairs, concerts, exhibitions, and sporting events. Only one of the Jews held here survived. A baby who was born in the camp was smuggled out to safety.

A sign commemorates the events that took place, informing us that the Gestapo Concentration Camp was built "to execute Jews and Gypsies. After the execution of Jews, it became a place of execution of captured Partisan and Chetnik fighters as well as the civilians caught in the war area between May 1942 and July 1944. What once was the biggest German concentration camp in occupied Serbia and southeast Europe today is one of the most important memorial places in Serbia."

But it doesn't look like one of the most important memorial places in Serbia. The inconspicuous sign stands at the edge of a small un-mowed lot. Around it, Roma live in low-income housing, their laundry hung out to dry. These families likely have relatives who were imprisoned here during the war. A stray dog wanders by. There's a little restaurant with outdoor seating where patrons enjoy the late afternoon, seemingly unaware of the spot's history.

It's been a draining day. That morning in the hotel Rebecca and I discussed how worried we were about my dad's legs, and I'm sure they're worse now. But none of us mentions it. My dad is not a complainer; what can't be remedied must be endured. He waits in the car while Rebecca, our guide, and I go to see the more prominent monument on the river. There is a second sign, this one in stone, telling us:

> This is the place where the Nazi concentration camp at the Old Belgrade Fair used to be during the occupation of Yugoslavia between 1941 and 1944. War crimes and genocide against around one hundred thousand patriots, members of Yugoslav national liberation movement, children, women and elderly, were committed here. Nearly half of the prisoners were killed either

in the concentration camp or at the mass execution sites like Jajinci, Bežanijska Kosa, Jabuka, and Ostrovačka Ada. Many of them were relocated to death camps throughout the German-occupied Europe. The victims were mostly Serbs, Jews, and Roma. This memorial is dedicated to all of them. It is also dedicated to the victims of the notorious Ustashi concentration camp of Jasenovac, victims of Hungarian occupation who were washed ashore in Belgrade, as well as the heroic resistance to the Nazi terror and all Yugoslav citizens, victims of genocide.

Belgrade on April 22, 1995, on the occasion of the day of commemoration of the victims of genocide and 50th anniversary of the victory over fascism.

Behind the sign is a giant gray sculpture, a broken open circle with two hands reaching skyward, one on each side of the split. We are the only tourists. I don't know what proper etiquette is when you live with a former concentration camp in your midst, but I'm bothered by a young skateboarder. He sits on the sign smoking, his baseball hat on backwards. He stares into space, perhaps focusing on music coming from his earbuds. To me, he represents a Serbia that hasn't erected a single monument with names of Holocaust victims and lets one of its most important memorial locations look like a vacant lot.

The sign was dedicated in the spring of 1995, almost the end of the communist era. Finally, the government acknowledged the genocide against Jews and Roma, not just against its citizens generally. It was three months before the Srebrenica genocide where the Bosnian Serb Army, along with the Scorpions, a paramilitary unit from Serbia, massacred more than 8,000 Muslim Bosniaks, primarily men and boys. Between 25,000 and 30,000 Bosniaks, women, children, and elderly were forcibly transferred. In 2005, Kofi Annan, the Secretary-General of the United Nations, called it the worst crime on European soil since World War II.[3]

We complete our day's touring with a quick trip to Zemun, once a separate city, now a suburb. It's on what was the Austro-Hungarian side of the Sava River. Historically the population there was predominantly Catholic, and most Jews were Ashkenazi. On the Belgrade side of the river, residents mainly were Serbian Orthodox, and the Jews were mostly Sephardic. Culturally it was two different worlds.

Zemun had a thriving Jewish community until the war. Its synagogue is now a restaurant. It's famous as the place where the grandparents of Theodore Herzl, the founder of Zionism, lived. We go to the cemetery to see his grandparents' graves, Rebecca Herzl (1798-1888) and Simon Herzl (1797-1879).

Here too is a monument to Jews killed in the Shoah, with their names listed in Cyrillic letters. Our second cemetery of the day is different, in part because Jews are buried in one section of a larger graveyard. We pass Christian and Muslim graves. For the first time, I see the graves of members of the Communist Party, with the communist star where a religious symbol would be.

We head back to the Hotel Moskva to shower and change before dinner. Back in our suite, I lie on my bed fully clothed, intending to rest for a minute, and fall into a deep sleep until Rebecca wakes me because Dragan is waiting for us. I could have slept until tomorrow.

Dragan picks us up for dinner at his apartment. We drive across the Sava River and into an entirely different place, New Belgrade, Novi Beograd. A city of 200,000 residents that was still blueprints when my grandmother left with her children for Israel. Instead of winding streets lined with old architecture, anonymous, uniform buildings tower over us. The space between them emphasizes their scale, unlike the skyscrapers of New York or even Boston, which stand shoulder to shoulder. Planned cities built during communism focused on shared spaces, such as gardens and parks, to promote communal living. The city was created for the thousands of people moving here from throughout Yugoslavia after the war. There are 72 *blokovi*, or blocks, each referred to by its number.

Surrounded by the Sava and Danube Rivers, New Belgrade was constructed on former swampland, which had been no man's land buffering the Ottoman and Austro-Hungarian empires. Sajmište Fairgrounds, which became the Semlin concentration camp, was built here in the 1930s. However, New Belgrade construction didn't begin until 1948. The enormous concrete buildings were symbols of the country's economic strength in the capital of multi-cultural, socialist Yugoslavia.

We arrive at Dragan's building, which is identical to the ones surrounding us. He drops us off and goes to find a parking space. The rain we had wondered about at the cemetery has arrived and we take shelter in the building's entryway. Shortly Dragan returns, shaking off his umbrella and folding it as we walk in together. We wait for the 1950s elevator that creaks and groans before stopping at the ground floor with a thud. Entering it is an act of faith.

Lejla opens the door and there is that triple kissing again. My father tries to greet her in Serbian to express his gratitude, but the words he can retrieve are in Hebrew. His brain seems to store his Serbian more deeply than his Hebrew. First in, last out.

We sit in their compact living room and look at more black-and-white family photos that are passed around. We lack a common language, but it doesn't feel uncomfortable. Past their balcony, past the rows of uniform high-rise apartments, there is a beautiful sunset.

Lejla shows us the exquisite and intricate lace she likes to make; Dragan's mother Nada taught her. Dragan tells us she wants to give us pieces: one for me, one for my parents, one for my brother and his wife. Knowing the hours she has spent, I feel uncomfortable and want to refuse. But to do so would be to insult her, so I graciously accept, trying to convey that I appreciate the time and skill that went into her beautiful work.

Dinner is delicious. Lejla knows we don't eat meat and seems to have made every vegetarian Serbian dish there is, and a bowl of steamed broccoli because she saw me eat it the night before. There is cornbread, cheese burekas, cheese with spinach burekas, cold roasted green beans with dill, slow-roasted beans, and ajvar, a roasted red pepper sauce. For dessert, we feast on homemade žito, a ground wheat and nut dish that symbolizes death and rebirth, served with whipped cream. I have eaten all these foods before when my mother has cooked them, but it's satisfying to find them all together here in Serbia, where they belong, and where I am starting to see we belong.

Lejla must have started last night by soaking the wheat and beans and then spent the day cooking. She fusses over us, offering us seconds and then thirds, worrying we are still hungry. Some things don't require a common language to convey. I couldn't have imagined a warmer welcome. Apparently, our being here doesn't seem as unlikely to them as it does to me. At the end of the evening, she worries we'll be cold and pulls coats out of her closet for Rebecca and me. I feel as if I've just been to visit a Jewish grandmother.

18

The following morning, Dragan picks us up at the hotel and drives us to a vast Serbian Orthodox cemetery. Today we visit the graves of my Christian family.

Dragan was a soccer star in his youth, and a pair of mini soccer cleats hang from his rear-view mirror. Dangling just below them is an Orthodox cross; its four points end in an oval with a point on top, a little crown. My mother once told me that my dad had cousins in Serbia who weren't Jewish. The implication was that they had somehow lost their Jewishness, possibly through communism or intermarriage, but that it had nothing to do with us or our story.

We are looking for two tombstones, one for Nada, Dragan's grandmother, who is my father's aunt, and one for Radmila, the great-grandmother Dragan and I share. Our guide told us yesterday we can honor them by buying flowers. While of course I know the Christian tradition, I have never brought a bouquet to a grave before. Dragan and my father argue about who will pay the old woman who sits outside the cemetery with plastic buckets full of blooms. The compromise is they will each buy a bunch.

We walk directly to a large stone with an Orthodox cross at the top. Six people are buried here, with their names, photos, birth, and death dates. There is room for four more. Dragan lights a candle. He places the flowers in a vase attached to the stone, stopping first to break the stems. He tells us in Serbian that this keeps people from stealing and reselling them. My dad translates. Every day we are here, he regains more Serbian. Perhaps you can never really lose your mother tongue.

The next grave is covered with flowers and surrounded by four active mourners. We don't acknowledge each other; it seems families attend to their dead with an illusion of privacy. A thriving rosemary bush is on our family grave. I know from studying herbs that rosemary is for remembrance. I point it out to Rebecca, who knows the reference from playing Queen Gertrude in Hamlet. "Look at my flowers. There's rosemary, that's for remembering. Please remember, love," she says, quietly quoting Shakespeare.

Dragan says he tried to plant other things, but they all died. He shows us the rock my aunt Shosh, who they call Ljiljana, her Serbian name, left on the grave last year. Cut flowers are beautiful. Does Dragan understand the Jewish tradition of leaving a rock? Are we the only Jews he's ever met? We place rocks at graves because of their permanence, and it works; Shosh's rock is still here. We are here in Dragan's country, in his family's space, and I want to follow his customs. Though he has been nothing but kind to us, I worry that he will think leaving a rock is strange or stereotypically cheap. But the language barrier prevents this discussion.

This is the Blagojević tombstone, my grandmother's sister Jelena's family. Here, Jelena, Dragan's grandmother is buried with her husband Blagoje and their three children: Nadeshda, nicknamed Nada, her oldest daughter, and Dragan's mother, Vera, her second daughter, and her son Lubomir, nicknamed Luba. They fled Belgrade with my grandmother and father after the Nazi bombing. Luba carried my father on his shoulders. Dragan's brother Boleslav, who died of heart issues in his fifties, is also buried here. My great-aunt Jelena died in 1988; she was alive for my whole childhood. She outlived all three of her children, who died in 1967, 1979, and 1983.

We set out to find Radmila's grave. Dragan has a piece of paper, but it only tells us what section. He calls his cousin Branko, who we have never heard of, for help. My dad rests on a bench, and the three of us walk up and down uneven rows until Dragan finds the stone. My dad comes over slowly and the four of us examine it. At the top in Cyrillic is carved Radmila, with her photo and the dates 1889-1969. Below her is a photo of Joseph, 1899-1934. Dragan tells us in Serbian, with my dad translating, that Joseph is Radmila's son, the one my grandmother was in mourning for when she got married, the one who might or might not have had a different father. Radmila after all, he tells us, had three or four husbands. But something is wrong with the dates; Radmila couldn't have given birth to Joseph at ten. Was she born earlier, or he later? Dragan is confused. Maybe Joseph was her first husband?

Radmila was born Catholic and converted to Orthodox when she married her last husband, Dragan tells us. At that point, she changed her name from Teresa to Radmila, which explains why her name is Teresa on my grandparents' marriage certificate. Nada, his mother, also converted when she got married. Just when I have gotten used to being Serbian Orthodox, I discover my grandmother was Catholic.

Our guide told us we could find out our family saint by asking Dragan, but he says saints pass through your father's line.

My father and Dragan sit together, two old men who are cousins but barely share a common language. Yet there is no doubt about the affection they feel for each other. My father invites Dragan to visit us at the Cape next summer.

Dragan brings us back to our hotel, with plans to meet later along with Branko, the cousin he called. We go for lunch across the street from our hotel. A dark-haired girl of about eight, a Roma or a Syrian refugee maybe, is panhandling through the outdoor seating until the waiter tells her to leave. I Facebook message a childhood friend of my kids, who randomly is also in Belgrade. I had seen a picture the day before of her posed in front of St. Sava. She joins us for a slice of now-cold pizza.

My dad goes to rest, and Rebecca and I walk around with our 17-year-old friend who is meandering alone through Europe. She tells stories of having to get off the train at night at the Hungarian border with the one other American for further inspection by the Serbian border guard. When she was coming into the city, she got off the train with her luggage in New Belgrade by mistake and started walking, only to realize she was miles away and needed a cab. She watched the meter running with no understanding of the currency, "goodness, were those euros?" To her relief, she realized later how cheap dinars are. Her days are unscheduled, wandering the city, trying to get to 10,000 steps on her Fitbit, looking for cheap things to do. She doesn't want to be out in the city alone at night, so she lies on her bed in the studio apartment a friend of a friend is letting her use, with her head angled off the bed to catch the Wi-Fi from next door so she can watch Netflix.

Our young friend has arrived casually, almost accidentally, in the city I have been wanting to visit since childhood. And we are here at the same time. I'd be so jealous if I were seeing her adventures on Facebook from the couch in my kitchen.

The physical pace of our time in Belgrade has been fairly slow. We are in the car a lot, and when we walk, we take breaks for my dad to catch his breath. But the emotional load is exhausting me. Three days here feels like three weeks. That night I wash out a shirt in the bathroom sink in our hotel room. I hadn't packed for three meals with cousins.

The last two nights Dragan's wife Lejla has directed me, with gestures, to pick my bag up off the floor. The first night, in the outdoor café at the Hotel Moskva, I thought she was worried that where I put it left it vulnerable to pickpockets. But she didn't want it on her living room floor either. My dad had translated, "No money on the floor." It must be some sort of superstition. Thinking back, my dad also had a thing about not leaving cash out or lying around. More than once, when I was a kid, he told me to put money away that I'd left on my dresser. It hadn't felt like a superstition, more an admonishment not to be careless, but now they seemed linked. The third night, I leave my bag in a drawer in the hotel to avoid another gestured conversation.

Branko and his son Nikola meet us at the hotel, along with Dragan. Only later do I realize that Branko is the grandson of my grandmother's brother Wilhelm. Dragan, Branko, and I are all equally related; we are Radmila's great-grandchildren.

Nikola is 24 and speaks excellent English. He tells us he's a graphic designer. He wanted to major in history but here all the young people do computer programming or graphic design because that's where the jobs are. He makes about 50 euros a day but could make 200 doing the same job in Western Europe. He lives with his sister Jelena, who takes in stray dogs.

We talk about Joseph, my grandmother's brother. Branko and Dragan know there was another brother, Joseph, but remember nothing about him. Only my dad knows Joseph had a son who fought with the Partisans and died with Žil, my grandfather's brother. Branko and Dragan have stayed in Belgrade, but their memories don't reach back as far as my father's.

Nikola excitedly tells us about the battle they died in, which took place in a parking garage. Stories we've known without context make sense here. There is a well-known Yugoslavian television show from the 1970s, *Otpisani*, which translates as "written off." They have an episode about this parking garage battle. Nikola is sure it must have English subtitles, but I can never find any. Later my dad watches the episode in Serbian. I watch about five minutes. It is over-dramatized with long views of expressions and suspenseful music, not unlike American shows from that era. Nikola tells us we should come back to Belgrade so he can be our guide. We friend each other on Facebook.

Lejla comes, and we walk down a narrow cobblestone street to dinner at a traditional Serbian restaurant. Patrons sit at long tables in the open air and musicians travel around, playing music for tips. We watch a group of men drinking and laughing together, casually touching each other in friendship in a way that groups of straight American men never would. The musicians come to our table and Dragan requests the song Shosh told him was their mother's favorite. My dad doesn't know it. I think again of everything my grandmother gave up when she moved to Israel and wonder at her motivations and regrets.

The food is traditionally Serbian, meat and fish, so Rebecca, a vegetarian, is left with a meal of baked potatoes. My fish comes with its head attached. My father sees my surprised face and quickly cuts off the head and puts it on his plate. He is thrilled to be eating an old favorite of his, the national dish of grilled ground meat, ćevapčići.

That night, 4,000 miles away back home, my younger daughter Sophie receives a school award at an event that features former Red Sox pitcher David Ortiz. Because of the six-hour time difference, I'm already asleep when it happens. I wish I could be there, but I'm right where I need to be—three generations rediscovering our past.

When we head to the airport, our trip still seems unfinished. Dragan meets us to say goodbye. I hug him with genuine affection and three kisses. So much has happened; it's hard to believe we met just four days ago.

We fly back to Heathrow. On our last day away, we take the Eurostar to Paris first thing in the morning. Paris is my father's favorite city. Enacting the scenes from my middle-school French book, we see the Eiffel Tower, take a boat ride on the Seine, and eat ice cream at an outdoor café. We visit the small Holocaust Museum at the tip of the Île de la Cité. At Nôtre Dame, with the new knowledge of our Catholic heritage, I take a moment to stand quietly, searching for connection. I feel nothing.

At Gatwick Airport the gates are down a level. As we wheel our carry-ons towards the escalator, I glance back at my father. A week of travel, a journey back to where he survived Nazi occupation as a preschooler, and a new heart medication that causes his legs to swell, on top of the arrhythmia that leaves him breathless after any exertion, are taking their toll. All trip I've been thinking about how people seem to age in spurts their whole lives. My kids seemed to grow in bursts, coming down for breakfast in pajamas that stopped above their ankle bone when it seemed they'd fit just fine at bedtime. This trek back two generations seems to have caused my dad to jump to some new level of aging. I suggest the elevator, but he insists he wants to navigate the escalator. After Rebecca and I start down, I see him balk at wheeling his suitcase onto the moving ramp. He shouts after us that he will take the elevator after all.

The elevator isn't where the escalator ends, and when we find it, he's not there. The monitors above our heads tell us the gate isn't posted yet, so we wait. Maybe he's behind us. He doesn't come. I doubt he will turn on his phone to connect with us, but I text him just in case. I leave Rebecca with the luggage to find out if there is another elevator, but there isn't. She leaves me to see if he might be sitting somewhere, he's not. I worry.

Finally, they post our gate, number 15. We don't know what else to do, so we head there. Through the plexiglass, on the other side of security, I see my dad comfortably seated, eating a granola bar. How did he get here ahead of us? He says he doubts we will believe his story. He looked at his boarding pass and saw the number 15, his seat number. He assumed that was the gate, not the seat, and walked there. The odds against this are fantastic. How many gates are there in the south terminal?

My family, living and dead, were lost to me. We went to Belgrade and, against all odds, found them just where you'd expect them to be, living in Belgrade and buried in the cemetery, just like my dad waiting at gate 15—not lost at all.

19

At Logan Airport in Boston, the agent at passport control must be looking at my father's place of birth. He asks if we were visiting family like it's the most normal thing in the world. We say we were. He knows nothing of the nearly 70-year gap.

"How was your trip?" well-meaning friends ask. After five or ten minutes of listening and responding appropriately, they move the conversation on to other topics.

But a whole world has opened for me that I need to process and explore. I message back and forth with my cousins in Serbia, wanting to get to know them better, hoping to glean more family information. My perspective has shifted now that Belgrade is a place I've been. I've seen the sights, talked to Serbs, and eaten the food. It's not a place I know well, but at least now we've met.

Itching to know more, I email Barbara at the museum, asking for information about Simon, who we discovered on the side of Bernhard's gravestone. "And do you know anything else about my extended family," I ask. She sends me 23 documents with the name Brill, everything in their archive.

I go through the new documents, finding a brother of my father's grandfather Heinrich. When I look to see if this newly discovered great-great-uncle Filip is older or younger than my great-grandfather, I see that the birthdates match: January 17, 1874. Twins! Filip is the father of Simon, whose inscription we found on the side of Bernhard's grave. This makes Simon my grandfather's first cousin. If the pair were identical, my grandfather and Simon would have genetically been like half-siblings. Simon is listed as a *zubni lekar* [dental clinic] and his mother Evgenija is an *udovica* [widow]. They were living at Andre Nikolića 29 in Belgrade when the war began.

The Nazis stole these everyday family stories my father should have heard growing up. They did not only take lives and homes and goods. They also removed narratives and people—the present and the past.

Simon's birth certificate shows he was born in Belgrade to Filip and Evgenija on December 19, 1911, and circumcised on December 27. My father thinks maybe Simon was the sick friend who was one of the reasons for my grandfather's reluctance to leave while there was still time. I learn Simon was killed in Banjica concentration camp, according to his death record, although he is not on its list of prisoners. Banjica was another German camp on the outskirts of Belgrade where Jewish, Roma, Partisan, Chetnik, and Serbian prisoners were held before being murdered by firing squad.

In the Yad Vashem database, both Evgenija and Simon are listed as victims by my father's uncle Bernhard. Did Bernhard also put up the marker for Simon? Why didn't he add one for Evgenija alongside it? Did he put one somewhere on one of her family's stones? Why didn't he make one for my grandfather Alexander? Did my grandmother's fervent wish that her husband would return—perhaps from Russia where it was rumored Jews would make their way back—prevent a second inscription? My grandmother never remarried; did she hold out hope on some level for her whole life?

I find Johanna, another sister of Heinrich and Filip's. She was born on June 30, 1872, and married Herman Vajntraub on March 11, 1904, when she was already 31. She then disappears with no record of children born, no cemetery plot, and no listing in the Nazi paperwork.

For as long as I can remember, I've wanted to fill in the family tree wiped blank by the Holocaust. We'd lost Filip, Evgenija, Simon, and Johanna, but now they are coming back to us. Though my father didn't know who they were, they likely knew him. They were probably at his parents' wedding and at his bris. They expected to get to watch him grow up in Belgrade.

There are other Brills too. I find Leopold, Elza, and a second Aleksandar, but I don't know how we're related. I draw little trees for the Brills I now have documents for but can't connect to our lineage.

I worry over Stevan Bril, son of the other Aleksandar. Stevan marries Jelena Trgovac, daughter of Edmund and Elizabeta, born Sabo at the Sinagoga u Kos on February 2, 1941. He is 22 and she is 17. Stevan's father and Josif Trgovac, Jelena's brother or uncle perhaps, are witnesses. Was it a hurried wedding without a formal portrait, a feast, or a wedding dress? Young couples would often marry before they escaped together. Was that the case for Stevan and Jelena? They don't appear on any of the German documents. What happened to them? I hope their common Serbian first names, the same as my Christian great-grandfather and great-aunt, hint at a level of assimilation that would allow them to pass. I wish they made it safely to Italy or lived through the war as Partisans, the two most common ways Jews from Belgrade survived.

I realize now the old answer I used to toss off when people asked whether I was related to this or that Brill doesn't suffice any longer. Before I'd respond that all the Brills in my family came from my father and his two uncles. But the documents suggest likely I am related to all the Belgrade Brills, and that they descend from my great-great-grandfather and his two brothers, who all came from Upper Hungary. Maybe Stevan and Jelena, or some other cousin, also survived against the odds. Stevan and Jelena would be in their nineties now, old but not impossibly so. I imagine them in the United States, Israel, Serbia, or perhaps Australia, where survivors also immigrated. They could have children, grandchildren, and great-grandchildren, whose heads are filled with harrowing war stories or who know nothing at all.

I read as many Holocaust second-and-third generation books as I can, seeking to understand how others have dealt with their family legacies of genocide. I pour over *Paper Love: Searching for the Girl My Grandfather Left Behind* by Sarah Wildman, *Three Minutes in Poland: Discovering a Lost World in a 1938 Film* by Glenn Kurtz, and *The Lost: A Search for Six in Six Million* by Daniel Mendelsohn.

The brutality, the improbability of any individual surviving, much less going on to live a functional life, is striking. The stories swirl together and reemerge in my dreams. I think of the details of the lives I'm reading about when I walk my dog Honey, drive to postpartum families' homes for lactation consults, stand in line at my local Whole Foods supermarket. The stories in the books feel almost like they've happened to people I know, to my own family. This is why I've avoided all details of the Holocaust for so long. *The Holocaust by Bullets*, the story of a priest who seeks to document mass shootings and mass graves, sits unread on my living room coffee table. I just can't.

I read in *Paper Love* that Jewish women in Nazi Germany who didn't have Jewish-sounding names had to take the middle name Sarah, and I reflect on my middle name being Sarah. When I was little, I loved that Sarah meant "princess." I am conflicted about my name until I read *Motherland: Beyond the Holocaust, A Daughter's Journey to Reclaim the Past*, by Fern Schumer Chapman. In her memoir about returning to Germany with her mother, Chapman relays this conversation with their local guide:

"'And do you know what I'm hoping my son and his wife will call the child?'

'What?' my mother asks.

'Maybe Joshua or Sara,' he says poetically. 'These are the Jewish names some Germans give their children to show their empathy with the Jews who suffered during the Holocaust.'"[1]

My parents named me Sarah after my maternal great-grandmother Sonia, following the Ashkenazi tradition of taking the first letter of a deceased family member and choosing a more modern, assimilated name that starts with that letter. It's a Jewish middle name, the "h" at the end being the giveaway. I'm back to liking my name.

Sophie helps me type up the family tree Dragan dictated to me, excited when we get to the generation where we can fill in her name and see a younger generation below her. I message my cousin Nikola the documents and pictures I have, as well as the tree, and he helps fill in some gaps. I watch the Genius series on Einstein, enjoying the plotline about his Serbian wife Mileva Marić, who is portrayed as the story's hero. Serbia gets its first female prime minister, and she is openly gay.

In 2017, the Holocaust is alive in the news and in my life. President Trump visits Poland and is criticized when he doesn't go to the Warsaw Ghetto. He's the first president not to go. A Louisiana congressman, Representative Clay Higgins, creates a video advocating an "invincible" American military inside the gas chambers at Auschwitz, despite the museum's request that silence be maintained. Sean Spicer resigns and Steven Goldstein, Executive Director of the Anne Frank Center for Mutual Respect, complains he should have quit months ago. "Spicer needed to leave in April, at the moment he said Hitler did not use chemical weapons on his own people. That was among the most offensive statements from any Presidential press secretary in our nation's history."

We hear from our guide that the property records for Solunska 8 only go back to 1935 and don't list a Brill owner. We've hit a dead end.

I turn 47. Like every birthday, my father reenacts the ritual of his annual retelling of my birth.

"June 12 was a Friday," he remembers. "Your mother's water broke early in the morning. We went to the hospital. The doctor tried to tell us it was too early and we should go back home."

On a health form, I list my grandfather's cause of death as murder for the first time. It seems I should offer more explanation, but there is no room on the short line allotted. Murder sounds more like his death was in a bar fight or a mugging gone wrong. Maybe I should have typed "genocide." I speculate if my answer will alarm the person reading it, but honesty about what happened to him seems newly significant.

I join some second generation, or 2G, groups on Facebook for the children of Holocaust survivors. Now in my Facebook feed, between photos of my friends' kids and political commentary on the Trump administration, I see posts from 2Gs about the Holocaust and its lasting repercussions. Many group members, born in the displaced persons camps immediately after the war, part of the drive to try to reproduce to make up for the lost millions, are old enough to be my parents. They post about being raised by traumatized survivors who said too much or too little about their war experiences. They share family photos, discuss commonalities among their childhood experiences, and search for what our legacy is and what we're handing down to our children.

I am confused the first time I see a reminder post like this: "If anyone had family taken from Kisvarda, Hungary, tonight is the Yahrzeit." Yahrzeit means time of year and refers to the tradition of lighting a candle in remembrance on the anniversary of a family member's death. It can be a little confusing because the deaths are tracked on the Jewish calendar while we live according to the Gregorian one, so sometimes a date can be in a different month altogether. I wonder how the poster can know when other people's family members died. Then it hits me: everyone was murdered at once. And in these villages where Jews intermarried for generations, in a sense one large family was murdered. My family is from a capital city where murders stretched out over months, and I don't have what they do: a day to mourn my grandfather.

We are the People of the Book and I'm not the only 2G in the group writing a memoir. The groups are huge and active but my queries to connect with others with Serbian roots get no responses. Could I be the only one there from Serbia?

I enroll in an online life coach training, where we are taught to practice asking each other, "Tell me about your area of greatest suffering." Knee-deep in Holocaust stories, the word suffering annoys me. I have no suffering. I suspect many in this group of predominantly middle-class, middle-aged, white American women don't either.

20

I've learned more about my father's family than I would have thought possible even a short time ago. It's satisfying. While it's not a complete picture, I've filled in quite a few gaps. Possibly I've gone as far as I can go. Then, on July 21, my dad forwards me eight emails with documents from Dragan's attorney son-in-law. A search I started the year before with an email to the Jewish Museum that I only half expected an answer to has gathered momentum as other forces feed it. I'm not sure if I would have chosen to know the content of the documents. I open them, not expecting how they will make my grandfather's last months more tangible, more visceral.

The documents are census records, the visa application for my grandmother leaving Yugoslavia for Israel, and the application form filing for my grandfather's death. Most significant are five forced-labor documents, with my grandfather's name, Alexander Brill, dated April 1941. I'm amazed that the Jewish Museum doesn't have documents this important.

I knew my grandfather slaved for the Germans, returning home at night, until the night when he didn't. But I didn't think about what my grandfather was actually doing, and I don't believe my father did either. Now, Google Translate tells us he was installing sewer pipes.

These sewers were replacing the ones destroyed in the German bombing. Did my grandfather stand in a trench, one man in a line of men, each with a shovel? I think of black-and-white photos I have seen of Jews doing this kind of labor, dressed in the suits and shoes that reflected their former lives. Men who recently worked in hospitals, law firms, or stores are now out in the elements working with their hands in the dirt. My grandfather was listed on his marriage license as a clerk. I don't know what his job entailed exactly. Still, it was inside work that would not have prepared him for hard physical labor, for being grimy, sweaty, exhausted, and blistered, for the smells of a city without a functioning sewer system.

One document, typed in Latin letters in Serbian, is a pass for Levii Isak, Arceti Jakob, Kavu Jese, Levi Hajim, Bril Aleksander, Almozlinovic Isak, Safer Tibor, Sonenberger Dexider, and Braun Ladiskav. It is dated: "21.-IV-1941." While my father was with his mother and her family in a nearby village, German soldiers with guns and dogs watched my grandfather dig ditches and install pipes. It is one thing to know your grandfather did slave labor for the Nazis and another thing to see written documents laying out the details. My throat tightens and my stomach clenches.

There is fascination and validation as well. It's no longer just fragmented family stories. What happened to my grandfather is documented historical fact. I didn't expect ever to see written proof, didn't even think that it existed, much less that it would arrive unbidden in my inbox.

Nazi lists were so powerful. In *After the Holocaust the Bells Still Ring*, Joseph Polak writes, "Typewritten meant official... Each name and its accompanying detail occupied a line; the approaching end of the line was signaled by the typewriter bell, and soon after it rang, the next line, with its next victim bell, so that bell tolled for you, and for each person after you. Six million bells rang in those years.[1]

I have seen my grandfather's name, Alexander Brill, written down so few times in my life. What is more familiar is my brother's name. Alex says being named for our grandfather is more meaningful because he was murdered in the Holocaust. So many people in this story have multiple names. My grandmother Rene Yellisavata Francezi became Regina Brill, like her deceased mother-in-law, and the whole time went by Delfa. Her mother was Theresa Francezi but remarried and converted and became Radmila. Across countries, whether his official name was Heinrich or Haim, my father went by Bubika, a name I never heard until we went to Serbia, where our cousins use it comfortably. When Sophie first heard this, she remarked to my dad, "They know who you are." All these multiple names, and here is the opposite, my brother with the same name as my grandfather, accounted for with a faint penciled checkmark on the list of sewer repairers.

I type in the Serbian words. Google Translate tells us the pass describes my grandfather and the other Jewish men as "water tankers, sewer-installers, and plumbers" and that "They are headed for work in the management of the water supply of P.G.B. address of the press, street 34. April 21, 1941, Belgrade." The form is illegibly signed. By whom? A Serb? Serbs were fighting the Germans but also collaborating with them.

The second document is in Cyrillic lettering, so Google Translate is no help. It is dated April 20, 1941, and bears the same stamp but a different signature. Men are listed under seven categories. With two and half years of schooling in Cyrillic 70 years ago, my father finds my grandfather's name: Alexander Brill. He's one of five on the list of water tankers, sewer installers, and plumbers. My father recognizes that another category is electricians.

I send our guide the documents for help with translation, and he writes back that the forced laborers are categorized as civil engineers, mechanical engineers, electrical engineers, chemists, electricians, locksmiths, tinsmiths, plumbers, and installers of sewage and water supply. Another typed document lists my grandfather and his brother, along with dozens of other men, many of whom they probably knew all their lives. Ašer J. Albahari lived a few doors down at Solunska 4, Hajnirh H. Fišer and Salaman M. Altarez across the street at Solunska 13, and Isak A. Albahar around the corner on the street my father would live on after the war: Kraja Petra. All are probably buried now in the mass grave at Jajinci where no sign lists victims' names. Likely they have no living descendants, no one to search out the details of their fate. I hope my listing them here is a small way to honor them.

German units entered Belgrade on April 12, 1941, six days after the bombing. They immediately began looting the property of local citizens, especially Jews, with ethnic Germans helping the soldiers. On April 19, under threat of death, Jews had to sign up at the Special Police Headquarters at Tašmajdan. The dates on the documents, April 20 and 21, and the location Tašmajdan, fit the historical context.

Dorde Alpar, a survivor who didn't register but witnessed male Jews reporting from the high ground above Tašmajdan, described it thus:

"Those who are there are being lined up in groups. Later I learn they are being sorted according to qualifications: doctors, engineers, merchants, tradesmen, students, and so on. Every tenth person is removed from the group, 122 of them, and taken to be shot as a reprisal for the burning of a truck. Among them is Raka Mandil, a 16-year-old schoolboy, a wonderful companion from the youth group of which I was a leader."[2]

On April 25, 1941, new orders said Jews were only allowed to buy food after 10:30 a.m. Public fountains (necessary after the bombing destroyed water pipes) could only be used by Jews after all Aryans had received water. Breaking these laws would result in being sent to a concentration camp.[3] After May 24, Jews, Roma, and anyone married to Jews and Roma could not be employed or use telephones, hotels, restaurants, cinemas, or theaters.[4]

On May 30, the Nazis proclaimed an Order Concerning Jews and Gypsies:

> A Jew in the sense of all orders already issued and those that will be issued by the Military Commander for Serbia, is any person who is descended from at least three Jewish grandparents. The grandparents are considered as Jews if they are racially pure Jews or belong to the Jewish religion or have belonged to it. Half-breeds from one or two Jewish grandparents, who have after April 5, 1941, belonged to or joined the Jewish religious community, are also considered Jews.[5]

Jews were required to register and wear yellow armbands on their left arms. They could no longer be public servants, lawyers, physicians, dentists, veterinarians, or pharmacists, and everyone between the ages of 14 and 60 had to report for forced labor. All Jews had to report their property within ten days. They had to give up their radios, cameras, refrigerators, and telephones. They could no longer own businesses. They couldn't ride on trams. On May 31, these sporadic decrees were codified in the Official Gazette of the Decrees by the Military Command in Serbia as "Orders Referring to Jews and Gypsies."[6]

Yugoslavia was no different from other places across the Reich. I remember believing as a child that since we didn't learn about it in Hebrew school, since five members of my family had survived there, it somehow wasn't as bad in Serbia as in other places. Having my grandfather's horrible experience confirmed in writing proves the opposite is true.

Each name is checked off with a faint pencil mark.

"Is anyone missing?" Sophie asks, looking up from her phone. She's drawn into the story, hopeful that someone escaped all those years ago.

Yes, one name is crossed off and another is circled. But a third name has been written in by hand and checked off. I can't read the Cyrillic names, but I see three together that are the same. Were they brothers? Father and sons? Is there anyone left who has searched them out? Claimed them as family?

Another form lists my grandfather as number 182 and his address as Solunska 8. His brother, Žil H. Bril, same address, is number 125. So Žil had been rounded up into that forced labor pool as well. Somehow, he fled and was able to fight and die in the resistance. Did he not report one day? There was a curfew at night, and you needed a pass during the day. How did he do it? My grandmother might have known, but now it's another story likely lost to history.

An internet search reveals Tašmajdan is the name of a Belgrade park, also called Taš. It has an extensive cave network that has been used since Roman times. During World War II, the Germans used the caves as a staging area for all Eastern Europe. The head of the German Air Forces in Serbia, Alexander Lohr, had his headquarters there. Hundreds of soldiers were equipped to spend months there without any surface contact. They had phone lines, a ventilation system, and a power generator. After the war, it was sealed off because the area was mined, but there is talk of turning it into a museum. In 2010-2011, Azerbaijan reconstructed the park as a gift to the people of Belgrade.

I find a black-and-white picture from the Bundesarchiv, the German archives, of the April 1941 registration at Tašmajdan. In the photo, the Jewish men of Belgrade are gathered together, waiting. They are dressed in jackets and shirts with collars. They stand, facing the photographer, except for one elderly man who sits. A boy of maybe 12 with a cap leans out and is blurred by the movement. A man near the front appears to check his watch as if he's late for an appointment. Before the end of the year almost all of them will be dead: worked to death or murdered in retribution for Nazi deaths, 100 for each dead soldier, 50 for each wounded one.

My grandfather, his brother, and cousin are likely somewhere in this crowd. It is probably the last picture of them. I think of the image of my grandfather holding my infant father, posing with his young wife, and try to spot his face. But I can't; beyond the first few rows, the faces blur.

Likely this is the April 19 registration. The men are not yet wearing yellow armbands imprinted with the word *JUDE*, Jew in German, and below it, the word in Serbian, *JEBPEJ(H)H* or Jevrei. Some armbands also had a Star of David. Yellow material had been stolen from Jewish textile shops, so it was not uniform; some was cotton, some silk, and the shade of yellow varied. [7]

A second picture taken at the same location shows some men standing in front of a table registering; they are wearing their armbands. My father's comment at the Jewish Museum in Belgrade echoes in my head. *How can there be pictures of this?*

We can decipher nothing from the Cyrillic letters on the application of death for my grandfather or the declaration of my grandmother's abdication of citizenship. It is dated 1949. She had left for Israel the previous December. Dragan tells us Jelena, his grandmother's name, is on it. She must have picked up the paperwork. My grandmother's ship was leaving, and she couldn't wait for documents. My grandmother turned her back on Yugoslavia, on a broken continent.

In Israel, she followed the custom of giving her children Hebrew names. She changed my aunt's name from Lilliana to Shoshana—first a lily, then a rose. My father went from Heinrich, his grandfather's name, which was now obtrusively German, to Haim. She started their new life by naming him literally "life."

Likely she couldn't imagine a grandchild nearly as old now as she was when she died grasping an identity she had jettisoned. But here I am, reclaiming my Serbian heritage, aching to fill in gaps, puzzling over documents and old pictures, searching for clues. If my grandmother had lived into her seventies or eighties, these might be stories I took for granted, details I never bothered to examine.

There are four census forms. One is for my father's uncle Bernhard and another for his uncle Žil, showing both living alone. A third is for his father, showing his mother living there as well. The fourth lists my father's grandfather Heinrich as head of household, living with his wife, born in Šabac, and all four boys, who are still minors, on February 29, leap day, 1924. On the forms, there is a category for *"vera"*, which means faith. It's one of the few Serbian words I know because it is the name of my father's cousin. His aunt named her children Nada (hope), Vera (faith), and Ljuba (love). All the documents list the *vera* as Ashkenazi.

I break my no-genocide-before-bed rule to have another go at the forms, one word at a time. In the home I have lived in comfortably for over 20 years, in the room where Sophie was born, I dream about the documents all night long. I dream I am translating but have no pen. As soon as I figure out one word, I have lost the previous. Papers are swirling and the harder I try, the more confusing it gets. I lie awake in the dark, thinking about the paperwork, about my grandparents, about reporting every morning with your neighbors to an occupier who forces you to dig ditches. When I fall asleep again, I am folded back into the same dream.

Another night I dream I am packing to go to a concentration camp. I research it like I'm planning a trip. I talk to a woman who is already there. The food is constipating, she tells me. Bring these laxative herbs. I am oddly devoid of emotion as I fold clothes the kids will need into their duffels. I pack snow pants and wool socks, although it is summer. I remember their phone chargers. I wake thinking of how I have brought back my childhood fears. I snuggle my sleeping dog, stare at the pre-dawn sky, and know I'm done sleeping. My mind turns to the women of Belgrade who turned in the keys to their homes, labeled with their addresses, and then reported to be interned at the Old Fairgrounds. I think of my grandmother living with her mother and her young children, knowing, as everyone in the city did, that her neighbors were prisoners on the other side of the river.

Sophie and I visit Rebecca, who has a summer internship on the Connecticut coast. It's a beautiful day and we sit on the grass outside her dorm and picnic, go to the beach, eat dinner at a clam shack. I want to tell her about the documents. I know she'd be interested, but the day is too idyllic, and I don't let genocide cast a shadow. What does it mean for my children, now young adults, to be third generation? What stories will go forward with them about the Holocaust? I tried to spare them from the brutality when they were little; now it seems essential for them to understand.

Googling about Serbia, a preoccupation that now seems to swallow my spare time, I find a story about a second restitution fund for Jews. It's unrelated to individual property ownership. Funds will be drawn from a central pool based on the number of applicants out of the estimated 1,000 survivors living abroad. My father wants to pursue it, not for the money but for the principle. I'm glad he wants to stand up and be counted.

My dad dictates and my mother hand writes:

> I was born to Jewish parents, Alexander and Regina Brill. My grandfather was killed in the bombing of Belgrade in April 1941. In the fall of 1941, my father was taken away by the Nazis. We did not know where he was and we never saw him again. In May 1942, my sister Ljiljana was born. During the war years, we lived under very difficult conditions. We hid in various locations and there was always a shortage of food. The Nazis were always looking for Jewish women and children. It was a terrible and frightening time for myself and my sister and our mother struggling to survive. After the war, we discovered strangers were living in our house on Solunska Ulica. We moved into one room on the third floor of the Jewish Community Center. In December 1948, we left Belgrade and immigrated to Israel.

My father sends a copy of his birth certificate with the application. There is a stamp in Hebrew on it, which he translates as "Ashkenazi Group Belgrade." I still don't understand the autonomy the Jewish community had in Yugoslavia in 1938. They were registering their own births. In Serbian it says: "Rabbinate Jewish Religion Local Authority." He also sends copies of my grandfather's forced labor documents.

My aunt had applied for restitution as well, but she was turned down since her application didn't prove she'd been born during the war. Unlike my father, she couldn't produce a Yugoslavian birth certificate since she'd been born to a family in hiding.

My father hears back from the general Serbian restitution fund, the SAVEZ Compensation Program for Holocaust Survivors.

"Thank you for all the documents that you have sent. I have reviewed them, and you do not need to send the birth certificate of your sister. The documents that you have sent are quite sufficient. They present a firm proof of your whereabouts during the Holocaust.... the enclosed documents that you have sent are so good that now they confirm not only your persecution story but also the story of your sister."

My father's story validated her application and allowed her to be approved as well. He forwards me this email with the note, "We're rich." He's joking of course. Is it satisfying to have a stranger confirm your experience 75 years later?

I find the first Serbian television series to be released in America. *The Scent of Rain in the Balkans* is about a Sephardic family living in Sarajevo and Belgrade. The title references a Serbian metaphor for impending disaster.[8] The story begins before World War I and continues through World War II. It is low budget and sappy, with overacting and dramatic music and lots of train station scenes of people leaving to find jobs or fight in wars. I love it.

I gather with my parents in their family room to savor each installment. We are amazed that this window into our obscure lost world exists. At the beginning of the episode, a voiceover announces in Serbian: "Knowing your family means learning everything about yourself." The translation sounds like something you'd find in a fortune cookie, but it resonates. This is why I keep digging deeper when someone else might just have walked away.

What is it about seeing our stories portrayed like this that is so immensely satisfying? This must be why people have told stories since the beginning of time. The characters walk by the statue of the hatless rider. They live through events I've studied. The villagers run from the encroaching army without even knowing which army it is. At one point, the youngest daughter is living in Belgrade during World War II. She considers following the order to report to the Staro sajmište concentration camp. She and a friend speculate about why the Germans are requiring this and conclude, "At least they can't kill us all."

21

I start working on getting Stolpersteine placed outside my father's childhood home in Dorćol. They would be a quiet but powerful reminder to everyone walking down Solunska, marking the space so people don't have the luxury of forgetting.

At first, I think of placing just one for my grandfather, but then I want to include his cousin Simon, and Simon's mother Evgenija. The Stolpersteine website talks about reuniting families by listing survivors and victims together. This would mean including my grandmother Regina, my father, my aunt Shoshana, and their uncle Monika. What about their uncle Žil who died fighting in the resistance? He is neither a victim nor a survivor. Would he be on the plaque? I decide to wait to ask my father and aunt if they want to be on a plaque until the project begins to take shape.

I picture all the Brill descendants from Boston, Los Angeles, Washington, DC, and Israel gathering in Belgrade's Dorćol neighborhood for the placement of the stones. I'm there with my father and my aunt, my kids, my brother and his kids, my dad's three cousins, their kids and grandkids. By my count, we are 25 direct descendants and there would be spouses there as well, most of whom have never been to Serbia. We fill the sidewalk outside Solunska 8 and spill out onto the street. It's a family reunion of sorts. My octogenarian father is the oldest, and there are cousins I've never met who are too young for school. The Nazis meant to keep my father and aunt from surviving the occupation. None of the rest of us were supposed to be born at all. But Hitler could not prevent this moment.

The international Jewish press would report on the first Stolpersteine in Serbia, in all of the former Yugoslavia. The local Jewish community, each of whom defied the odds by existing, the Israeli ambassador to Serbia, and the Serbian press would attend. Residents and passersby who appear to know nothing of Dorćol's Jewish roots could not miss this crowd. Perhaps they would cross the street to see what the fuss was about. And when it was over and we were all scattered in our homes, the shiny stones would remain. We'd have a permanent reminder of our family, specific people with names and birthdays, and all the Jewish residents of Dorćol who have no descendants to mark their final voluntary residence. My grandfather and his home are gone, but the spot where he lived is marked by the first Stolperstein in Serbia, the first marker there that names a victim of the Holocaust.

I email Anne, Demnig's assistant for placement of stones outside Germany. She tells me these would be the first stones placed in Serbia and any country in the former Yugoslavia. I need to get permission from Belgrade's mayor. I find an email address online, but my request receives no response. I email the Belgrade synagogue and the Belgrade Jewish community for help but stop short of asking the Jewish Museum for another thing.

I message my cousin Tanja, Dragan's daughter. We are both around the same age but separated by a generation; my grandmother and her great-grandmother were sisters. We chat about the forced labor documents and the document where my grandmother renounces Yugoslavian citizenship, which her great-grandmother signed, since my grandmother was already in Israel.

She writes: "When I saw the documents with names, dates of birth and death, I get emotional. These were real people, my cousins who lived here in my hometown."

I ask her what she knows about what happened to her great-grandmother during the war. She responds:

"Jelena died when I was 17 years old, but then, like all teenagers, I didn't have much interest about that time. Now I eat myself because she would certainly have had interesting stories of those days and about all the members of her family. But we can't do anything about that now, so we must learn our family history through papers and documents. I only remember her story about that morning when Belgrade was bombed on 6 April 1941. She had just woken up to send her husband Blagoje off to work. He was a taxi driver. It was early in the morning when bombs started falling. They had to hide. When I was little, I imagined how she must be feeling on that cold April morning when her whole life is about to change. She had a hard life."

I remember looking at her grave and realizing she outlived all three of her children.

With Tanja's help, my father hires a Belgrade attorney to help with a property search. He tells my father his family never owned Solunska 8. His parents must have been tenants.

Anne, the coordinator for the Stolpersteine project, emails to let me know she's coming to Boston. The first Stolperstein exhibit outside of Germany will be at Boston City Hall. The Stolpersteine are literally coming to me.

We meet for coffee at Brandeis. The library café is a stone's throw from Sophie's freshman dorm. We chat for hours; it's like I'm meeting an old friend. Anne doesn't usually travel to where the stones are placed. But she tells me she'll come to Belgrade if I succeed in getting permission for my family's stones. That there aren't any in Serbia makes it more critical that we do this.

Anne remarks that six million is a number no one can comprehend, but we can understand one individual or family. She is working towards the first North American Stolperstein and the first one in English. She was contacted by a woman in Quebec whose father, a Polish immigrant, went back to fight for Poland and died in a camp. His stone will be outside his last voluntary residence in Montreal. The first English stone will be in the Channel Islands, which Churchill didn't try to defend and which Germany occupied.

We talk about my inadequate Holocaust education in public schools in suburban Boston and her inadequate Holocaust education in England. Anne feels Germany does a better job of teaching school children about the genocide than anywhere else. Part of her job involves education. Her Boston visit includes the German School and Malden High, whose student vandalized the New England Holocaust Memorial in Boston, inspired by the violent, racist events in Charlottesville.

What does a genocide that happened over 70 years ago mean for today? Anne tells me about a Canadian border guard at the airport in Toronto who asked her the purpose of her trip. While holding her passport in his hand, he remarked, "Hitler wasn't that bad until 1936," an oddly specific form of denial, disturbing in part because it suggests study of the topic.

Anne criticizes an official who, earlier that week, at a forum at Boston City Hall, praised Germany for the work it was doing recognizing its past. She disagrees with that kind of self-congratulatory attitude; you don't get points for doing the right thing after doing the incomprehensible. I had been at that event with my parents and hadn't even registered his comments, but I immediately agree with her point.

Hungry to be able to imagine what my family experienced, I search the internet for firsthand accounts from other Jewish families in Serbia. Centropa's website tells the story of a Sephardic family who lived in Belgrade for centuries. They were all killed except for two sisters and their mother. Those sisters, now old women, are ten years older than my father, old enough to remember their lives before the war. They recall how their mother, who had converted to marry their father, was often at odds with her mother-in-law, who insisted that if she were going to eat ham sandwiches, she had to do it out in the street. Did I have a ham-sandwich-eating grandmother?

Reviewing early 20th-century Yugoslavian history in *Life in Dark Ages: A Memoir*, I realize how closely it might tie in with my grandfather's name. King Alexander became the crown prince of Yugoslavia when his older brother George renounced his right to the throne on March 27, 1909. My grandfather was born a few months later, on July 5, 1909. My great-grandparents, following the Sephardic tradition, had named their oldest son Bernhard after his paternal grandfather. My grandfather should have been named Baruh after his maternal grandfather. Did his parents forsake tradition to name him after the future king?

Serbian and then Yugoslavian history is colorful and violent. Few leaders seem to die in bed. King Alexander's father, King Peter I, came to power in a violent coup that killed the ruling king and queen. King Alexander became heir to the throne when his older brother was declared unfit after killing his valet; some believe Alexander orchestrated the event. Alexander was educated in St. Petersburg at the court of Nicholas II and maintained a royal dictatorship that was fiercely anti-communist after the Czar and his family were executed by the Bolsheviks. Following World War I, Woodrow Wilson encouraged the creation of the Kingdom of Yugoslavia. Alexander tried to protect his newly formed country from German and Hungarian aggression with the Little Entente, a treaty between Yugoslavia, Czechoslovakia, and Romania. In 1934 he was assassinated in Marseille, in what was one of the first assassinations to be filmed.

Through the US Holocaust Memorial Museum, I get family documents from Bad Arolsen, the German archives. Bad Arolsen contains information on 17.5 million victims of the Nazi regime. Its primary purpose was to reconnect families. Records on those who sought information were added to the files of those they requested information on. But it had a massive backlog of searchers, and people were dying without answers. The 11 countries that govern it—the United States, the United Kingdom, France, Germany, Italy, Belgium, the Netherlands, Greece, Poland, and Luxembourg—kept it closed to researchers and reporters from 1955 to 2008. Finally, in 2008, it was partially opened to investigators for online searches. At that point, key wording was changed. "Died" became "murdered," and "evacuated to the east" became "deported."[1]

The information comes quickly. The museum has a fast track for the families of victims. As I'm waiting at Brandeis for Sophie's dance show to begin, I get a call from Bashi, a researcher clarifying details to improve the search. I step out of the auditorium into a quiet hallway to hear her better. She says she's watching her young grandson, who interrupts our discussion. "Please be a good boy while I'm on the phone," she says. It's like I'm chatting with someone I know, not a faceless museum employee. It seems for both of us, tracking down the Jewish past in Nazi Europe seeps into our nights and weekends.

22

The official papers from Bad Arolsen legitimize and reaffirm family stories. My response to German documents is more visceral than to the Serbian ones; I feel it in my stomach. German is a far easier language to get translated. I post them in a 2G group on Facebook and have a translation before bedtime. Some of the forms relate to my grandmother's efforts to get restitution money in the early 1950s.

The new yield includes a vital date, November 13, 1941, the day my grandfather was transported from the camp in Belgrade. The United States hadn't even entered the war yet.

It is chilling how the Germans recorded this kind of thing. My grandmother surely did not know what I know now: November 13 was her husband's death date, his Yahrzeit date when he should be remembered with the Kaddish and a candle according to Jewish tradition. I put it into an online Hebrew calendar and learn it was a Thursday, the 23rd of the Hebrew month of Cheshvan.

Coincidentally, both my grandfathers have Yahrzeit dates in the same week. And it is the week my nephew will celebrate his bar mitzvah this year. Now both Yahrzeit dates can be announced at his synagogue when he is bar mitzvahed. It will sound so normal and obscure the 76 years that passed before we found it out.

From Bad Arolsen, via the US Holocaust Memorial Museum, comes the typed list of surviving Jews from the Autonomous Relief Committee

Belgrade, part of the Union of Jewish Communities of Yugoslavia, compiled in 1946. For decades it wasn't well understood that Arolsen also housed postwar material. Each survivor is listed, last name first, with their birth year and city of birth. Here's a record created by leaders of a traumatized community, a head count of who was left when Jews emerged from hiding and returned to Belgrade. My father and aunt, numbers 426 and 427, are the only children listed on the section I receive.

I submit a request for Hanna, my father's aunt by marriage, who was my grandmother's friend. Hanna and my father were quite fond of each other. I remember meeting her when I was five. I threw up in the cab on the way from the motel to her house in Los Angeles. When we got there, she had strawberries, my favorite, but I couldn't eat them because of my sick stomach. She kindly wrapped them up for me to take with me. I thought her old, but the documents show she was born in 1919, so she was 55.

Hanna assumed a false Christian identity and moved from Fornas, Czechoslovakia to Budapest, where she was known to no one. She found work in a shoe factory where she met her future husband Bernhard, who was doing the same thing. In 2001, she submitted her false papers to the US Holocaust Memorial Museum. Her alias was Kristin Palna. The document has her picture, showing a young woman with dark curly hair, alongside a handwritten pass and an official stamp.

On their restitution requests from Germany, Hanna, her husband Bernhard, and his brother Monika all have invented stories. The wording Google Translate spits back is identical. They all wore the Jewish star on an armband from the time of the occupation. The brothers lived in occupied Belgrade, then made their way through some villages and lived in the Jewish ghetto in Budapest. Hanna started in Czechoslovakia before arriving in the Budapest ghetto. The stories are fabricated to meet the requirements for restitution. While they are Holocaust survivors under the definition used by Yad Vashem and the US Holocaust Memorial Museum, Jews who survived in occupied Europe, they didn't meet the more stringent requirements for German restitution. None of them ever received any money.

Seeing my family's past mapped out across the generations helps me see my place in it. I encourage my mother to buy funeral plots in Sharon Memorial, where my maternal grandparents, great-grandparents, and aunt and uncle are buried. We have talked about it before, but this time, she sets up an appointment to purchase six plots to cover her, my father, my brother and his wife, me, and some imaginary future spouse. At the last minute, I decide to buy four more for my kids and their future spouses. It feels slightly morbid, but I reason I'm giving them an investment they can always sell if they don't want it. The cemetery salesman—what do they call themselves?—calls to remind me that spouses can only be buried there if they're Jewish.

My father receives $380 from Serbia, the first of his annual restitution payments. He expects the payments to go up every year as people die. It seems increasingly unlikely he will get property restitution.

The Serbian government compensated the Jewish Community in Belgrade for all unclaimed Jewish property. This self-administration follows the Serbian pattern of allowing each group autonomy over their own affairs. When heirs come forward to claim restitution for stolen property, the community is responsible for distributing the money owed. In the meantime, they can use the funds for community purposes, so there is a disincentive for them to help with restitution. Rather than operating a database where survivors and descendants can submit their ancestors' names to see if there's a property match, they are required to present the address of the stolen property. All the addresses where we know our family lived before the war come up as owned by other people during our search. My father is sure his grandfather owned land in the village they went to after the bombing. His mother told him his father used to go there to collect rent. He's frustrated there is no central database in Serbia and thinks they only want to appear to be trying to get into the EU.

My father now speaks about newly discovered family facts with a familiarity that implies he has grown up knowing this.

"My grandfather was a twin," he reminds my mother. "His son Simon and my father were life-long friends. My mother told me they wanted to run away together. My uncle Monika or uncle Bernhard put up the marker to him and his mother on the side of my great-grandfather's stone with the words 'victims of fascism.' We don't know what happened to my grandfather's twin. He should be buried in the cemetery in Belgrade or on the Nazis' lists. Maybe, like my grandfather, he was killed in the bombing."

I want to say that this is a gift for him as he heads into his eighties, but really it is restitution. He has gotten back what is rightfully his. He and my mother buy a Kiddush cup for my nephew as a bar mitzvah gift. "This is for Jonah, ben Alexander, ben Haim, ben Alexander, ben Heinrich, ben Bernhard," he says proudly, marking the y chromosome and the family name handed down over five generations, 150 years, from Slovakia to Serbia to Israel to the United States.

The Serbian student at Brandeis I've hired to translate the Bad Arolsen documents by Thanksgiving sends them in mid-January. Here is my great-grandfather's signature on a residency document. He has no grave or death certificate, no surviving photographs or letters, nothing he owned has been passed down. My father is the only one who remembers him now, and that is with the haziness of a toddler's recollections. But here is a record of his existence.

The documents list family members living at various places in Belgrade in the 1930s, although thus far we've not been able to turn up ownership records for any of them. One document is dated 1930, which can't be right because my father is listed on it, and he was born in 1938. The document lists him with the right birth date and month and his year of birth as 1838. An odd mistake for my great-grandfather to make.

The death document for my grandfather answered the question of death/disappearance simply as "as a Jew." It lists his potential lifetime earnings as 1,500,000 dinars, just over $15,500 US dollars today. My grandmother lists herself as a housewife and asks for 700,000 dinars but is given 400,000. My father, age seven, is listed as a student, asking for 200,000 and given 168,000. My aunt Shoshana, who would have been three when the document was filled out on September 20, 1945, is listed as a child, age four, asking for 200,000. She is awarded 204,000.

The family would have received 780,000 dinars or roughly half the estimated lifetime earnings. This money was not related to the Nazi genocide but to the death of a Serbian wage earner during the occupation. The County War Commission awarded it five months after it was filed, on February 14, 1946. It likely would have been paid out as a pension over time, something my grandmother forfeited when she renounced her citizenship and left for Israel.

This age discrepancy concerning my aunt makes me ponder if she might actually have been four or closer to it in September 1945. Without a birth certificate, my grandmother could have chosen a birthdate for her later. While I'm not sure what incentive she would have had to make her younger than she was, an earlier birthdate would make my father's memory fit. He vividly recalls her being born while they still lived at Solunska 8. His retelling of the night she was born starts with remembering peeking out to watch German soldiers march in pairs down his street.

"They had long rifles," he tells me. "Longer than modern guns. They wore helmets and had curved metal plates on chains around their necks. Perhaps those were for identification or to show they were on duty."

From his viewpoint at the window, he was looking down on their heads. If they had glanced up, the patrolling army would have seen a small, vulnerable, dark-haired boy.

The night his sister was born, his mother couldn't go to the hospital because of the curfew. Two of those German soldiers brought a female doctor to their home. My dad was asleep in his father's bed. Waking after the baby's birth, he said, "My sister is here." Leaving his mother to wonder how he knew it was a girl.

I had used his clear memory of place to establish they were still living in Dorćol in May 1942. I see now that was impossible. Jewish women and children were imprisoned in Sajmište concentration camp, the old fairground across the river, by the previous winter. Those who survived influenza, exposure, and starvation were gassed in the mobile van by May. Knowing my aunt was born at Solunska 8 means understanding my grandmother changed her birthdate.

I pull up on my phone the one picture I have from the war, the one where my father and aunt stand on the street. From their clothes I can tell it is spring or summer. If my aunt were born in May, as now seems impossible, she would be about a year or two in the picture. I peer at it. She is standing solidly on her own two feet, clearly a toddler, and while my dad has told me she walked early, I don't believe she is a year old. She is too robust. But it is also hard to believe she is two. She has hardly any hair. She looks about a year and a half, matching an older birthdate.

At a local Indian restaurant's lunch buffet, I show my parents and Rebecca the image. The little boy in the picture "looks so much like Papa now," Rebecca comments. "And also, Uncle Alex and Jonah." She hands my mother the phone.

My mom examines the image. "Not a year old, even if she did walk early. Not two either," she pronounces.

My dad barely glances at it. "I don't know, and I don't care," he says, not angrily, but with a finality that closes the topic. "And don't ever mention this to your aunt."

Another document lists where in Dorćol my father's mother and uncles were living on various dates in the 1930s. Inexplicably there are two other names on the list. One is Pelagija Francezi, an unknown person with the same maiden name as my grandmother, living at 2 Mutapova, a neighborhood near where St. Sava Church now stands. A different document lists my great-uncle Solomon as having been born in Velika

Plana, implying the family was living about 60 miles away from Belgrade in 1915. Several documents list where Ernestina Nakman lived on various dates, although if and how we are related is unknown.

At the bottom, in all capital letters, the exit document proclaims:

> By a decision made by the Ministry of Internal Affairs of Socialist Federal Republic of Yugoslavia from 20.5.1949, an announcement of Socialist Federal Republic of Yugoslavia citizenship denouncement has been accepted for the below listed:
>
> Bril (Regina) Jelisaveta, clerk from Belgrade, 71 Seventh July Street, born in Belgrade on 9.9.1914 from father Stevan Francezin and mother Radmila born Blaž, and underage children Bril Hajnrih born on 23.8.1938 and Bril Ljiljana born on 5.2.1942 in Belgrade. The appointed ceases to be a citizen of Socialist Federal Republic of Yugoslavia and Socialist Republic of Serbia on 11.8.1948 when she filed a citizenship denouncement to the Ministry of Internal Affairs. We request the appointed to be erased from the Citizens Book of the Socialist Republic of Serbia, and regarding immovable property, a procedure for transferring ownership of the nationalized immovable property of foreign citizens should be initiated (Socialist Federal Republic of Yugoslavia from 23.6.1940)
>
> DEATH TO FASCISM, FREEDOM TO THE PEOPLE!

Here is the evidence that remains 70 years later of my grandmother packing up her two young children, renouncing her ties to Yugoslavia, and moving to a six-month-old country in the Middle East that is at war with its neighbors. She must have believed emigrating would mean a better future for her children.

Another document, six months after her move, announces:

> Based on the carried checkup I have determined the appointed has no immovable or movable property in the territory of this region.
>
> June 8, 1949

The Yugoslavian bureaucracy certified they left nothing in Belgrade. My grandmother could never have imagined her grandchild would one day hold a copy of this document in her hands, translated from Serbian to English, and ponder what could have moved her figuratively and literally. I inherited nothing from my grandmother, but I've found something she left behind.

Much later, my mother finds a clue in the exit document I've overlooked. I'd read my aunt's birthday as May 2 and not noticed anything was amiss, although she celebrates on May 5. Unlike Americans, Europeans list the day first and then the month. The document proclaims her birthday to be on the fifth day of the second month, not May 2 but February 5.

23

My father and I decide to plan a second trip. I'm hoping another visit will trigger new childhood memories. I'm keen to see some of Serbia outside the capital. I want to solidify our family connections. I'm thrilled my 18-year-old daughter Sophie will have a chance to see where her grandfather is from, with him there to explain.

Going back the next year is easier. We are going to a known place. I can picture the airport, the hotel, the palačinki stand. My dad seems less excited this time and it requires a bit more persistence to pin down travel dates. But once we get our plane tickets, he seems eager, happy to have a more leisurely second trip with time to drink cappuccinos and people watch.

I think again of the line at the beginning of every episode of *The Scent of Rain in the Balkans*: "Knowing your family means learning everything about yourself." When we first discovered that my grandmother was born Catholic, Sophie found this new knowledge significant. "To me, being Jewish is more about ethnicity than religion," she explained. "So, knowing that I'm not all Jewish matters. Being less Jewish, coming from this Serbian family, makes me more Serbian." I also feel our Serbian roots more strongly now.

As we prepare to return to Belgrade, I set a news alert for Serbia. Much of what I read is slightly weird or unsettling. Clocks in Europe are running behind because Serbia did not fill in the gap left by the amount of electricity being produced for Kosovo. A Kosovo-Serb politician named Oliver Ivanović is assassinated in a drive-by shooting. A pregnant Bulgarian cow named

Penka meanders across the border into Serbia, and when she wanders back, the European Union wants to kill her because she does not have paperwork verifying her health. Online protesters, especially in Britain where there are many EU skeptics, ultimately succeed in saving her life.

Many people know close to nothing about Serbia. The most frequently searched questions about Serbia include: How much milk does Serbia consume annually? Is Serbia part of Russia? Does Serbia still exist? What do Serbians speak? What was Serbia called before? Is Serbia in the Middle East?

I email a tour guide named Snežana about researching our family history and taking us on a family heritage tour. At her request, I send many of the documents I have amassed. My dad balks at the price of 550 EUR, which he finds too expensive for Serbia. He doesn't want to be taken advantage of.

I'm intrigued by the bits of information Snežana gathers as she researches our family history. She asks me where the surname Francezi came from, telling me that in certain areas of the Pannonian Plain it was a common nickname given to all French settlers by their non-French neighbors. In another email she tells me we might be related to Jennie Lebel, the author of the one book in English I have found on Serbian Jewry. I am surprised at how excited that makes me. I get a little rush thinking about being part of the web of Jews in Belgrade, being anchored in a place, being from somewhere. Maybe I am related to this author whose book launched me on this search.

In another email, Snežana writes she has located where Radmila, my great-grandmother, was born. We can go there when we visit my other great-grandmother's birthplace of Šabac. She reveals that Radmila's third husband, Milosavljevic, died during World War II. Radmila was widowed twice, in each of the world wars. I picture her and my grandmother, both widows, caring for my young father and aunt, running a farm, and watching German officers ride their horses. I'm curious when Radmila married Milosavljevic and converted to Orthodoxy. Did she convert the children as well, which means my grandmother would have been twice a convert? Snežana has dropped enough breadcrumbs that we commit to a family heritage tour.

There's no PayPal to Serbia, so payment is via Western Union. I've never sent money this way. "PROTECT YOURSELF FROM FRAUD", their website warns. "Only use Western Union to send money to friends and family. Never send money to someone you have not met in person… After the money is paid, Western Union may not be able to give you a refund, even if you are the victim of fraud, except under limited circumstances." Is what I'm doing sketchy? Our guide last year was recommended by the Jewish Museum and didn't ask for payment in advance. Is Snežana a scammer? I click submit, but my card declines to send cash to a faceless person in Serbia. I click the green button on the fraud detection email, and my second attempt goes through.

Snežana continues to research my family. She writes that my grandmother's mother Radmila is becoming a mystery. It's odd how many errors there are in the documents, and she can't verify where my great-grandmother was born.

Radmila's birth was recorded in the state system as Tereza Sami, born on January 9, 1882, in Pančevo. Her father was Blaza and her mother was Marija. Snežana assumed she might have been Croatian because there's an area near Pančevo where Croatians settled during colonization in the 18th century. Blaza and Tereza are Croatian first names. Marija could be a Croatian name. Radmila's second husband was Croatian, so "it would fit," she writes.

The only detail that worried Snežana was the unusual surname, Sami, which was not recorded anywhere else. She guessed this was another error, so she went to the Church of Saint Karl Boromejski in Pančevo, where all Catholic births are recorded. The pastor went through all the original books, checking each entry. There is no entry in the original church books with the name of Tereza Sami. There is no other Tereza with father Blaž, nor mother Marija, born between 1877 and 1885. And there was not a single person with the surname Sami recorded in the original books. So, it seems Radmila was definitely not born in Pančevo. There is no record of her birth in Belgrade. There is a slight possibility that she might have been born in Slavonia, a Croatian province.

"I do trust the pastor as he found other persons I was looking for and gave me certificates of births and deaths for another ancestry case," Snežana assured me. "He confirms he has never found the Sami surname in any document. Also, no record at all in any books for Prede and Francezi. We could not find the surname Blin in any records either."

Radmila's husband Stevan Francezi, my great-grandfather, was most probably a Croat because of his last name, a very rare Croatian surname found only in Slavonia. Before her third marriage, Radmila's name was Tereza Prede Francezi. Prede likely was the surname of her first husband, with whom she had a son. Her third marriage certificate says Radmila Prede Francizi. When Tereza married Antonije Milosavljević on May 31, 1920, she converted to the Orthodox faith, changed her name to Radmila, and accepted Milosavljevic, her husband's surname. The marriage certificate reveals her husband Antonije was born in Maštalište, but it does not say where Radmila was born. Antonije died on May 3, 1942. Radmila died on June 12, 1969, one year to the day before I was born.

The next step, Snežana writes, is to check Croatian records and see if Radmila might have been born in Slavonia, where her second husband Stevan Francezi probably came from. Maybe finding a record of his birth would give us information on his wife. So far, she could not find any record of his death during the war and no record of his existence in Serbia. But his son and daughter were born in Belgrade, so he must have lived there for some time.

Snežana found Radmila's two sons and granddaughters based on existing birth and death records in the state system: Joseph Francezi—no data recorded except the burial record (the same years as on the gravestone) 1889 —died on December 14, 1934. Wilhelm Francezi—born on March 29, 1904, married to Živka, died on July 5, 1981, in Belgrade. At the time of his death, he lived at 5 Ledinačka Street and was divorced. Wilhelm's daughter Bosiljka Francezi, my father's first cousin, was born on July 29, 1933. She died on October 19, 2004. At the time of her birth her parents lived in Borča, Slatina 12d in Belgrade. Another Jelena, Jelena Francezi, Bosiljka's sister, was born on July 26, 1929, in Belgrade and died on February 26, 2005. She never married.

Snežana asks if anyone in my family has ever mentioned the towns of Erdut, Vinkovci, Osijek, or Dalj because the surname Francezi can be traced only in those places. So far, she assumes Radmila might have been Croatian or German and definitely Catholic. Her sons' names, Josif and Vilhelm (Slavic transcription) are German. She checked all the first names and surnames of the French families who colonized in Banat, but the surnames Sami, Prede, and Blin are not listed anywhere.

Our family mysteries have sucked in Snežana. "Please let me know," she writes, "if any of this data makes any sense or rings a bell. I hope we will find where Radmila was born, but we must count on the possibility that we might not find it. It has become a challenge. If there is any additional information you can provide me with, it might be helpful."

It's all very confusing. I write my cousin Tanja to ask about our family heritage. She messages back: "We are not Croatian."

"The Serbs hate the Croats," my father says.[1]

I ask my cousin Nikola. He responds:

> My father and I agree your researcher might be on the wrong path because she is looking for the origin of our last name Francezi in the Balkans. A legend about our family goes like this: some Italian guy named Francisko or Francesko (who knows when, maybe in the 18th or 19th century) married a German girl and their children came to Serbia with that last name Francezi. We think they came from the Austro-Hungarian or Prussian Empire, so they can't be traced to today's Croatia. All their children were German and married either other Serbian Germans (here we call them Volksdeutsche) or Serbians.
>
> Towns like Erdut and Vinkovci were populated with Serbians, but my father never heard of them in relation to our family. But he's heard of Pančevo.
>
> We will try to find some more info about all this soon. My sister told me she remembers our grandmother told her one of our ancestors was maybe married to someone from France.

Nikola's casual use of "Volksdeutsche" makes my stomach tighten. My internet searches on German migration to Serbia felt academic until I read his Facebook message. Volksdeutsch was Hitler's term for Germans living outside of Germany; they didn't hold citizenship but could be counted on to aid German soldiers and fight alongside them. This one loaded word moves up the timeline from a centuries-old past in Germany for my family to implied participation in the fight against the Allies.

Being Jewish, I learned in childhood, was the answer to not only questions about religion but also ethnicity. It didn't matter where your family was from; Jews were the same, and the details—Romania, Lithuania, Ukraine, Serbia—were incidental. A grandmother who was born Catholic changed that. Her ethnicity and childhood were something entirely different from what I'd thought. Her family line was something else entirely from that of my other grandparents.

Now, finding out I'm Volksdeutsch robs me of some of the righteousness being Jewish has bestowed. It seems I have family roots on both sides of the Holocaust.

I wonder if not just having Catholic family, but a grandmother who was German, explains how my dad was able to live in plain sight on the horse farm on the outskirts of Belgrade. Was my great-grandmother a collaborator? Was this why my grandmother left Europe forever and settled in Israel? For the first time, I consider abandoning my meddling with family history.

In response to my worried reply, Nikola assures me Volksdeutsche is just the term used in Serbia. Wilhelm, he writes, refused to fight with the Wehrmacht because he considered himself Serbian. Wilhelm is my father's uncle and Nikola's great-grandfather. He served in the Army of the Kingdom of Serbia in the early 1920s, and during World War II, he was part of Belgrade's illegal resistance movement, providing logistics under the code name Mile.

Nikola sends me pictures of a February 15, 1937 newspaper article about Wilhelm's house collapsing, with his English translation. My father remembers meeting Wilhelm only once. They went to say goodbye to him when they were leaving for Israel. Wilhelm's alcoholism led to his divorce and created a split between him and his sisters, one of whom was my grandmother.

I look on my phone at the pictures of the blurry black-and-white images from the old newspaper article. This is nothing I could have found through research. One photo shows furniture and other possessions now outdoors. It's hard to make out what they are, blurry gray objects, but in the right-hand corner is a white chicken. The second picture shows the family in front of the rubble. The mother, in a long coat, holds a young daughter. They both wear kerchiefs. The father holds another daughter. Two more children stand nearby. Although it is February, neither has a coat, and their pants come only to their knees. Such poverty. Such misery.

Nikola had thought the house had been destroyed as retaliation for being in the resistance during the war, but the date shows it happened earlier. He translates the headline as "House of poor worker Wilhelm Francezi was ruined while he was asleep with his wife and children." The article explains that the house was built with "the hard sweat of this worker" who worked in a bed factory and had four children. "Despite misery and trouble in the Francezi family, there was happiness and pleasure. There was hope for a better life. Six months ago, he and his wife built their one-room house, which survived a storm with heavy rain and wind. But when the water that got in froze, the house collapsed. A wardrobe kept the roof from falling on the sleeping family. When they escaped, they realized one son was missing. They looked for him with their neighbors. They found him under a pile of bricks; the bed frame had protected him. In the commotion, someone with a heart of stone stole a big blanket from the ruined house. 'What to do now? Jump in the river?!? No, that is not a solution. Who will feed everyone but me?' says Wilhelm, who couldn't continue the sentence. Two big tears slipped down his skinny face while his kids shivered and stared at the remains of their house."

Bosiljka and Jelena, the little girls in the photo, are my father's first cousins. They would have been able to fill in so many gaps in our family story and were still alive well into my thirties. They lived into this century when technology like email and cell phones shrank the world. If only I'd started my search sooner, less would have been lost.

24

"Do you know where the Anne Frank House is?" my dad asks the Uber driver. We have a few days in Amsterdam before we fly to Belgrade.

"Everyone in Amsterdam knows where it is, including the Germans 70 years ago," the driver responds in a friendly voice.

It is the biggest attraction in a city famous for attracting partiers with its coffee shops that sell marijuana instead of coffee, its red-light district, and its famously permissive attitudes. Unlike in Belgrade, we study the Holocaust in organized groups here. Fifty visitors are allowed entry every 15 minutes. The tickets are released two months in advance. The day I went online to purchase them, there were 135 people in line ahead of me. When I saw the confirmation screen showing I'd reserved three slots, I felt like I had scored concert tickets.

The Anne Frank House is now surrounded by businesses that cater to tourists. We could easily eat Dutch pancakes, book a bus tour at the visitors' center, or hop on a waiting canal boat. When I was here in the 1980s, we entered through the original front door and I could understand after I made my way up a steep flight of stairs how confusing the building had been, how the entrance had been hidden behind a bookcase. Now we enter through a glass-enclosed addition. As we line up with other tourists clutching printouts of their tickets, we could be waiting at any popular museum in the world.

The Anne Frank walking tour we take later that day awkwardly tries to appeal to partying tourists in its marketing. "This tour makes it super easy to pack in a little daytime history in between exploring Amsterdam's vibrant nightlife." About 60 of us wait to be divided into groups for our walk. Our tour guide is Bec, an Australian spending a year in the Netherlands. We meet her outside the Amsterdam Jewish Museum, a vast, modern space with double-door security that doesn't allow you to enter through the foyer door until the outside one has closed behind you, reminding me of the design that keeps butterflies from escaping at our local butterfly museum. A combination ticket here gives access to the museum and the Portuguese Synagogue across the way, unlike in Belgrade, where you can only see the synagogue if you know someone who can let you in.

We learn the Franks thought Amsterdam would be a safe place to flee to since the Netherlands had been neutral in World War I. Otto Frank quietly prepared their hiding place after the Nazi occupation, bringing sheets, towels, and other household supplies a little at a time in the bag he carried with him to work. We see the Auschwitz Memorial and the Jewish Quarter, rebuilt in the 1960s because the Dutch pulled apart empty Jewish houses during the Hunger Winter, desperate for anything they could burn for warmth. The buildings were so devastated that liberating Canadian soldiers thought they'd been bombed.

Towards the end of the tour, we stop at two Stolpersteine that mark a husband and wife outside their last voluntary residence: Andries van Gelder and Duifje van Gelder-Van Bever. Both were born in 1884 and murdered in Auschwitz on November 27, 1942. Stolpersteine are always in the local language. I learn a Dutch word, *vermoord*. It means murdered.

Bec explains the monuments. The rest of our tour, mostly older American women, seem to be learning about them for the first time. They act interested. Then a man who appears to have come across our group and been listening to Bec approaches us. He explains he got these stones for his grandfather and step-grandmother. He lives in Antwerp and only happens to be visiting today. Bec asks him questions and people thank him for getting the stones. Afterward, Sophie and I agree that thanking him is an odd response. But the intensity of their reaction spurs me to want our family's Stolpersteine more.

Tanja and Dragan pick us up at the Tesla Airport in Belgrade two days later. It seems normal to go over for Sunday lunch. We meet Tamara, Tanja's sister. She works in IT securities and speaks excellent English. She loves sports, including American football, and knows more about the Patriots than we do.

She has a friend in Boston who manages a Staples store. She wants to visit her and go to a game in Foxboro.

It is so different returning to Belgrade and seeing family we know. It's hard to remember until recently I barely knew we had family in Serbia, that we only met for the first time last year.

"How will it work if they only speak Serbian?" Sophie had asked nervously when I told her we were going to Dragan and Lejla's apartment for lunch.

"It somehow does," I reassured her, remembering the warmth I felt wrapped in last summer. "Papa understands enough Serbian and Dragan understands enough English."

For lunch we eat *kajmak*, a cultured yogurt dish found only in Serbia, roasted peppers, slow-cooked beans, meat, broccoli, cucumbers and tomatoes, spinach *borek*, cheese *borek*, potatoes, vegetable soup, and strawberry shortcake. I eat until well past full and then somehow find room for Christmas bread. Later Dragan will tell us Lejla was worried we didn't like her food since we hardly ate anything.

Back home, I will read about this Serbian culinary aggressiveness in a book Tanja gives me, *A Guide to the Serbian Mentality*. I learn Serbs believe there is no place with such wonderful food as in their homes, and "that you—being lean—have just barely escaped hunger," and they will do their very best to serve you.[1]

We are staying at the Hotel Moskva again. Its name is reminiscent of the Cold War and the Iron Curtain, still vaguely threatening to my American ears. Sophie and I sit in the outdoor café and people watch. Groups of young men and families gather in front of the hotel, trading football cards. Four young men about Sophie's age wait for drinks at the bar, tumbling over each other as joyful, affectionate, and uninhibited as puppies. People walk by unrushed, engaged in conversation.

Five years ago, when we visited Israel, Sophie commented on how nice it felt to be surrounded by people with tight curls like hers.

"Do Serbs have a look?" I ask Sophie.

"Not really," she decides.

Thousands of years at a crossroads, accepting influxes of people from elsewhere, has created a diverse-looking population.

Later, buying bottled water and local cherries in a convenience store, the clerk addresses me in Serbian. Do we look Serbian?

We start by touring the city, mostly revisiting sites we saw last year so Sophie can see them too. When we step outside our hotel, my dad remembers more than last time, "I walked here with my mom and Shosh. There was a streetcar then. We would go visit my aunt Jelena near where St. Sava is now."

In the car with our guide for Belgrade, my dad spots the zoo where he learned to swim. "There was a polar bear that had its own pool, but the animals were killed in the war. After the war, kids swam in the bear pool."

"Did you also swim in the river?" I ask.

"Three or four times, not a lot. There were many drownings where the rivers meet, and the currents are strong."

"Belgrade is located on the site where 120 rivers meet," our guide says. "One hundred rivers empty in the Danube and 20 empty into the Sava. This important location resulted in numerous sieges and occupations. Belgrade has been destroyed and rebuilt 40 times. The Nazis were the last occupiers. They planned to stay for 1,000 years."

"Let's go see the king's palace," my dad says. "I remember it as a big place. There used to be a fence on the street."

On the way, he points out a building at Students Square that was a prison where his uncle was held immediately after the war.

This is news to our guide, which is surprising until I imagine someone from my hometown showing up and pointing out places where things existed 70 years ago. Later he will look it up and confirm that it was the notorious Glavnjača jail. It was a place of police investigation and a symbol of repression under five different political regimes. My father lived there for the last three: the Yugoslav Royal, the Nazi occupation, and the communist regime.

Near the prison was an ice cream shop and a park he walked through to go to school.

"Kalemegdan is straight ahead," he remembers, apparently enjoying himself. "We used to sled on this street, watching out for traffic and trams. There wasn't much. We had wooden toboggans." Passing the Opera House, he remembers going once with his mom but doesn't recall what they saw.

We go back to Solunska 8 where he lived with his parents and uncles before the war, so Sophie can see it.

"Which way did you go towards your grandfather's during the bombing?" I ask my dad, seeking clues of the location of the property we had sought restitution for.

"This way. Let's go. It's hot." He's getting tired. I worry if he's drinking enough water but know he might be short with me if I ask.

Before the war, a synagogue was literally in my father's backyard, although he doesn't remember it. I consider whether my great-grandmother Regina prayed here. Since Nazi bombers destroyed it at the beginning of the war, the site has been uninhabited. When we visited last year, there was a cement basketball court. Now a company wants to begin construction. They are paying for an archeological dig, a prerequisite for the permitting process.

We go around the corner and talk to the archeologist. He is supervising two young men as they chisel away at the pale, packed soil and put the resulting dust in metal wheelbarrows. Three others rest in the shade, watching. One has wrapped his shirt around his head. The operation looks ragtag, nothing like the well-organized gridded system and careful sifting I have seen elsewhere.

"We haven't found much of interest yet," the archeologist tells us. "But I'm optimistic. This site dates to the 1500s. We know it was the first synagogue built by Sephardic Jews, not long after they were driven from Spain."

Later, we stand in the lobby of the Jewish community center, by the residents' mailboxes, thinking about what to do now. This time, I am determined to make it upstairs to get closer to the last place my dad lived in Belgrade. Not like last time when the elevator was broken, and my dad was too tired for the final staircase.

My dad eyes the old glass-and-steel elevator. "As a child, I rode up and down for fun. They kept coal down in the basement."

A man unlocks the door to the apartments, and after he's walked through my father catches it to keep it from closing. Sophie eyes me to see if this is okay, but I'm happy we've found a way up.

My dad hesitates. "What are we going to see? A door?"

And just like that the plan is changed. We are so close, but my dad's unexpected resistance stops me in my tracks. Does it no longer seem worth the effort of a flight of stairs, or is it something else that keeps him from wanting to get closer to where he, his mother, and his sister shared one room in an apartment with other survivors?

We go into the Jewish Museum instead. It's hot. If the museum has air conditioning, they aren't running it. The exhibits are dusty and faded.

A display near the end is titled "Eleven Heroes," but one face has been covered with tape. Ten true heroes and one fallen one? There is no explanation about the implied scandal and no one to ask.

I think of the museum in Amsterdam with its audio tours, videos, and prominent positioning. From the outside, no one would know this museum was here.

At Kalemegdan, the ancient fort, we hear a group of Israelis speaking Hebrew and my dad starts talking to them. When I glance back, they are taking their picture with him. We've entered the fortress the back way from the street rather than across the drawbridge. From this perspective, it looks like city parks anywhere. As we walk through a passageway, we bump into my dad's Israeli cousin Aci, his wife Rachel, their friends, and our guide from last year. We knew Aci and Rachel were coincidentally in Belgrade, but we hadn't realized they were the ones who had booked our guide before we could reserve time with him. And having our paths literally cross feels like a God wink.

When we revisit the Jewish cemetery, it seems more cramped, perhaps from being more familiar to me. We quickly find the graves of my father's grandmother and great-grandparents. It's almost exactly a year since we were here the first time. Around a year after a family member's death, Jews often return to the cemetery for an unveiling, where the gravestone is seen for the first time. Although my father's grandmother has been dead for over 80 years, today is also an unveiling of sorts, as we see her restored stone for the first time.

It has been nicely remade; her picture is more easily discernible. I scan her face looking for family resemblance, but can't say I see any.

My father has had his great-grandparents' graves restored. I take a picture of Sophie beside one; our family now spans six generations. We know so little about their lives. My great-great-grandmother's grave identifies her only as the wife of a doctor. Surely, she had her own passions and skills. I weed Bernhard's grave. It seems a futile gesture since no one will be here to weed it when the plants return. I don't know if we will ever be back. Some of the surrounding graves are in disrepair. There is no one left to tend them.

None of our family who are buried here were born in Belgrade. Regina came from Šabac and her in-laws were from Upper Hungary, now Slovakia. They have no siblings here and, surprisingly, no children either. The final resting places of all my great-great-grandparents' children are unknown. My great-grandfather, killed in the Nazi bombing, is likely in a mass grave somewhere. One of the slave-labor jobs Jewish men were forced to do was disposing of the decomposing bodies in the rubble. But he was the youngest; where are his siblings and half-siblings buried? Some of them had undoubtedly died before the war began.

We were hot and tired at Kalemegdan but have perked up here. We stop at the Holocaust memorial, located at the far end of the cemetery. From outside the wall, we can hear children at play. I suspect they have never been on this side of the wall and know nothing of this part of their history that happened before their grandparents were born.

On our return to our hotel, our guide's car starts stalling at red lights. The first few times, he can restart it, but then it quits altogether. It coasts down a slight hill until it rests at the side of the road. Our guide starts to apologize but my father has had enough. He gets out, so Sophie and I follow. Without hesitation, he follows the map in his head through a market, up a hill, around a corner, and back to our lodging. He doesn't need a guide or a GPS in the city he's from.

25

Our new guide, Snežana, picks us up for what I've been calling grandmother day. We are going to visit the birthplaces of my dad's grandmothers. His Sephardic grandmother, who died before he was born, came from Šabac, a port city on the Sava. His Catholic grandmother was from Pančevo, an industrial city with a large ethnic German population.

Snežana tells us apologetically that her glasses broke the day before. She holds them in place with one hand while she reads us our day's itinerary. They give her a disheveled look. But as she starts to recite the day's plan, she's focused. In clear, academic English, she conveys how seriously she takes our quest and how intrigued she's become with our family story.

My dad, already suspicious that she's overcharged him, that he's been taken advantage of because he's American, interrupts to ask, "Why are you so interested in this history? Are you Jewish?"

I hear the implication that if she's not, then what could she know? He shows her none of the warmth and instant connection he shared with our guide the year before. Snežana calmly and defenselessly explains she's Christian but has helped many Jewish families. My dad seems to soften a bit.

Snežana has new information on my grandmother Regina's father's family. She found the death certificate for Pelagija Francezi, who is my grandmother's paternal grandmother. Her parents were Filip Živić and Cveta Janicijević. Now we have two more family names we can trace. Pelagija was born in Mala Plana, in central Serbia, in an area called Šumadija, which means forestland. It was once heavily forested, although it would have been mostly cleared in her time. It is very fertile; apples, grapes, plums, and other fruit are grown there. Pelagija's birth date is unknown, but we learn she died on July 18, 1947. My father would have been almost nine, but he doesn't remember her. There's no record of her in Belgrade's cemeteries. Perhaps she returned to Mala Plana and was buried there.

"Pelagija is a typical Serbian name," Snežana tells us. But I know her family came from elsewhere since my DNA shows no Balkan heritage. "She probably met her husband in Belgrade. He was probably from Croatia. She probably converted from Orthodox to Catholic when she married him."

A census record shows that in 1937, the year before my father was born, my grandparents Regina and Alexander lived with Pelagija on Mutapova Street, near where the massive St. Sava Church is now.

Snežana says, "When a widow remarried, she wouldn't take her children from the first marriage to her new home. They would go live with their father's parents, the grandparents who had lost a son." Serbian culture is strongly patriarchal.

My grandmother living with her grandmother after she was married suggests this. It looks like her paternal grandmother was the person she was closest to, closer than to her own mother. Our relationship couldn't be more different; I was cheated out of meeting her and only began to refer to her as "my grandmother" in middle age.

I thought my grandmother had no family on her father's side because her father died in World War I before she was born. Now a census record paints a very different picture. She was likely raised by her paternal grandparents, or at least her paternal grandmother. That grandmother, Pelagija, died in 1947. Did that loss play into my grandmother's decision to leave for Israel in 1948?

When I ask my dad, he replies: "Definitely not. If anything, my mother influenced my uncles to go. She hated that people had allowed this to happen. She felt Europe was condemned. That was the driving force to get out of here. Of course, I don't know if she would have made that decision if she knew what she was going to."

On our way out of Belgrade, Snežana points to a building still damaged from the NATO bombing in 1999, the year Sophie was born. My dad and Sophie have sore throats, so she offers Serbian candies called Negro. They were invented by a Jewish man, Jozsef Ruff, who lived in Subotica. After the war his company was nationalized, and he became an employee. He emigrated to Israel, where he was miserable. He wrote to ask if he could return but was told no, they were better off without him.

The wrapper has an image of a chimney sweep, and the slogan is "the chimney sweep of the throat," which doesn't quite translate culturally. The image seems fittingly Serbian though. This isn't Disney's Mary Poppins' chimney sweep. Something stuck in your throat? This man will get rid of it with a long, wire brush. The recipe is an industrial secret. Anise with a liquid center—delicious.

On the way to Šabac, we pass vast fields of freshly cut grass, drying under blue skies. The sweet, earthy smell sneaks into the car, although the windows are rolled up against the heat and noise. I think of breaking open bales for the horse I owned as a teenager, breathing in the smell of summer in the winter darkness. Haying everywhere is an act of faith. Farmers must believe dry weather will hold long enough to bring in their harvest. Rain now would ruin it.

I picture my nervous great-grandmother Regina, just 18, the age my daughter is now, traveling in a horse-drawn wagon past these fields in the other direction, towards the capital. I know from her marriage certificate it was June, just like now. She left her home and family for a new life in a strange city with her young husband, who had different traditions and spoke Yiddish instead of Ladino. Perhaps she was happy about the match, chatting nonstop to try to calm her nerves as they trotted along at the beginning of her exciting adventure. Her dowry, likely bought with the funds from the sale of the house we will see this morning, was in big trunks behind her in the wagon bed. I see her thinking of the silver candlesticks, feather pillows, quilts, and towels she had carefully packed. For married life, she would have needed four sets of dishes, one for meat, one for dairy, and two more to be used only on Passover. Or maybe she'd cried that morning, hugging her father hard, and rode quietly, remembering the childhood she was leaving behind. I know so little about her, but I see what she couldn't: five sons, one of whom would die in infancy, a life that ended when her youngest was only nine, before she would know her first daughter-in-law took her name, Regina, to honor her. Before she could meet her five grandchildren. Later, I learn that travel in 1906 was probably down the river rather than by road, so I try to imagine a view of hayfields from the water instead.

Snežana was unable to uncover much about the Ruso family in Šabac. There were two men with that surname, one of whom was my great-great-grandfather. The deed still exists, showing he bought a house for his daughter when she was a baby and later sold it when she was a teenager, probably for her dowry. His relationship to the other Ruso man, who had two sons, is unknown. My great-grandmother likely had siblings, but no record of them exists. Although Jews in Šabac date back to at least 1572, I have to let go of the idea that my family lived there for generations, as that too is unknown. It's also unclear if there was still family remaining in 1941, part of a Jewish population of about 80 who perished along with the Jews in the Kladovo transport.

Šabac, a port city on the Sava known as Little Paris, was a trading center that attracted a Jewish community. Our first stop is the cramped Jewish cemetery outside of town, across the road from the much larger Orthodox one. The grass is overgrown, and some graves are broken. As with so many other Jewish cemeteries across Europe, there are no descendants left to tend the graves. Like Dorćol, Belgrade's Jewish neighborhood, Šabac is now a community without Jews. The restored synagogue[1] is a community music hall. There is no record of Rusos buried here, but it is unknown who are in the damaged graves. Are we related to the nameless and forgotten dead?

The house my great-grandmother owned is two stories but narrow. It sits right up against the sidewalk, with no breathing room between it and its neighbors. It's a civic building now, so we can go through a doorway into a surprisingly quiet courtyard hidden from the main street. There are potted flowering plants, climbing roses, and a grape arbor. We sit in the shade at a long table, drinking coffee and herbal tea, feeling welcome despite lacking a common language.

The city's museum is large, clean, and modern, occupying two floors. We are the only visitors. I wonder who comes here. Few people speak English. Our museum guide explains the exhibits as Snežana translates. Here, the story of Šabac contains no mention of the local Jews, their synagogue, which is one of the few left in the country, or the Kladovo transport, arguably the most well-known event in the Holocaust in Serbia. Back in the van, Snežana explains that Serbs are still struggling with their complicity.

On the way out of town, we circle around, looking for the warehouse where some Jews from the transport spent the winter. The physical remnants of this Holocaust story, undocumented in the local museum, seem to have been torn down.

We stop for lunch at an open-air restaurant on the river. There are no vegetarian dishes. The waiter argues with Snežana in Serbian. He's reluctant to bring me risotto without prawns. They are the main part of the dish. The vegetarian risotto I eventually get is tasty and ample enough for two.

My dad keeps trying to have Sophie sit in the middle row of the van so she can see better, although this places him in the rear, where he has difficulty hearing Snežana. At lunch, I encourage Sophie to get into the van before him to claim the rear seat. "Knock him down if you have to," I joke.

After lunch, we head to Pančevo to explore my grandmother's maternal family. My great-grandmother Radmila's marriage certificate shows that she was born there on September 1, 1882. We cross a bridge built by Russians 75 years ago to use for 20 days. I'm glad I learn this after we are safely back in Belgrade.

We hear church bells ringing on the square. This will be only my second time in a Catholic church. The priest who unlocks the door is young and friendly. On the wall near the entrance, he is listed as the most recent priest on a plaque. It was placed last year for the 300th anniversary of the church's founding in 1717. It has the oldest records in Serbia. He pulls out a book to show me the writing, beautiful calligraphy in Latin. This must have been Radmila's childhood church, although he and Snežana searched and couldn't find her baptism record.

The domed ceiling above the altar is painted gold and turquoise. There are statues and oil paintings. The priest bends to open a long wooden box below a massive oil painting. In it lies a statue of Jesus.

The small courtyard has a well with a bucket.

"We had one on my grandmother's farm like this," my dad remembers. "And an outhouse." During the occupation, he remembers his grandmother slaughtering and rendering pigs and force-feeding geese, but mostly he remembers endless cornbread. My father will eat almost anything, but not more cornbread.

"Welcome, this is your home," the priest says.

26

Branko and his son Nikola pick us up outside the hotel. We are headed to a café on the Danube on the outskirts of the city, close to where they live.

We've made the plan via Facebook Messenger. "It might be cold on the river," Nikola messaged me. "You might want to bring jackets, especially Bubika." I'm touched by his use of my father's childhood nickname, which he left behind when he emigrated to the US, and I'm reminded about the respect and concern Serbians have for the elderly.

Nikola sits in back with Sophie and me. Branko has more English than I remember, but it's heavily accented and terse.

"My dad sounds like a Russian mobster," Nikola says.

Sophie and I giggle.

The café is crowded, and Nikola knows many people there. Patrons are talking, drinking, and smoking, but no one is eating. Seven o'clock is too early for dinner.

Nikola's sister Jelena was married a few weeks earlier. They show us photos and videos on their phones. Nikola is a graphic designer, and he made the best man and maid of honor nametags with an image that includes a button. There is a Serbian expression I learn: "as necessary as a button."

I ask Branko about Radmila. He was born in 1960, so he was nine when she died. He moves his hands wide to show she was round, which my dad confirms. She was a hearty woman who drank a beer for breakfast every day, according to my aunt, and outlived three of her slim children. What would she have thought of me, her American great-granddaughter, who knows so little about being Serbian? I'm not even sure if she knew my dad had married an American; after my grandmother died, I don't think she got any more updates about my father.

Nikola translates that Branko still has a milk cup she gave him. I'm unsure exactly what a Serbian milk cup is; I envision a child-sized metal cup with a handle. But I am irrationally jealous he has this cup, that he knew our great-grandmother. The jealousy is tempered a bit when I remember she died a year to the day before I was born. It is time as well as geography that separated me from my milk cup and my memory.

Radmila was part of a community known as Danube Swabians, Germans who settled 400 years ago along the Danube in what is now Serbia, Romania, Hungary, and Croatia. They were mostly farmers who maintained their culture, language, and identity.

"Did Radmila speak German?" I ask. The question feels disloyal to my dad, although everyone at the table is descended from his grandmother. Although Nikola and Branko aren't Jewish, ethnic German heritage in Serbia could be a shameful thing to acknowledge, given the brutality of the Nazi occupation.

"She probably did," Nikola translates Branko's answer. "But her children William and Regina, our grandparents, didn't." This makes sense considering the new information that they were likely raised in large part by their paternal grandparents, Radmila's in-laws. Branko also confirms our grandparents were full siblings; only their oldest brother had another father.

Nikola asks what a flight to the US from Belgrade costs and is pleased by the answer. I explain about websites that alert you when fares drop. We discuss visas.

"Come in March," I encourage him. "We will go see how they tap the maple trees to make candies like the ones we brought you. Or come in the summer and we'll go to the beach. We can visit Boston. People say it is the most European American city and there is lots of history there." I know from our last visit he likes military history, so I add, "Lexington and Concord are neighboring towns and important early Revolutionary War sites."

The next day, a hired driver takes my dad, Sophie, and me, along with Dragan, Lejla, Tanja, and her husband out of the city on a day trip. We plan to see a castle on the Danube, take a boat ride, have lunch on a farm, and learn about an ancient archeology site.

At the castle, we can't park because of a rule they made yesterday about calling ahead for groups. The man who enforces this regulation has a weathered face and is missing some of his front teeth. My dad suggests the guide pay him 1,000 dinars, about ten dollars, to resolve the issue, but the guide points out there are cameras everywhere. Though the matter is unresolved, my cousin's husband opens the van door and our group files out.

Here in Serbia, there is no Uber, no Starbucks, no UPS, no Hard Rock Café. Anthony Bourdain never did a show here. Amazon doesn't ship here. We are in a relatively remote area on the Romanian border. As we walk towards the castle, we pass a group of teenagers walking towards us. I catch a snippet of conversation. An American voice says, "I'm not going to lie. It was hard to switch from Dunkin Donuts to Starbucks at first. But I got used to it and now I prefer Starbucks." Dunkin Donuts started in New England. I strain to hear if she has the familiar Boston accent. I am embarrassed for Americans that she is traveling through Eastern Europe, representing us and loudly discussing her coffee-drinking challenges.

It is fun to be out with family. We see cruise ships make their way down the Danube. We see Romania across the river. Lunch is traditional: elderflower drink, chicken soup, various meats, smoked cheese, bread, potatoes, pastry with jam, and shots of traditional plum brandy called slivovitz.

I tell Tanja what we learned yesterday about Regina's grandmother. It all makes sense to her. She knows about the tradition of leaving the children with the dead father's parents. She translates to Dragan and Lejla, who confirm the picture they have is of Pelagija and her husband. Dragan had thought it was Radmila's parents; now we know they are her in-laws.

On their last night in Belgrade, my cousin Aci and his wife Rachel, who are visiting from Israel, tour a cave and she falls down some stairs, breaking her ankle. The next day, while she rests with her foot up in their hotel room, Aci and I take a cab to the cemetery. He wants me to show him family graves. His Serbian is fluent, so taking a cab for our visit, my third to this cemetery, seems easy. Aci left as a baby. He learned to speak Serbian in Israel and listening to him chat with the cab driver, I wonder how often he has spoken his mother tongue with a stranger.

I think of the medical school mantra: see one, do one, teach one. On our first visit, the place was foreign, and we needed our guide, the cemetery keeper, and the information from the museum to find each stone. Returning this year, we knew the general location of the graves and could find them with some searching. This time, I walk towards each one directly, in a cemetery that seems to have grown smaller. It feels surreal. I am the guide, telling Aci about his grandmother and great-grandparents, pointing out the Holocaust memorial and the World War I monument, and sharing the story of the Kladovo Transport.

Aci is a nickname for Alexander. He was named after my grandfather by his father, my grandfather's younger brother. His father, the Partisan who rose in Tito's government, was on the first ship to Israel with his wife and Aci. He was turned away from serving in the Israeli military, which didn't accept soldiers from communist countries. He never recovered. He worked as a security guard, learned little Hebrew, and pined for the Old Country.

We wash our hands as we leave, and I think for the third time that this is likely my last visit. We hail a cab and head for the only Israeli restaurant in Belgrade for a falafel lunch.

It's still dark when we leave the Hotel Moskva for our 6:30 a.m. flight the next morning. The 1980s Pat Benatar song "We Belong" is playing on the radio. "We belong to the light. We belong to the thunder. We belong to the sound of the words we've both fallen under."

The cab driver addresses my dad, and for the first time he replies in Serbian. I'm guessing by the words I can pick out: "Dorćol—Solunska—Beograd," that he is responding to the standard question whether he has been here before.

He proudly answers, "I am from here."

Back home, I feel spurred on by our visit and our encounter with the man who got his grandparents Stolpersteine in Amsterdam. I email Snežana, asking for suggestions of who in Belgrade I can contact for help. Two organizations never respond to my queries. But on my birthday, I receive an email from Sonja, the director of Haver Serbia. My timing is perfect. They have considered taking on this project for several years, but it's been on the back burner. Now, with my prompting, they are ready.

The day we arrange to Skype, my Facebook feed is filled with news articles and friends' posts detailing the horror of immigrant adults and children being separated on the US-Mexican border. Toddlers and babies, some of whom are breastfeeding, are being held in Tender Age Camps. Parents are told their children are being taken for baths and never returned. Caretakers are not allowed to hug or comfort crying children. Many young children speak only their indigenous languages and not Spanish. There is no plan in place for reunification.

The 2G groups on Facebook discuss if what is being done should or should not be compared to the Holocaust. The debate is uncivil. We share similar histories but there's no agreement about what it means for the present. I think of the old expression, "two Jews, three opinions."

A meme goes by declaring if you ever wondered how you'd behave in Nazi Germany; you are doing it right now. It is a shameful time to be an American. My quest for a Stolperstein for my grandfather simultaneously feels inconsequential at a moment when children are being taken from their parents by my own government and more relevant than ever. We haven't evolved past the lessons of the Holocaust.

Sonja asks if I speak Serbian, another validation we are from Belgrade. She tells me in Serbia they are 25 years behind. But at least to some extent they are ready to address their past, in part because they seek entrance to the European Union. She'd like to put a call out to other families from Serbia who might be interested in a stone. Belgrade hasn't had a mayor for three months, since the winner of the last election hasn't yet been declared, but she thinks it will happen soon. Then they can seek permission. She can start to work on the project in three months. She doesn't feel the urgency I do.

At a Shabbat dinner before a trip to California for his cousin's grandson's bar mitzvah, my father reminisces about his bar mitzvah and remembers putting on the tefillin. Tefillin are foreign to me since they generally are worn by Orthodox men, and my father is not religious. We don't have any photos of that day, but I visualize a 13-year-old version of my father, tall and skinny, wrapping the straps for prayer around his arm.

"I wrote something to read to the congregation, but I started to cry and couldn't do it. I ripped it up. But the rabbi picked it up and read it for me." My father tears up at the memory. My mom and I exchange glances. This is new to me, and it seems to her as well.

"What did it say?" I ask.

"It was about my father and the war."

Of course, my adolescent father would miss his own father, though he couldn't remember him, on his bar mitzvah day. I never realized there was continued discussion about him and about the war once they were in Israel. My father said more than once that such things weren't talked about. But actually they were, and in a very public way. I want to ask more questions. I'm working to form one about what else he remembers or what he wanted to say about his dad. But my dad has moved on to talking about their upcoming trip and I don't steer the conversation back.

I dream I get a surprise visit from my cousins from Belgrade. Weirdly they visit me on my college campus. I introduce them to friends I haven't seen in over 20 years. "These are my Serbian cousins," I tell each one. All are surprised I am Serbian. "Yes, being Serbian roots me to a place in a way that being Jewish doesn't," I try to explain.

For the 2018 World Cup, 23 and Me sends me genetic information so I can know who to cheer for. They call it "Root for your Roots." My strongest match, really my only match, is with Germany. I'm given a meme with Germany circled on a map of Western Europe and the German flag. The copy says "I have ancestors who lived in Germany within the last 200 years. *Los geht's Deutschland!*" It's an in-my-face reminder of what is somehow still a surprise: the place I am from, the ethnicity that is written in my DNA, is German. Beyond that, 23 and Me can only look at my 67 percent Ashkenazi heritage and wonder if perhaps my people are from Poland or Russia. Since I have 254 Neanderthal variants, similar to levels in Spain and Portugal, those countries are listed as distant matches. Serbia comes up as a wild card. The copy reads, "I may not be from there, but this team is gonna Serbia up some quality soccer!"

On our first trip to Serbia, our cousin Dragan gave us a picture showing my dad as a toddler. He sits on the table while the adults around him, my grandmother, great-grandmother, and great-aunt, gaze at him adoringly. Serbs love children. My grandmother could have looked at me that way. I'm her only granddaughter. I thought of my father's expression when pride and love burst from his face. He's so comfortable with physical and verbal expressions of love with his children and grandchildren. In my family, unconditional love has flowed down the generations. This is the legacy my grandmother passed down.

In my childhood, we referred to them as "dad's mother" and "dad's father," implying to me that since they had died before I was born, they had no connection to me or me to them. But now, having immersed myself in family history, trying to catch what I still could before it vanished forever, I claim them as my grandparents. They belong to me.

The picture that started my quest was the one of my dad and his little sister Shoshana taken during the war. In the black-and-white image, they stand on a city street. She's in a light summer dress, her legs bare, with short socks and leather shoes. He wears European short pants with suspenders, knee socks, and laced leather boots. His shirt, my aunt told me once, like her dress, was made from scraps of the train of my grandmother's wedding gown.

They pose for the photographer. At least part of my grandmother still believed the rumor that my grandfather had been deported to a work camp and could still be alive. Was the photo to record this moment for him?

What my future aunt and the boy who will grow up to be my dad are not doing is hiding. It's the inconsistency of this picture that made me want to know more. Later, I noticed they each wear a small bell around their necks.

"Yes," my father remarked off-handedly in the family room after a Shabbat dinner, "those bells have something to do with Easter." Since Orthodox Easter was on April 25 in 1943, this is likely the date of the photo. In Serbia, Christian children wear bells at Easter to announce the coming of Jesus, but also to symbolize hope and faith, exactly what was needed in Belgrade in 1943. The picture shows my father and aunt's Christian heritage that enabled them to survive. The answer to my quest to understand his survival was in plain sight the whole time.

EPILOGUE

The Covid Pandemic made the world beyond my neighborhood seem far away. In 2020, it was hard for me to imagine flying again. Serbia was effectively once again rendered out of reach.

In late 2021, I learned that more than four years of work would finally pay off. Though the Serbian government was refusing to place Stolpersteine for my father and other survivors, permission was granted for our family to have three stones. My grandfather Alexander, his cousin Simon, and Simon's mother Evgenija, along with seven other Holocaust victims, would receive memorials.

As I booked our flights, travel restrictions, mandatory Covid testing, and vaccine requirements were still part of international travel. My parents, my daughters, and I had not had Covid, but I was especially worried my father would get gravely ill in Belgrade.

"Bring plenty of Euros," my cousin advised, though the Serbian currency is the dinar. "You'll need them to get a doctor's attention in the hospital if one of you gets sick."

I felt grateful for Europeans' love of outdoor dining. We'd be outside as much as possible and try to stay masked indoors. I purchased travel air filters and packed KN95 masks along with the new dress I planned to wear when I made my short speech about my grandfather at the installation, on what happened to be my grandfather's 113th birthday.

In July 2022, my father, Rebecca, and I returned to Belgrade for the installation of the capital city's first Stolpersteine. We were surrounded by the Jewish community and other Serbians, including survivors and the community leaders from Haver Serbia and elsewhere, who made the moment possible. Also, our newly discovered cousin Viki was there that day.

The year before, while we were still waiting for approval to place Stolpersteine in Belgrade, the first commemorative stones in Serbia were placed in Zrenjanin. Jews from the former Yugoslavia met virtually to celebrate. Earlier that year, the US Holocaust Memorial Museum had interviewed my dad via Zoom. Someone who saw the video that the museum posted of his testimony invited us to the community's gathering. After my father shared some of our family story, one of the attendees mentioned, "You know, I know another great-grandchild of Dr. Bernhard Brill. She lives in Croatia." A few weeks later, we connected with this long-lost cousin Viki.

After believing all other Jewish family members were lost to genocide, finding Viki was a gift. She told us that her mother was Simon's sister. This meant her grandfather and my father's grandfather were twins. Simon was her uncle and Evgenija was her grandmother. Viki knew their tragic fate. Simon tried to escape with false documents to Romania but was captured and transported to the Nis concentration camp in southern Serbia, where he was imprisoned.

Since he was a dentist, he was sometimes allowed to leave the camp on Sundays. On the street in Nis, Simon met his ex-girlfriend and her husband. They invited him to lunch and mailed his letters. Viki shared two postcards that Simon sent to her older siblings and her mother. After the mail stopped, Viki's mother assumed Simon had been killed, feasibly as a result of a Partisan attempt to liberate the camp. It was Viki's mother who had his photograph and inscription placed on the side of Bernhard's grave.

Evgenija was imprisoned at Sajmište, the concentration camp at Belgrade's fairgrounds where most Jewish women and children were held. When they reported under threat of death in late 1941, they turned over their house keys, and each brought a single suitcase. If Evgenija survived that brutal winter, the Germans gassed her in early 1942 in a mobile truck as it drove through the city.

There was only one survivor of Sajmište, a baby born there and smuggled out. We met her at the installation. Viki's mother's husband was not Jewish and he was able to save his wife and children.

On the day of the Stolpersteine installation, the weather was sweltering. Many survivors did not come because it was forecasted to be over 100°F. We drank warm water and fanned ourselves with our programs as representatives from the German and Israeli embassies and members of the Serbian-Jewish community spoke about the Holocaust and the significance of this moment. No one from Belgrade's city administration or the government of Serbia was there to mark the day.

We went to four locations outside victims' homes in the old city. Where my grandfather lived, I shared a bit about him, the story of an individual and his family. I wanted to make visible one human being among Belgrade's 10,000 murdered Jews, among the Holocaust's 6,000,000. My interpreter repeated my words in Serbian.

For a moment on Solunska Street, on that sultry day, my father held his father's stone, and it was our family's. And then he handed it to Gunter Demnig who placed it where it belongs, in the ground outside my grandfather's last home. It isn't just for my grandfather but for all murdered Jews from Belgrade and for the city itself.

The history is no longer hidden. Now it is in plain sight. It is a reminder to all who pass by that before the Germans came this was a vibrant Jewish neighborhood. It is not enough, of course, but it is something.

After Mr. Demnig installed the Stolpersteine, the weather shifted. A breeze lifted the oppressive heat. As we reached our hotel, thunder boomed, and rain washed down the streets. The downpour would set the stone dust, and water the seeds we had just planted.

"Now, the stones are really in the ground," Rebecca said.

The Nazis wanted to murder all nine million European Jews and to wipe out any evidence that they had ever existed. They tried to erase all traces of Belgrade's Jewish community. They nearly succeeded. But on that hot July day on Solunska Street, my father, my daughter, and I were evidence that my grandfather existed. That the Jewish people exist. Each of the six million Jews who were murdered is more than just the way they died. By marking the last voluntary residence of Holocaust victims and survivors, Stolpersteine help us celebrate their lives. The stones will help keep the memory of my grandfather and other Holocaust victims alive.

PHOTOS

The Hotel Moskva, Belgrade, Serbia, 2017

Haim and Rebecca outside Kalemedgan, 2017

The new building at Solunska 8 in Belgrade, where Haim lived, 2017

Cousins Nikola, Julie, Haim, Branko, and Rebecca at the Hotel Moskva Café, 2017

Dragan and Haim in Belgrade, 2017

Haim next to his great-grandfather Bernhard's stone in the Sephardic Cemetery in Belgrade, 2017

Rebecca and the stone of Rosa, Bernhard's wife, 2017

Monument to the Jewish Victims of Fascism, Sephardic Cemetery in Belgrade, 2017

Raising the stone of Regina, Haim's paternal grandmother, 2017

Skateboarder sitting on the memorial at the Staro sajmište concentration camp, 2017

Catholic church in Pančevo, Serbia, 2018

Sophie eating a palačinki at the Hotel Moskva, 2018

The Topovske šupe concentration camp in a state of disrepair, 2022

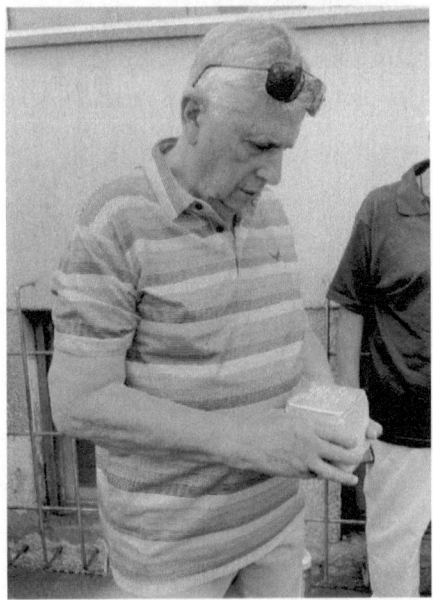

Haim holding his father's Stolperstein, 2022

Gunter Demnig installing Alexander Brill's Stolperstein, 2022

Alexander's Stolperstein, newly installed at Solunska 8, 2022

Julie and Haim on Haim's 80th birthday, 2018

Haim on his 85th birthday with his wife Martha, his children Julie and Alex, his daughter-in-law Johanna, and his grandchildren and his granddaughter's fiancée

NOTES

Chapter 1

1. Snyder, Timothy. "So much worse than Auschwitz: 'People not very different from us murdered other people not very different from us at close quarters.'" *Salon Magazine*, October 3, 2015. Accessed August 18, 2024.
2. Ibid.
3. Timothy Snyder, *Bloodlands: Europe Between Hitler and Stalin* (New York: Hachette Book Group, 2010), p. 200.
4. Marianne Hirsh, "Postmemory" Accessed August 1, 2024, https://postmemory.net
5. John J. Sigal and Morton Weinfeld, *Trauma and Rebirth: Intergenerational Effects of the Holocaust* (New York: Praeger, 1989), p. 6.

Chapter 5

1. "The JUST Act Report: Serbia," U.S. Department of State. Accessed February 24, 2024, https://www.state.gov/reports/just-act-report-to-congress/serbia/
2. Jennie Lebel, *Until 'The Final Solution': The Jews in Belgrade 1521-1942* (Bergenfield, NJ: Avotaynu, 2007), p. 284.
3. Ibid.
4. Paul Mojzes, *Balkan Genocides: Holocaust and Ethnic Cleansing in the Twentieth Century* (New York: Rowman & Littlefield, 2015), p. 83.
5. Lebel, p. 334.
6. Snyder, p. 412.
7. Ibid, p. 395.
8. "Electrician Stumbles Upon Holocaust Time Capsule Inside Amsterdam Home's Crawl Space," *Haaretz*, April 19, 2017.
9. Joseph Polak, *After the Holocaust the Bells Still Ring* (Brooklyn, NY: Urim Publications, 2015), p. 101.
10. Jane S. Gerber, *The Jews of Spain: A History of the Sephardic Experience* (New York: Simon & Schuster, 1994), p. 161.
11. Geraldine Brooks, *People of the Book: A Novel* (New York: Penguin Books, 2008), p. 27.
12. Gerber, p. XIV.
13. Idem, p. XXIV.
14. Accessed August 22, 2024, www.lostsephardicworld.org

Chapter 6

1. Steve Friess, "When 'Holocaust' Became 'The Holocaust,'" *New Republic*, May 17, 2015.

Chapter 7

1. Dvora Hacohen, *Immigrants in Turmoil: Mass Immigration to Israel and Its Repercussions in the 1950s and After* (Syracuse, New York: Syracuse University Press, 2003), p. 60.
2. Yael Allweil, "Israeli Housing and Nation Building: Establishment of the State-Citizen

Contract 1948-1953," *Traditional Dwellings and Settlements Review*, Vol. 23 (No. 2) Spring 2012, pp. 51-67.

Chapter 8

1. Noah Lederman, *A World Erased: A Grandson's Search for His Family's Holocaust Secrets* (Lanham, MD: Rowman & Littlefield Publishers, 2017), p. 2.
2. Tulila Catalan & Marco Dogo, *The Jews and the Nation-States of Southeastern Europe from the 19th Century to the Great Depression: Combining Viewpoints on a Controversial Story* (New Castle upon Tyne: Cambridge Scholars Publishing, 2016)
3. In 2014, Spain published a list of 5,000 Jewish names, including Ruso, as part of a new law to allow those who can prove Sephardic descent to apply for Spanish citizenship. The Spanish government is trying to atone for the "historic mistake" it made when it expelled Spanish Jews. There are an estimated 3.5 million people of Sephardic-Jewish descent. To get citizenship, they would also have to show a "special link" to Spain, such as "past study of Spanish history and culture, doing business in Spain and involvement in conservation of Spanish culture." ("Welcome home, 500 years later: Spain offers citizenship to Sephardic Jews," Henry Chu, LA Times, October 1, 2015). In July 2016 Spain granted citizenship to 220 Jews. ("Spain Grants Citizenship to 220 Sephardi Jews, *The Jerusalem Post*, July 8, 2016).

Chapter 10

1. Lebel, p. 280.
2. Idem, p. 281.
3. Ernest Powell, *Life in Dark Ages: A Memoir* (Lanham, MD: National Book Network, 1995), p. 226.
4. Stevan K. Pavlowitch, *Hitler's New Disorder: The Second World War in Yugoslavia* (London: Hurst Publishers Ltd., 2008), p. 151.
5. Powell, p. 82.
6. David A. Norris, *Belgrade: A Cultural History* (Oxford: Oxford University Press, 2008), p. 125.
7. Sonja Ciric, "Charles Simic, poet and essayist: A smoked ham for poetry," Accessed August 11, 2024, https://www.b92.net/o/eng/insight/eng/comments?nav_id=102520
8. Roger Cohen, *Hearts Grown Brutal: The Sagas of Sarajevo* (New York: Random House, 2001), p. 4.
9. Aleksander Gaon, *We Survived... 2: Yugoslav Jews on the Holocaust* (Belgrade: The Jewish Historical Museum, 2005), p. 474.
10. Idem, p. 446.
11. Idem, p. 344.

Chapter 13

1. In my recipe box at home is my mom's palačinki recipe, written in her neat, round handwriting. She gave it to me when I moved into my first off-campus apartment, along with the pan we used to make them. It dates back to the time when we thought margarine was healthy.

Chapter 14

1. Norris, p. 125.
2. "Jews in the Balkans" Accessed August 22, 2024, https://lostsephardicworld.org/exhibition/jews-in-the-balkans/

3. Elon Gilad, "500 Years Later: The Mysterious Origin of the Word 'Ghetto'," *Haaretz*, March 29, 2016.
4. Lebel, pp. 230-231.
5. Powell, p. 23.
6. *The Kingdom of Yugoslavia in the Second World War: What Really Happened in Western Europe 1941-1945?*, Episode 3, "Soldiers, Revolutionists and Quislings."
7. Lebel, p. 264.
8. Idem, p. 266.
9. Idem, pp. 269, 272-273.
10. Idem, pp. 274-275.
11. Grieshaber, Kirsten. "Plaques for Nazi Victims Offer a Personal Impact." *New York Times*, November 29, 2003, www.nytimes.com/2003/11/29/arts/plaques-for-nazi-victims-offer-a-personal-impact.html
12. Eric Westervelt, "Stumbling Upon Mini Memorials to Holocaust Victims" Accessed August 11, 2024, https://www.npr.org/2012/05/31/153943491/stumbling-upon-miniature-memorials-to-nazi-victims

Chapter 15

1. "Virtual Jewish World: Yugoslavia" Accessed October 5, 2024, https://www.jewishvirtuallibrary.org/yugoslavia
2. After Tito split with Joseph Stalin in 1948, Stalin made at least 22 assassination attempts on his life. In 1953, when Stalin died, a letter from Tito was found in his office saying, "Stop sending people to kill me. We've already captured five of them, one of them with a bomb and another with a rifle. If you don't stop sending killers, I'll send one to Moscow, and I won't have to send a second." Some speculate that Tito successfully poisoned Stalin.
3. Dominique Lapierre & Larry Collins, *O Jerusalem! Day by Day and Minute by Minute: the Historic Struggle for Jerusalem and the Birth of Israel* (New York: Simon & Schuster, 1972)
4. Lebel, p. 317.

Chapter 16

1. Norris, p. 125.
2. Lebel, p. 245.
3. Idem, p. 248.
4. Idem, p. 184.
5. Idem, p. 250.
6. Schmuel Specter & Geoffery Wigoder, *Encyclopedia of Jewish Life* (New York: NYU Press, 2001), p. 100.
7. Lebel, p. 172.
8. Idem, p. 174.
9. Idem, p. 175.
10. Miroljub Mijušković, "Scattered Memories of the Jews of Šabac," Accessed August 13, 2024, https://muse.jhu.edu/article/620928/summary
11. See Shmuel David's *Two Princes and a Queen* for a detailed retelling of life during the transport. It was a series of rumors, false hopes, and disappointments. Many times, the group was told to pack and be ready to travel, only to have plans delayed and eventually canceled. David's father was one of the few from the group who was born in Belgrade. He managed to survive and emigrate to Israel in March 1941.
12. Bogdan Bogdanović was not only an architect. During World War II, he fought as a partisan and served as Belgrade's mayor from 1982-86. After his death in 2010, his wife received special permission from the Jewish community for him to be buried in the Sephardic Cemetery, where his monument to Jewish victims of fascism stands.

Chapter 17

1. Norris, p. 125.
2. Powell, p. 14.
3. "May we all learn and act on the lessons of Srebrenica," says Secretary-General, in a message to anniversary ceremony, United Nations Press Release, November 7, 2005. Accessed August 22, 2024, https://press.un.org/en/2005/sgsm9993.doc.htm

Chapter 19

1. Schumer Chapman, *Motherland: Beyond the Holocaust, A Daughter's Journey to Reclaim the Past* (New York: Penguin Publishing Group, 2001), p. 178.

Chapter 20

1. Joseph Polak, *After the Holocaust the Bells Still Ring* (Brooklyn, NY: Urim Publications, 2015), pp. 25-26.
2. Gaon, pp. 99-100.
3. Lebel, p. 284-285.
4. Idem, p, 290.
5. Idem, p. 292.
6. Idem, pp. 292-294.
7. Idem, p. 286.
8. Stephanie Baric, "Asio Querida: TV Spotlights Sephardim in the Balkans," *Lilith* magazine, Summer 2017, p. 7.

Chapter 21

1. Susan Slyomovics, *How to Accept German Reparations* (Philadelphia: University of Pennsylvania Press, 2014), pp. 107-108.

Chapter 23

1. During World War II, the fascist Ustasha-Croatian Revolutionary Movement, which ruled Croatia, murdered hundreds of thousands of Serbs and thousands of Jews and Roma.

Chapter 24

1. Momo Kapor, *A Guide to the Serbian Mentality* (Belgrade: Dereta, 2017), pp. 22-25. *Kajmak* is special. It's made by skimming freshly boiled milk. There is an "international kajmak smuggling ring conducted by Serbs who risk everything to bring this dairy product to their countrymen around the world," writes Momo Kapor. "Like some drug smuggler, I, too, have carried kajmak, this precious foodstuff, through the strict customs control at New York's Kennedy Airport… I packed kajmak in circular tins of 'Nivea' cosmetic cream."

Chapter 25

1. Since our visit in 2018, the synagogue has become the Museum of Šabac Jews. It is part of the National Museum.

ABOUT THE AUTHOR

Julie Brill has been collecting family stories since she was a little girl. She is a lactation consultant, childbirth educator, doula, and the author of the anthology *Round the Circle: Doulas Share their Experiences*. Her essays have appeared in various publications, including *Haaretz*, the *Forward*, *Balkan Insight*, *Kveller*, *Cognoscenti*, and *Hey Alma*. She shares her family's experiences in the Shoah with middle and high school students through Living Links. The mother of two grown daughters, Julie lives near Boston, Massachusetts.

You can connect with her on her website:

juliebrill.com

ACKNOWLEDGMENTS

Thank you to my family for their interest and loving support. To my daughters Rebecca and Sophie who traveled to Serbia with me and rehashed stories as we looked for clues and tried out hypotheses. To my mother Martha and my brother Alex who came along on this journey of discovery. And of course, to my father Haim Brill who shared the painful stories that made this book possible and who was always willing to go back over details so I could get them right. This book was very much a family project. I love you all.

Thank you to Liesbeth Heenk and Amsterdam Publishers for believing in *Hidden in Plain Sight* and helping share my family's story and the story of the Serbian Jews.

Thank you to my Serbian cousins for being such generous hosts and for your help with connections and translations. And to Emil Kerenji who was always willing to answer questions and provide expert guidance. Thank you to Sonja Viličić for your support of my family and this book and for the ongoing education you provide on the Holocaust in Serbia.

Over the eight years I worked on this project, many writing teachers and fellow writers provided encouragement and feedback. Thank you to authors Sarah Wildman, Tova Mirvis, Linda K. Wertheimer, Tamara MC, Susan Shapiro, Lauren Markham, Diane Zinna, Judah Leblang, Katrina Anne Willis, Robert Laubacher, and Patty Mulcahy. Thank you to Professor Stephanie Knapp and her Emerson College Fall 2022 Book Editing Class for their thoughtful suggestions. Thank you to Peter Selgin for the beautiful cover and for your patience during its creation. And to Paula Jordan and Brian Scheick, thank you for your friendship and thoughtful feedback on this project. I'm sorry for those I left out.

AMSTERDAM PUBLISHERS HOLOCAUST LIBRARY

The series **Holocaust Survivor Memoirs World War II** consists of the following autobiographies of survivors:

Outcry. Holocaust Memoirs, by Manny Steinberg

Hank Brodt Holocaust Memoirs. A Candle and a Promise, by Deborah Donnelly

The Dead Years. Holocaust Memoirs, by Joseph Schupack

Rescued from the Ashes. The Diary of Leokadia Schmidt, Survivor of the Warsaw Ghetto, by Leokadia Schmidt

My Lvov. Holocaust Memoir of a twelve-year-old Girl, by Janina Hescheles

Remembering Ravensbrück. From Holocaust to Healing, by Natalie Hess

Wolf. A Story of Hate, by Zeev Scheinwald with Ella Scheinwald

Save my Children. An Astonishing Tale of Survival and its Unlikely Hero, by Leon Kleiner with Edwin Stepp

Holocaust Memoirs of a Bergen-Belsen Survivor & Classmate of Anne Frank, by Nanette Blitz Konig

Defiant German - Defiant Jew. A Holocaust Memoir from inside the Third Reich, by Walter Leopold with Les Leopold

In a Land of Forest and Darkness. The Holocaust Story of two Jewish Partisans, by Sara Lustigman Omelinski

Holocaust Memories. Annihilation and Survival in Slovakia, by Paul Davidovits

From Auschwitz with Love. The Inspiring Memoir of Two Sisters' Survival, Devotion and Triumph Told by Manci Grunberger Beran & Ruth Grunberger Mermelstein, by Daniel Seymour

Remetz. Resistance Fighter and Survivor of the Warsaw Ghetto, by Jan Yohay Remetz

My March Through Hell. A Young Girl's Terrifying Journey to Survival, by Halina Kleiner with Edwin Stepp

Roman's Journey, by Roman Halter

Beyond Borders. Escaping the Holocaust and Fighting the Nazis. 1938-1948, by Rudi Haymann

The Engineers. A memoir of survival through World War II in Poland and Hungary, by Henry Reiss

Spark of Hope. An Autobiography, by Luba Wrobel Goldberg

Footnote to History. From Hungary to America. The Memoir of a Holocaust Survivor, by Andrew Laszlo

Farewell Atlantis. Recollections, by Valentīna Freimane

The Courtyard. A memoir, by Benjamin Parket and Alexa Morris

The Mulberry Tree. The story of a life before and after the Holocaust, by Iboja Wandall-Holm

The Boy in the Back. A True Story of Survival in Auschwitz and Mauthausen, as told to Fern Lebo by Jan Blumenstein

Beneath the Lightless Sky. Surviving the Holocaust in the Sewers of Lvov, by Ignacy Chiger

Run, Mendel Run, by Milton H. Schwartz

The series **Holocaust Survivor True Stories** consists of the following biographies:

Among the Reeds. The true story of how a family survived the Holocaust, by Tammy Bottner

A Holocaust Memoir of Love & Resilience. Mama's Survival from Lithuania to America, by Ettie Zilber

Living among the Dead. My Grandmother's Holocaust Survival Story of Love and Strength, by Adena Bernstein Astrowsky

Heart Songs. A Holocaust Memoir, by Barbara Gilford

Shoes of the Shoah. The Tomorrow of Yesterday, by Dorothy Pierce

Hidden in Berlin. A Holocaust Memoir, by Evelyn Joseph Grossman

Separated Together. The Incredible True WWII Story of Soulmates Stranded an Ocean Apart, by Kenneth P. Price, Ph.D.

The Man Across the River. The incredible story of one man's will to survive the Holocaust, by Zvi Wiesenfeld

If Anyone Calls, Tell Them I Died. A Memoir, by Emanuel (Manu) Rosen

The House on Thrömerstrasse. A Story of Rebirth and Renewal in the Wake of the Holocaust, by Ron Vincent

Dancing with my Father. His hidden past. Her quest for truth. How Nazi Vienna shaped a family's identity, by Jo Sorochinsky

The Story Keeper. Weaving the Threads of Time and Memory - A Memoir, by Fred Feldman

Krisia's Silence. The Girl who was not on Schindler's List, by Ronny Hein

Defying Death on the Danube. A Holocaust Survival Story, by Debbie J. Callahan with Henry Stern

A Doorway to Heroism. A decorated German-Jewish Soldier who became an American Hero, by W. Jack Romberg

The Shoemaker's Son. The Life of a Holocaust Resister, by Laura Beth Bakst

The Redhead of Auschwitz. A True Story, by Nechama Birnbaum

Land of Many Bridges. My Father's Story, by Bela Ruth Samuel Tenenholtz

Creating Beauty from the Abyss. The Amazing Story of Sam Herciger, Auschwitz Survivor and Artist, by Lesley Ann Richardson

On Sunny Days We Sang. A Holocaust Story of Survival and Resilience, by Jeannette Grunhaus de Gelman

Painful Joy. A Holocaust Family Memoir, by Max J. Friedman

I Give You My Heart. A True Story of Courage and Survival, by Wendy Holden

In the Time of Madmen, by Mark A. Prelas

Monsters and Miracles. Horror, Heroes and the Holocaust, by Ira Wesley Kitmacher

Flower of Vlora. Growing up Jewish in Communist Albania, by Anna Kohen

Aftermath: Coming of Age on Three Continents. A Memoir, by Annette Libeskind Berkovits

Not a real Enemy. The True Story of a Hungarian Jewish Man's Fight for Freedom, by Robert Wolf

Zaidy's War. Four Armies, Three Continents, Two Brothers. One Man's Impossible Story of Endurance, by Martin Bodek

The Glassmaker's Son. Looking for the World my Father left behind in Nazi Germany, by Peter Kupfer

The Apprentice of Buchenwald. The True Story of the Teenage Boy Who Sabotaged Hitler's War Machine, by Oren Schneider

Good for a Single Journey, by Helen Joyce

Burying the Ghosts. She escaped Nazi Germany only to have her life torn apart by the woman she saved from the camps: her mother, by Sonia Case

American Wolf. From Nazi Refugee to American Spy. A True Story, by Audrey Birnbaum

Bipolar Refugee. A Saga of Survival and Resilience, by Peter Wiesner

In the Wake of Madness. My Family's Escape from the Nazis, by Bettie Lennett Denny

Before the Beginning and After the End, by Hymie Anisman

I Will Give Them an Everlasting Name. Jacksonville's Stories of the Holocaust, by Samuel Cox

Hiding in Holland. A Resistance Memoir, by Shulamit Reinharz

The Ghosts on the Wall. A Grandson's Memoir of the Holocaust, by Kenneth D. Wald

Thirteen in Auschwitz. My grandmother's fight to stay human, by Lauren Meyerowitz Port

Dreaming of the River, by Pauline Steinhorn

The series **Jewish Children in the Holocaust** consists of the following autobiographies of Jewish children hidden during WWII in the Netherlands:

Searching for Home. The Impact of WWII on a Hidden Child, by Joseph Gosler

Sounds from Silence. Reflections of a Child Holocaust Survivor, Psychiatrist and Teacher, by Robert Krell

Sabine's Odyssey. A Hidden Child and her Dutch Rescuers, by Agnes Schipper

The Journey of a Hidden Child,
by Harry Pila and Robin Black

The series **New Jewish Fiction** consists of the following novels, written by Jewish authors. All novels are set in the time during or after the Holocaust.

The Corset Maker. A Novel, by Annette Libeskind Berkovits

Escaping the Whale. The Holocaust is over. But is it ever over for the next generation? by Ruth Rotkowitz

When the Music Stopped. Willy Rosen's Holocaust, by Casey Hayes

Hands of Gold. One Man's Quest to Find the Silver Lining in Misfortune, by Roni Robbins

The Girl Who Counted Numbers. A Novel, by Roslyn Bernstein

There was a garden in Nuremberg. A Novel, by Navina Michal Clemerson

The Butterfly and the Axe, by Omer Bartov

To Live Another Day. A Novel, by Elizabeth Rosenberg

The Right to Happiness. After all they went through. Stories, by Helen Schary Motro

Five Amber Beads,
by Richard Aronowitz

To Love Another Day. A Novel,
by Elizabeth Rosenberg

Cursing the Darkness. A Novel about Loss and Recovery, by Joanna Rosenthall

The series **Holocaust Heritage** consists of the following memoirs by 2G:

The Cello Still Sings. A Generational Story of the Holocaust and of the Transformative Power of Music, by Janet Horvath

The Fire and the Bonfire. A Journey into Memory, by Ardyn Halter

The Silk Factory: Finding Threads of My Family's True Holocaust Story, by Michael Hickins

Winter Light. The Memoir of a Child of Holocaust Survivors, by Grace Feuerverger

Out from the Shadows. Growing up with Holocaust Survivor Parents, by Willie Handler

Hidden in Plain Sight. A Family Memoir and the Untold Story of the Holocaust in Serbia, by Julie Brill

The Unspeakable. Breaking my family's silence surrounding the Holocaust, by Nicola Hanefeld

Eighteen for Life. Surviving the Holocaust, by Helen Schamroth

Austrian Again. Reclaiming a Lost Legacy, by Anne Hand

The series **Holocaust Books for Young Adults** consists of the following novels, based on true stories:

The Boy behind the Door. How Salomon Kool Escaped the Nazis. Inspired by a True Story, by David Tabatsky

Running for Shelter. A True Story, by Suzette Sheft

The Precious Few. An Inspirational Saga of Courage based on True Stories, by David Twain with Art Twain

Dark Shadows Hover, by Jordan Steven Sher

The Sun will Shine Again, by Cynthia Goldstein Monsour

The series **WWII Historical Fiction** consists of the following novels, some of which are based on true stories:

Mendelevski's Box. A Heartwarming and Heartbreaking Jewish Survivor's Story, by Roger Swindells

A Quiet Genocide. The Untold Holocaust of Disabled Children in WWII Germany, by Glenn Bryant

The Knife-Edge Path, by Patrick T. Leahy

Brave Face. The Inspiring WWII Memoir of a Dutch/German Child, by I. Caroline Crocker and Meta A. Evenbly

When We Had Wings. The Gripping Story of an Orphan in Janusz Korczak's Orphanage. A Historical Novel, by Tami Shem-Tov

Jacob's Courage. Romance and Survival amidst the Horrors of War, by Charles S. Weinblatt

A Semblance of Justice. Based on true Holocaust experiences, by Wolf Holles

Under the Pink Triangle. Where forbidden love meets unspeakable evil, by Katie Moore

Amsterdam Publishers Newsletter

Subscribe to our Newsletter by selecting the menu at the top (right) of
amsterdampublishers.com

www.ingramcontent.com/pod-product-compliance
Lightning Source LLC
LaVergne TN
LVHW091547070526
838199LV00024B/564/J